A LIFE OF
VICTORY

Ulf Ekman

Word of Life Publications

A LIFE OF VICTORY
First published in English, 1991
Second edition, 1993

ISBN 91 7866 247 8
ISBN 1 884017 07 X usa

Printed in Finland for Word of Life Publications
by TryckPartner AB

Word of Life Publications
Box 17, S-751 03 Uppsala, Sweden
Box 46108, Minneapolis, MN 55446, USA
Box 641, Marine Parade, Singapore 9144

Acknowledgments
Unless otherwise indicated, Scripture quotations are
from the *Holy Bible, New International Version,*
Copyright © 1973, 1978, 1984 International Society.
Used by permission Zondervan Bible Publishers

Scripture quotation noted NKJV are from the *New King James
Version* of the Bible, copyright © 1979, 1980, 1982 Thomas
Nelson Publishers, Inc.

Contents

SALVATION

*For God so loved the world that he gave his
one and only Son, that whoever believes in
him shall not perish but have eternal life.*

John 3:16

1

Saved!

I want to introduce you to the Person who is the center of the Gospel, someone you have perhaps often avoided: Jesus Christ.

He has constantly tried to approach you to bless and transform your life, but you have kept your distance. Uncertainty has held you back and you have carefully changed the subject. But don't do that now! There are many pretexts for not believing in Jesus, yet none of them are valid and none of them will make you happy.

If Jesus came into your room now, you'd be ashamed and all your arguments would drop to the ground, like dead leaves in the fall. At least find out who He is and what He wants.

Deep inside, everyone knows that God exists. However, believing that He exists is not the same as knowing Him. You need to know God personally. He is not hidden! He is longing for an opportunity to reveal Himself to you.

Everyone knows that God exists and they also realize that things are not as they should be. They all see that something is wrong. Everyone has problems. Millions of people are plagued with anxiety, dissatisfaction, a sense of futility and a guilty conscience. Everyone has some kind of conflict or sense of guilt. Psychiatrists do all they can to relieve people's feelings of guilt but how can that help if the actual guilt remains? Someone must do something about the guilt itself!

Man died—Inwardly

The Bible plainly states that you are not here on the earth by chance. You are not a grain of sand, flung into the midst of a meaningless universe. You are created by God. He loves you and has made you for a purpose. He has a wonderful plan for your life and He wants to help you achieve your potential in Him.

The Bible tells us that although man was created by God, he rebelled against Him and fell into sin. He went his own way, away from God and lived only for himself.

When man sinned, he violated God's Word. God had declared that the consequence of sin would be death. Man sinned and died. First, he died inwardly. When man was in fellowship with God, he enjoyed a life of power and abundance, peace and harmony, health and joy. This died as he estranged himself from his Creator and went into darkness. As the darkness engulfed him within, he died spiritually. Externally, he continued to function, but internally, where he should have been filled with God's presence and glory, he was dead.

Mankind's worst sufferings can be traced to that fall. The basic problem is not drinking, swearing, fighting, lying or stealing. Nor is it depression, anxiety or fear. The deepest problem is that you are dead on the inside. God's life is elsewhere and you can neither produce it, nor attain it, yourself. It must come to you from without. You must be born again!

This is exactly what Jesus said to a well-known religious leader of His time, *Nicodemus, you must be born again! Born from above!* Religion is not enough, nor are high ideals. Personal aggrandizement won't do. Even good deeds are insufficient. You must receive God's life from above and be born again. You must receive a new life altogether!

God sent Jesus to the earth for this very purpose. He came to remove all the hindrances, so you could be born again and restored to fellowship and life with God. This is why Jesus died on a cross at Calvary, in Jerusalem, nearly 2,000 years ago. He did not die as an unsuccessful revolutionary, or as a despised prophet. He didn't die as a persecuted founder of some religion. He wasn't a martyr for the sake of His doctrines and ideas. He died for you!

Jesus Paid your Debt

When Jesus came to earth, He already knew He had come to die. He knew from the beginning that He was God's innocent Lamb, come to take away the sin of the world. He knew He was to redeem us from the curse that had fallen on mankind through sin. He had to deal with the consequences of sin—with spiritual death. God loves us all so much, the Bible says, that He gave His one and only Son to die for us.

Jesus had to die because the consequences of sin is death. The penalty for your sin fell on Him and He took the sentence in your place. **Jesus died instead of you.** He paid the debt that you and I owed, by dying on Calvary, so we could be redeemed and set free.

By giving His life, Jesus redeemed you. He took everyone's sin, mistakes, loneliness, poverty, anxiety, sickness and slavery. He bore it all in His own body. When He died on the cross, it all died with Him. On the third day, when He was raised

10

from the dead, He was the Victor over sin, death and all of its consequences.

Through His death and resurrection, Jesus unlocked the way for all who would believe in Him to partake of God's life again. Without God, everyone lives with a guilty conscience, under condemnation. Now, condemnation need no longer have any power over us. It was totally removed when Jesus paid our debt.

Jesus rose from the dead so we could be justified. Therefore, through Jesus' sacrifice for us, we can come to God, the Father, without a sense of guilt or condemnation. Jesus has taken His righteousness, His life and His position of security and boldness before the Father, and given it to us. We have been justified and made righteous in and through Jesus' death and resurrection.

Through Jesus, we have received a completely new position before the Father. Through Him, the Father looks on me just as if I'd never sinned. He loves me because I am His child. He answers my prayers and supplies my needs from His riches in glory. This is a total revolution. This is what new birth means. This is what it is to be a Christian!

When you realize that your own efforts are worthless, that you cannot improve yourself although you try; when you see that your new year's resolutions usually don't last the week, and that you can't even manage your own affairs (you are perhaps simply surviving, but you're not living to your full capacity); when you realize that something basic is missing— you are ready for help from outside. You are ready to be saved.

The Door to God is Open

To be saved means "to be helped", "to be rescued." What you cannot do for yourself, Jesus does for you. When you say "I know I am not innocent before God, I have gone astray from Him," remember that Jesus took your guilt and your rebellion upon Himself. When you see that Jesus died for you and you lay claim to the benefit of His death, then something happens! When you see that Jesus was raised from the dead so you could come back to God, salvation will become a reality in your life. By His death and resurrection, the door to God is open—the payment has been made, the curse is broken and the sin atoned for. You cannot do this yourself, but you can accept and receive by faith what Jesus has done for you.

When you accept Jesus' death on Calvary and His resurrection as something God has done for you, something wonderful happens. God sees that you accept Jesus' redeeming sacrifice for yourself! Then, because of Jesus, and only because of Him, not because of anything you have done, the Holy Spirit comes into you, and you are born again.

God steps into your life and transforms you on the inside. A miracle takes place and you become a new creation. A new person is born inside you. God's power starts to work in your life and His blessings begin to flow. You begin to feel that God has accepted you. You see how He begins to talk with you, lead you and do wonders in your life—all because of Jesus!

This is what it means to be a Christian. It does not mean having an interest in religious activities and ideas about life. It is the power of God transforming your entire being and making you a channel for His blessings to others.

God wants to meet every need in your life. There is no area in which He cannot perform a miracle or bless you. When Jesus walked this earth, He was always doing miracles. He healed the sick, liberated those who were possessed and bound by the devil and fed and satisfied 5,000 people with five small loaves and a couple of fish. He drew upon the stores of heaven and showed that God is kind and good and meets mankind's needs with His riches.

Jesus does just the same today. He has never changed. He is a living Savior, who will restore and bless you in every way and give you a totally new life.

He loves you and can help you in a way that no one else can. Hundreds of thousands of people throughout the world know this personally and God wants you to know it too. Don't run away from this any longer! Accept Jesus and receive Him as your Savior and Lord.

2

The Curse is Broken

No one really knows the full extent of the disaster that took place in Eden at The Fall. Sin spread judgment and death like a plague, from person to person and generation to generation. Everyone was affected. No one escaped.

God had breathed the breath of life into man (Gen 2:7) and he came alive in spirit, soul and body. God's abundant life flowed through him and he became God's companion. But all this was broken when he fell into sin. God had warned him that if he ate of the fruit on the Tree of Knowledge, he would *surely die* (Gen 2:17).

When he sinned, Adam died. His spirit died, his soul was estranged from God and his body became subject to the laws of corruption, one day to die forever. Death entered every part of his being. Where there was once life, there was now death. Where there had been plenty, there was now lack. Where there had once been blessing, there was now a curse.

Sin entered the world and became the root cause of mankind's problems. Romans 5:18 tells us that by the offence of one man, judgment came upon all men to condemnation.

Sin spread throughout the world in each successive generation. None escaped. That is why we read in Romans 3:10,11, *There is no one righteous, not even one; there is no one who understands, no one who seeks God.* Since the Fall, there has been no exception. *All have sinned and fall short of the glory of God* (Rom 3:23). God's glory, His presence and blessing, departed and all the world became guilty before God (see Rom 3:19).

No matter how hard he tried, man lacked the ability to become what God had originally intended him to be. He was spiritually dead and on the way to physical death, to finally die forever in eternal separation from God, in hell.

Mankind's fate was tragic. He was originally created as a morally responsible being, to live with God forever, to serve and honor Him. However, he rebelled against God, wilfully sinned and died. He then received a substitute lord—Satan, and it was his death-nature that now entered man.

Man was Unable to Deliver Himself

Ephesians 2:1-2 states, *As for you, you were dead in your transgressions and sins, in which you used to live when you followed the ways of this world and of the ruler of the kingdom of the air, the spirit who is now at work in those who are disobedient.* In other words, we followed Satan. We belonged to his kingdom and we were his slaves.

In John 10:10 Jesus says, *The thief comes only to steal and kill and destroy; I have come that they may have life, and have it to the full.* Satan steals, kills and destroys. He can pass on nothing but death—it is the only inheritance he can give. Jesus came to deliver us from this dominion of captivity and death.

Man cannot save himself. None of the superficial improvements that people attempt, can ever solve the basic inner problem. They are spiritually dead and under the curse of sin that lies upon the entire human race. This curse must be broken and life must flow into them again, from an outside source.

As we have said before, man can't do this himself—a dead man can't resurrect himself—someone else must come and do it for him. Someone must break the curse. No living person can ever do it because we are all under the same curse. Therefore, God sent His only Son, Jesus. In Hebrews 2:14 it says, *by his death he might destroy him who holds the power of death—this is, the devil.*

What actually happened when Jesus died? Galatians 3:13,14 tells us that *Christ redeemed us from the curse of the law by becoming a curse for us, for it is written: "Cursed is every one who is hung on a tree." He redeemed us in order that the blessing given to Abraham might come to the Gentiles through Christ Jesus, so that by faith we might receive the promise of the Spirit.*

When Jesus died, He took on Himself the full curse that had come upon humanity through sin, and He was made a curse for us.

What exactly is a curse? The root of the word means "to expel, abandon, excommunicate and doom to destruction." Throughout the Bible, we see that obedience to God brings blessing, while rebellion, sin and disobedience incur a curse; or in other words, man cuts himself off from the life found in God.

A curse is always associated with death. The curse of the law meant death for those who broke the law. Deuteronomy 28:15 states, *If you do not obey the Lord your God and do not carefully follow all his commands and decrees I am giving you today, all these curses will come upon you and overtake you.*

People could only avoid the curse on this earth by keeping themselves within the bounds of the covenant, which God had made with Abraham. As long as they kept the covenant of Abraham they were protected, but if they went outside it, the curse would come into effect.

God's Overwhelming Victory at Calvary

In the Old Testament, the people had to keep to the law. When anyone transgressed it, he would offer a trespass offering. Even so, they always carried a sense of guilt and insufficiency before the law, knowing they were transgressors but that the blood of the sacrifice would temporarily cover their sin. Yet even this system, did not solve the sin problem. A sacrificed calf or goat could never solve man's dual problem; it could never break the curse over him and grant him new life.

For this very reason, Jesus died on Calvary where He bore the curse and all of its consequences.

When Jesus died, the curse was annihilated and its power over the human race was broken. Since Jesus was not under the curse himself, He could take it upon Himself and remove it from mankind. Jesus was innocent, so God was able to raise Him from the dead and through Christ, provide reconciliation for the whole world.

Colossians 2:14,15 says, *Having canceled the written code, with its regulations* (the condemnation of the law leading to the curse), *that was against us and that stood opposed to us; he took it away, nailing it to the cross. And having disarmed the powers and authorities, he made a public spectacle of them, triumphing over them by the cross.*

Through his death and resurrection, Jesus paid the debt and broke the power of sin and death. The curse was annulled and Satan was disarmed and defeated. Jesus gained an overwhelming victory over Satan, through His death on Calvary and His resurrection. No more meaningful word can ever pass your lips than the word, **victory**!

In Christ, God won an all-out victory over Satan and the curse upon the human race was broken once and for all.

We must realize that there are only two states in which we can live: blessing or curse, life or death. *This day I call heaven and earth as witnesses against you that I have set before you life and death, blessings and curses. Now choose life, so that you and your children may live* (Deut 30:19).

15

God wants you to live. He wants you to have a part in His eternal, bountiful life! Jesus came to give you abundant life. Through Christ, God broke the curse and poured out the blessing.

Blessing is Yours—Life to the Full

When you see what Jesus did for you on Calvary and confess Him as your Savior and Lord, you become born again and God's life flows into you. In Galatians 3:14, we read that we are to be blessed and receive the Holy Spirit by faith. When you are born again, you receive the Spirit of God who gives you everlasting life, abundant life—God's life.

This life from God is a blessing that affects you in every way. In Deuteronomy 28:1-14, we see that blessings overtook the people and came upon them. They were "struck" by blessings in every area of their lives.

In Ephesians 1:3, we read, *Praise be to the God and Father of our Lord Jesus Christ who,* **has blessed us in the heavenly realms with every spiritual blessing** *in Christ.* All the good that God has, He has given to us in Christ. He has not withheld any good thing from us.

He who did not spare his own Son, but gave him up for us all – how will he not also, along with him, graciously give us **all** *things* (Rom 8:32).

God made Jesus go through everything for us, so we could partake of everything **in Him**. He has freely given us **everything** through Jesus. What does **"all"** mean? It means that, through Jesus, God's life, blessings, help and riches flow down from heaven over every area of our lives. Where death once ruled, life has now come!

Romans 5:20,21 says that *the law was added so that the trespass might increase. But where sin increased, grace increased all the more, so that, just as sin reigned in death, so also grace might reign through righteousness to bring eternal life through Jesus Christ our Lord.*

Where sin once held sway and produced death, righteousness now reigns, producing everlasting life from God, in every area of human existence. Jesus embraced every aspect of human life on the cross. He took our sin, our sickness, our loneliness, our anxiety and our poverty. All this was part of the curse that came upon Jesus on the cross. That is why there is blessing in Christ in all these areas today!

Blessing is more than a pat on the shoulder. It is heaven's abundant life flowing to you so that prosperity and success become your daily reality. Where there was once a desert and death, there is now a flourishing, well-watered garden.

Remember that you are blessed! Thank God for it and live in it daily. Jesus paid a great price to give it to you!

The Christian life is not a book of rules to be slavishly followed. It is life to the full—life flowing copiously from heaven. It doesn't consist of a thousand activities and endeavors to please God. It is fellowship with the Father who has begotten you and through Christ, you have a tremendous security as His child. You have life in Him, and His life flows through you.

His life is supernatural, so your life becomes supernatural too. His life is His power, so your life becomes strengthened by His power too. When His life comes into contact with people, signs and wonders and mighty deeds take place. That is why miracles take place through any believer, who is filled with the life of God.

Your life as a believer does not just consist of a longing for God. It is intimacy with him and results in His life flowing through you to other people. His power will pulsate out through you to those with needs and His life and blessing will be conferred upon them. You will observe God performing miracles in their lives and they will become gloriously blessed, liberated and totally restored.

John 1:4 states, *In him* (Jesus, the Word) *was life, and that life was the light of men.* In John 14:6 Jesus says, *I am the way and the truth and the life.* Jesus is life, and everyone can have life in Him.

This life is Christianity. All the rest is just religiosity and helps no one. God's power alone can help people—and that power is available to all who lay claim to what Jesus accomplished on Calvary. There, He broke the curse and established a new order in which God's life and blessing are poured out to all who confess Jesus as their Lord.

3

The Cross

The most essential part of the Gospel—the cross—is often surrounded in confusion. If we do not understand what happened there, we will not know who God is or what it means to be a believer.

The cross is the power behind the Gospel. Without it, the Gospel would be rendered powerless to transform people's lives.

Today, a number of new "spiritual" movements have arisen which use a terminology misleadingly similar to that of the Bible. They speak of a "new birth," of "being filled with the spirit," of "the inner man," of "revelation" and of "guidance." All these expressions are, in fact, Biblical, and it is dangerous if Christians stop using them for fear of being taken for new so-called "spiritual" movements.

It is a satanic strategy to make us step down from all that God has given us in the Gospel. Satan wants to stop us—and is attempting to do so through ungodly movements that try to steal Biblical expressions and give them another meaning. But we will never stop speaking these truths! On the contrary, we must preach the fullness of the Gospel even more radically.

If occult movements speak of "healing," we must preach healing all the more, because it is only through **Jesus' wounds** that we are truly healed. Now is not the time to retreat in fear. We must preach the Gospel more boldly than ever, so that men and women see that Jesus alone has something to give them.

All these new "spiritual" movements avoid the **cross of Christ.** They can't stand hearing about **the blood** and they don't understand **redemption**. All false religions are repulsed by the wounds and the blood of Jesus, and they invariably launch their attacks against these realities. This is hardly surprising since it is only through the blood, the cross and the redeeming death of Jesus, that Satan is overcome. He desperately attacks it because the blood is the weapon that defeated him. Therefore, he always tries to institute bloodless religions and philosophies, founded upon "deep knowledge" instead of on the redeeming work of Calvary.

Paul says in 1 Corinthians 1:17,18, *For Christ did not send me to baptize, but to preach the gospel—not with words of human wisdom, lest the cross of Christ be emptied of its power. For the message of the cross is foolishness to those who are perishing, but to us who are being saved it is the power of God.*

Jesus Came to Die!

The message of the cross is foolishness to the devil, but to us it is the power of God leading to salvation. Even Paul, when he came to the Corinthians, said that he *resolved to know nothing...except Jesus Christ and him crucified* (1 Cor 2:2).

What actually happened on the cross? Why is it so powerful? To the casual observer, it was just a Jewish teacher accused of agitation, revolt and heresy, dying a criminal's death. Many people had similarly been crucified before and many would be afterwards. To the secular historian, He was just one among many others. But to God, He was altogether different.

Jesus came to earth as a sacrificial lamb. John the Baptist said of Him, *Look, the Lamb of God, who takes away the sin of the world!* (John 1:29). Jesus purposely came to die! He was conceived by the Holy Spirit and born of the virgin Mary. He was the Word that was made flesh. He was one hundred percent God and one hundred percent man. *He was both the Son of God and the Son of man.*

The Holy Spirit descended on Him like a dove. *God anointed Jesus of Nazareth with the Holy Spirit and power, and...he went around doing good and healing all who were under the power of the devil, because God was with him* (Acts 10:38). He taught and preached. He performed signs and miracles. He healed the sick and drove out evil spirits.

As God's Son, He showed the people who God really was—how good He is and what His will is. He was *the radiance of God's glory and the exact representation of his being* (Heb 1:3). When the people saw what Jesus did, they saw God.

Jesus was also the Son of man. When the people saw what He did and heard what He said, they saw what a man should be. They saw God's original intention for the human race. **However, Jesus did not just come to live among men, do good and be an example**—He came to die for them.

Man had left God and fallen into sin (Rom 3:23). Through sin, death had entered the world (Rom 6:23) and by his rebellion, man had lost contact with God. First, he died spiritually (Eph 2:1), then physically and so, eternally. Without

God, he was lost forever and through the sin nature, hatred, loneliness, lying, rebellion, sickness and poverty came into his daily life.

His conscience began to tell him that he was not innocent before God and a sense of guilt, fear and anxiety became his daily food. Bound by sin, he was enslaved to the prince and god of this world, the devil. It was impossible for him to escape.

What Happened on the Cross?

No one was strong enough, wise enough or good enough to settle the debt with God. No one could manage to deliver himself from the prison he was in. Someone had to help him. Someone had to pay his ransom money.

Humanism, religiosity and new "spirituality" object to this. The flesh refuses to accept the fact that it cannot save itself. The unregenerate person wants to be his own savior. He tries a thousand ways, from rock music to yoga, from free sex to self-denial, from careerism and humanism to socialism and pacifism. But he never succeeds.

Man cannot repair his breach of God's command or pay his debt and so God sent His own Son, Jesus, who came to die.

Romans 6:23 says, *the wages of sin is death*. Either a man himself dies and is lost forever, or someone else dies in his place. Where? On the cross!

If an ordinary person were to die, the price would never be paid because man can never pay his own debt. God Himself could not die to pay the price, because it was man who had sinned. Therefore, Jesus came as both God and man. He was wholly man and could die as man's representative. He was also wholly God, not beset by mankind's sin, and so He could die in our place.

Jesus died as our substitute on the cross. He was innocent, but He took the debt of others on Himself. Jesus willingly bore other people's sins and guilt and became a sacrificial lamb, a sin offering.

*God made him who had no sin to be sin **for us**, so that **in him** we might become the righteousness of God* (2 Cor 5:21). *He himself **bore our sins in his body** on the tree, so **that we might die** to sins and live for righteousness; by his wounds you have been healed* (1 Pet 2:24). *For Christ died for sins once for all, the righteous for the unrighteous, **to bring you to God**. He was put to death in the body but made alive by the spirit* (1 Pet 3:18).

We were guilty and we should have died on that cross but Jesus died there and paid the debt for us. The **cross** was the place for this **wonderful** exchange. Do you see it? It is vital that you do!

His blood was shed as a sin offering, paying the price for your sin. He gave His life and died, so that you could live. His blood is the ransom money that has redeemed us from the devil's slave market where we were held captive (1 Pet 1:18,19).

The Blessed Exchange

In Gethsemane, Jesus decided to tread the path of obedience and be sacrificed for man's rebellion. He was taken, found guilty, scourged and crucified. Everything God wanted to release you from was laid on Him.

Surely he took up our infirmities and carried our sorrows... He was pierced for our transgressions, he was crushed for our iniquities; the punishment that brought us peace was upon him and by his wounds we are healed (Isa 53:4-5).

The cross is the garbage dump of all time: The sin of the whole world—its hatred, rebellion, bitterness, fear, anxiety, loneliness, sickness, poverty and death, were all cast upon Jesus there. He took it all and went with it into death.

There, Jesus settled the debt of sin forever. By His death, He annihilated it and all of its consequences and broke its power and right to rule the world:

The cross is the place where your debt was paid.

The cross is the place where the power of sin was broken.

The cross is the place where the power of sickness was broken.

The cross is the place where the power of poverty was broken.

The cross is the place where enmity with God was broken.

When Jesus died on Calvary He reconciled you with God. His blood is the basis on which the Father pronounced mankind to be righteous. The redemption, Jesus' death on the cross, is the ground for God's forgiveness of the world. He now declares that the debt is paid! Whoever calls on Him, pleading the blood of the cross, has the right to become a child of God. He can be justified, born again and have fellowship with the Living God.

Jesus died—**so you** could have everlasting, bountiful life and fellowship with the Father as His child.

Jesus was made sin—**so you** can have forgiveness and be made righteous (2 Cor 5:21).

Jesus took your sickness—**so you,** by His wounds, could be healed (Isa 53:5; 1 Pet 2:24).

Jesus became poor—**so you,** through His poverty, might be rich (2 Cor 8:9).

Jesus took your anxiety—**so you** could have peace (Isa 53:5).

Jesus was made a curse—**so you** could be blessed (Gal 3:13,14).

God wants you to see that **Jesus died for your sins and was raised again for your justification**. God's demand for justice was satisfied on the cross, through Jesus' death. He died so you can live . He paid the price to obtain your release. He was made a curse so you could be blessed with every spiritual blessing in the heavenly realm (Eph 1:3).

You show gratitude for the cross and believe in it, by accepting and receiving all that Jesus' death bought for you. We do not live in the time of the Old Testament. We live after the cross, in the age of the New Covenant. We live in a day when the blood of Jesus constitutes the basis of a better covenant.

The Cross—A Blessing for the Whole of Life

The blood that Jesus shed on the cross is the covenant blood. It is the guarantee and cornerstone of a better covenant, founded upon better promises, through Jesus (Heb 8:6).

*Christ is the mediator of a new covenant, that those who are called may **receive the promised eternal inheritance**— now that he has died as a ransom to set them free from the sins committed under the first covenant* (Heb 9:15).

The New Testament contains promises and blessings for every area of life. Jesus shed His blood, paid the ransom and defeated the devil. Therefore, there is now a basis for God's blessings to come over your life. Victory is available for you and a life in the Spirit awaits you.

Jesus died so that you could experience the blessings of the New Covenant. Even today, He is sitting at the right hand of the Father interceding for you, praying that you may receive all that he wants to give you through His death (Rom 8:34; Heb 7:25).

He paid an astronomical sum on the cross for you, and He wants the full benefit of that salvation to be yours. He took upon Himself such a crushing burden that we will probably never fully understand what He really went through. He tasted the depths of sin and misery, so you and I could taste the heights of blessing.

Don't resist what He offers you. Honor Him instead, by accepting and receiving what He has made available to you by His death. It gives Jesus infinite joy when we honor the cross, by receiving what He has provided for us. His blessings are precious—they cost Him His life. Do not treat them lightly, but receive them with an earnest and grateful heart!

THE BAPTISM OF THE HOLY SPIRIT

You will receive power when the Holy Spirit comes on you; and you will be my witnesses in Jerusalem, and in all Judea and Samaria, and to the ends of the earth.

Acts 1:8

4

The Power of the Holy Spirit

In Acts 1:8, we read that Jesus said: *You will receive power when the Holy Spirit comes on you; and you will be my witnesses in Jerusalem, and in all Judea and Samaria, and to the ends of the earth.*

Jesus knew that His disciples could not accomplish what He had commanded them to do by their own human power. The life He had promised them, and which God was about to give them, was a supernatural life, a life from above. That is why in John 3:6, Jesus says: *Flesh gives birth to flesh, but the Spirit gives birth to spirit.* In other words, when a person is regenerated, he is born again; he is born from above, or born of the Spirit (John 3:3).

Jesus talked about this in John 7:38-39, when He said: *Whoever believes in me, as the Scripture has said, streams of living water will flow from within him. By this he meant the Spirit, whom those who believed in him were later to receive. Up to that time the Spirit had not been given, since Jesus had not yet been glorified.*

The Age of the Spirit

After Jesus died, He rose again and ascended into heaven. Thus, a new age began; it was known as the Age of the Church, the Age of Grace or the Age of the Spirit. It is a period of time during, which the Holy Spirit is made available to every person in every nation, in a way He never was during Old Covenant times.

Under the Old Covenant, the Spirit of God only came on those who held one of three offices: the king, priest or prophet. These three positions of authority were anointed by the Spirit of God and He acted solely on behalf of those who stood in these positions. The Day of Pentecost removed these limits and the Holy Spirit no longer came on just a few people in one nation. Now, He was given to every person in any nation, who called on the Name of Jesus. He was not only present with them on certain special occasions, He was now in them and constantly working through them.

This is what Jesus had promised when He said *streams of living water will flow from within*. He was explaining that the Holy Spirit would continually flow out from a person's inner man or heart. In John 14:17, Jesus continued talking about the Holy Spirit, the Spirit of Truth, and said: *The world cannot accept him, because it neither sees him nor knows him. But you know him for he lives with you and will be in you.*

The news of the New Covenant Age is that the Spirit of God now enters into people and lives in them. How? Through the new birth. When anyone repents from his heart, confesses his sin, proclaims Jesus as his Lord and Messiah and turns his back on this world, he becomes born again. God's Spirit removes his old heart of stone (his old sinful nature), creates a new person within and gives him a new heart.

Within this newborn inner man, God sets up His home. The inner man of anyone who is born again becomes God's "holiest place," the place of His abiding presence. God does not live in a person's old heart, but in a new one that He Himself has created. This becomes the place of God's presence—and it all happens at the new birth.

The Baptism of the Holy Spirit

The new birth is a life-changing experience but there is even more for the new Christian! Jesus declared in Acts 1:5: *...in a few days you will be baptized with the Holy Spirit.*

Jesus was speaking here about baptism in the Holy Spirit. He said it was an empowering for supernatural service for Him. This is something more than the inner life with Him that is available through the new birth. Baptism in the Spirit is the power of God equipping the believer for supernatural service.

The disciples experienced this power as the Holy Spirit came upon them on the Day of Pentecost:

Suddenly a sound like the blowing of a violent wind came from heaven and filled the whole house where they were sitting. They saw what seemed to be tongues of fire that separated and came to rest on each of them. All of them were filled with the Holy Spirit and began to speak in other tongues as the Spirit enabled them (Acts 2:2-4).

This was the fulfillment of the promise that John the Baptist had made when he said, *I baptize you with water for repentance. But after me will come one who is more powerful than I, whose sandals I am not fit to carry. He will baptize you with the Holy Spirit and with fire* (Matt 3:11).

While the disciples were praying, the fire of God fell on them and they were baptized with the Holy Spirit. As an outward sign and manifestation, they began to speak with tongues: *All of them were filled with the Holy Spirit and began to speak in other tongues as the Spirit enabled them* (Acts 2:4).

When the disciples were filled with the Holy Spirit, God's spiritual gifts then began to be manifested in their lives.

The Spiritual Gifts

Paul describes the spiritual gifts in 1 Corinthians 12:4-11. They may be divided into three categories:

1. The Knowledge Gifts: the word of wisdom, the word of knowledge and the gift of discernment of spirits.

2. The Power Gifts: the gift of faith, the gifts of healing and the gift of miraculous powers.

3. The Oral Gifts: the gift of prophecy, the gift of speaking in different kinds of tongues and the gift of interpretation of tongues.

Each of these nine gifts is supernatural. They are all God's supernatural abilities manifested in his children by the Holy Spirit. When the disciples were baptized in the Holy Spirit all these gifts began to work in and through them.

5

Speaking in Tongues

The first of the nine gifts of the Spirit to be manifested at Pentecost was speaking in tongues. Speaking in tongues is not an ecstatic babbling, but a spoken language, either human or angelic (1 Cor 13:1). The difference between this and natural language is that the speaker does not understand what he is saying.

On many occasions, people have come to me and said, "You spoke in Bengali," or "Swahili," "Tibetan" or some other language. On the Day of Pentecost, people gathered around and heard about God's mighty acts in their own languages, though the disciples themselves did not understand what they were saying. They were speaking in new tongues.

Tongues For Every Believer

When a believer is baptized in the Holy Spirit, God gives him the ability to speak in tongues. This particular gift is the outward manifestation of the baptism in the Holy Spirit.

God wants every believer to be baptized in the Holy Spirit. Paul says in First Corinthians 14:5, *I would like every one of you to speak in tongues.* When giving the Great Commission, Jesus said, *These signs will accompany those who believe: In my name they will drive out demons; they will speak in new tongues* (Mark 16:17).

The baptism in the Spirit is not an experience for a few chosen spiritual specialists. It is the norm for every believer. God wants every Christian to speak in new tongues.

Notice that as the hundred and twenty disciples were assembled in the upper room, *all of them were filled with the Holy Spirit and began to speak in other tongues* (Acts 2:4). Everyone began to speak in other tongues! God's will is still the same today. He wants us all to speak with tongues!

Speaking in tongues is the doorway to the other gifts of the Spirit. When it is opened, like a floodgate, rivers of living water begin to flow, and other currents start to flow with it. Rivers of healing, supernatural wisdom and supernatural power, also emerge.

Throughout the Acts of the Apostles, we see examples of the supernatural life that began to flow from the disciples' inner man. At their baptism in the Holy Spirit they were *clothed with power from on high* (Luke 24:49), and the gifts of the Spirit began to be mightily manifested in their lives.

Different Functions of Speaking in Tongues

Speaking in tongues, however, is not limited to just one purpose. It has several different functions. First Corinthians 14:4 tells us that one of these other functions is to build us up. When you pray in tongues, your spirit prays (1 Cor 14:14). Your inner man is edified, strengthened, made sensitive and purified, as you speak in new tongues.

When you pray in tongues, you are talking to God. It is a wonderful way of communicating with Him and of exalting and praising Him. You can speak mysteries to the Living God that are far beyond your own understanding (1 Cor 14:2). Your inner man is conveying your love and appreciation to God from deep inside.

If you pray in tongues, you will also become an intercessor. Romans 8:26 says, *The Spirit helps us in our weakness. We do not know what we ought to pray for, but the Spirit himself intercedes for us with groans that words cannot express.* The Holy Spirit takes hold of your inner man, puts desires within you, and then helps you to pray them out by speaking in tongues with "groans that words cannot express."

There are things that your mind does not understand, but God knows about these matters and the Spirit moves you to pray. The will of God is then released through your Spirit-led prayers in tongues. Your mind does not get in the way or limit your prayers, because you are praying directly from your spirit. The Holy Spirit can then lead you to pray in tongues in many ways, rather than just one way.

There is tremendous variation in the Spirit to meet the many different needs and situations that confront mankind.

Appreciate and Use Tongues

Do not let anyone despise such a unique spiritual gift. First Corinthians 14:39 tells us, *Do not forbid speaking in tongues.*

The devil, of course, does not like people to be baptized in the Spirit, nor does he like God's spiritual gifts. He tries to stop the flow of God's power, wisdom and presence both within you and around you. Therefore, he often makes fun of tongues and ridicules it to hinder or limit its use.

People can go to excesses in anything, but do not let the fear of that hinder you from speaking a lot in tongues. Paul told the Corinthian believers, *I thank God that I speak in tongues more than all of you* (1 Cor 14:18). So the apostle Paul frequently spoke in tongues! So did Peter. It was the same with Jesus' mother, Mary, who was in the upper room and was baptized in the Spirit, together with the other disciples (Acts 1:14).

Do not let anyone hinder, limit or ridicule the gift God has given you. Learn how, when and why you are to use it, and never neglect it. First Timothy 4:14 states, *Do not neglect your gift, which was given you* but *fan into flame the gift of God, which is in you through the laying on of my hands* (2 Tim 1:6).

How Can I be Baptized in the Holy Spirit?

1. You must be hungry for God. Paul says in First Corinthians 14:1, *Desire spiritual gifts.* Indifference and spiritual lethargy will receive nothing from God.

2. Refuse deliberate sin, compromise and worldliness in your life. Confess it and ask for cleansing in the blood of Jesus (1 John 1:9).

3. Make a clear confession of Jesus as your Lord and Savior. Tell Him that as His servant, you will serve Him all your life but that you need His power to do so (Acts 1:8).

4. Ask the Lord to baptize you in the Holy Spirit, as He has promised. You do not need to wonder whether He wants to do it or not. Luke 11:13 says, *If you then, though you are evil, know how to give good gifts to your children, how much more will your Father in heaven give the Holy Spirit to those who ask him!* God is longing to give His Holy Spirit to you.

5. Receive the baptism in the Holy Spirit by faith. Baptism in the Spirit has less to do with feelings than many people think. It is primarily a spiritual experience, not an emotional one. Many people are baptized in the Holy Spirit without any special sensations. Later, however, feelings may grow and many kinds of tongues may be manifested.

6. Open your mouth and begin to speak. Remember what Acts 2:4 says: *All of them were filled with the Holy Spirit and began to speak in other tongues as the Spirit enabled them.* The disciples were filled with the Spirit but it was they who did the talking. The Holy Spirit gave them the language and the words, but they had to open their mouths, move their lips and let the sounds come from their vocal chords!

You must do the same! The Holy Spirit will inspire you, but He will not speak for you—that is your job. He will give you a language that is not your mother tongue, or religious phrases, but words from the Spirit of God, coming from your inner man. Then, you are responsible to speak them.

Sometimes, when people are baptized in the Holy Spirit, rivers of tongues will immediately rise and flow from them. Others begin with just simple expressions. Tongues vary so it does not matter which way you begin, but it is important that you start. Then, the language will gradually develop and increase. The tiny rivulet will become a stream and eventually, a mighty river of many different kinds of tongues.

A Precious Gift from God

The baptism in the Holy Spirit is a precious gift from God. When tongues begin to flow from your inner man, you will find that you have received a powerful instrument that God wants to use in many ways. Take care of what God has given you, and also allow the Holy Spirit to lead you to use His other gifts.

As we mentioned before, these gifts include the interpretation of tongues, prophecy, the word of knowledge, the gifts of healing and so on.

You will see how God's Spirit flows through you more and more in blessing, restoration, healing and freedom for countless men and women. The same Spirit that was on Jesus is now resting on you. You have the same anointing so that you can do the same works He did (John 14:12-13).

SPREAD THE GOSPEL!

Go into all the world and preach the good news...

Mark 16:15

6

The Powerful Gospel

Throughout the world, an increasing number of people are awakening to the fact that God is real as He reveals His peace, love and power to them. His glory is being manifested more than ever in their gatherings, and He is showing them His nature through signs and wonders. His Word is not simply being quoted—it is also being confirmed by His miraculous power. Believers are learning to be led by the Holy Spirit and the supernatural is becoming the norm for them as God is making Himself known!

The first disciples said, *We have seen his glory* (John 1:14). They saw the glory of God revealed through the life of Jesus, through what He said and did. This same glory is becoming increasingly visible in the Body of Christ today. God wants to show the world who He is, and what He wants to do. He is more than willing to reveal His love and power so the world will believe in Him.

When the Spirit of God is at work and people everywhere are being drawn to Jesus, the devil is usually active. His aim is to hinder as many people as possible from hearing the Gospel, believing it and becoming saved. He is trying to stop the Gospel from spreading, so that people will never see God's glory. He employs a number of different methods to reach his aim—and we must be familiar with them, so we can stop him from accomplishing his goal. *For we are not unaware of his schemes,* Paul says, in 2 Corinthians 2:11.

Romans 1:16 declares that the Gospel, is the power of God for salvation to everyone who believes. His power is revealed in and through His "good news". In 1 Corinthians 1:17, Paul says, *For Christ did not send me to baptize, but to preach the gospel—not with words of human wisdom, lest the cross of Christ be emptied of its power.* He continues, *My message and my preaching were not with wise and persuasive words, but with a demonstration of the Spirit's power, so that your faith might not rest on men's wisdom, but on God's power* (1 Cor 2:4).

The enemy wants to rob the Gospel of its power, one of the ways he does this is by mixing it with so much wisdom and worldly opinion that it becomes impotent. The opinions of this world have always been diametrically opposed to the revelation and knowledge of the Gospel. But power can only be found in the Gospel. Therefore, if the devil can rewrite, abridge, edit and censor God's Word, to make it more "human," it will immediately lose its attraction and be left with nothing but short epithets on general, good behavior. The devil will then have managed to empty the Gospel of all its message and power.

Satan has busied himself with this task throughout each generation and sadly, in many cases, he has succeeded. But, praise the Lord, God is changing this!

No Miracles Without Holiness

A wave of Holy Spirit revelation based on the written Word is sweeping through the world today. Hundreds of thousands are beginning to receive the Word of God, believe it and act on it as never before. All over the world, the Holy Spirit is restoring faith in the Bible and the full Gospel. Men and women are tired of hearing the Scriptures explained away and attending services where the glory and power of God are conspicuous by their absence. People are being drawn to Jesus as soon as they are presented with the genuine article—the original Gospel—not a watered down counterfeit. Everywhere, people are beginning to believe that Jesus says what He means, and means what He says.

The result, of course, is a direct confrontation in the spirit realm with the prince of this world. But this is nothing new. The disciples in the Book of Acts constantly experienced such confrontation and wherever he traveled, Paul found people rising up against the preaching of the Gospel. There was trouble everywhere. In Acts 16:20 they said, *These men...are throwing our city into an uproar.* Why? Because Paul had preached Jesus and cast a clairvoyant spirit out of a young woman. When you preach Jesus, lay hands on the sick or cast out evil spirits, you upset the devil's camp. The balance of power in the spirit realm is shifted, and God's Kingdom gains the upper hand.

Another method the enemy uses to prevent the glory of God—God's manifested presence—from spreading, is to tempt believers to maintain worldly lifestyles. You cannot stand with one foot in the devil's camp and the other in the Kingdom of God. You cannot serve two masters. You cannot offer the members of your body as weapons for both righteousness and unrighteousness.

When God wants to perform miracles and bring revival, He always begins by waking up and cleansing His people, so that they can believe and obey Him. When God wanted to do a new thing and bring the children of Israel into the promised land, He said, *Consecrate yourselves, for tomorrow the Lord will do amazing things among you* (Josh 3:5).

A Wave of Cleansing

When God wants to perform miracles and manifest His presence and power, His people must first be purified and consecrated to Him. God cannot use a people with divided loyalties, who are unclean through sin, or dominated by the spirit of this world. Sin in the camp will always block the power of God. When believers sink to this world's moral standards, the power of God can never be unleashed among them.

You adulterous people, don't you know that friendship with the world is hatred toward God? Anyone who chooses to be a friend of the world becomes an enemy of God (James 4:4). This does not concern outward sins only like sexual laxity, theft, murder or the love of money, but it also includes more "respectable" sins such as jealousy, ambition, squabbling, back biting and a critical spirit and a judgmental attitude.

As believers, we do not have the same standards as the world. When the world criticizes and condemns, we acquit. Where the world finds fault and complains, we commend and encourage. As Paul says in 1 Corinthians 4:12-13, *When we are cursed, we bless; when we are persecuted, we endure it; when we are slandered, **we answer kindly***. Paul had a different standard—he answered kindly and was conciliatory. He spoke words from the Living God, instead of current popular opinions.

There is tremendous power in the Word of God. In times of criticism and siege, you must not begin to mull over all the negative things happening around you. Meditate instead on the Word and declare what it has to say about the matter. When you speak it forth, the Word of God will release its own power to change those circumstances. Thus, your tongue becomes an instrument for the Lord to do His deeds and manifest His glory. He wants your mind and tongue to be channels for His Gospel, which is the power of God for salvation—not a gutter for sewage distribution.

There is a wave of cleansing passing through the Church today. Unscriptural, religious thinking with its traditions and worldly behavior are giving way to purity, holiness and faith, so that the glory of the Lord can be revealed.

The Bible talks about the Church as the Lord's army but an army without clothing, food and ammunition is unserviceable. An army of starving, shivering soldiers is unfit for duty. An army torn by internal strife, without a clearly defined target, which does not take its task seriously, is useless.

The Lord has long inspected His troops with the intention of preparing them for the struggle for God's power and glory that lies ahead. *For our struggle is not against flesh and blood, but against the rulers, against the authorities, against the powers of this dark world and against the spiritual forces of evil in the heavenly realms* (Eph 6:12). We must be equipped and armed by the Lord to reach out effectively with the Gospel, so that the masses can be saved.

God has told us at Word of Life Church and Bible Center that our task is to **"Arm God's people with His word of faith, train them to use the spiritual weapons He has given them and send them out in victorious battle for the Lord."** That is the commission God has given us and we praise Him that we already see thousands in Sweden, who have received the Word of the Lord and are walking in faith as never before. Christians everywhere are realizing the power in the Name of Jesus, in His blood, in the Word of God, in prayer and praise and worship.

Believers around the world are discovering their position in Christ and realizing their authority to tread on all the power of the enemy. More than ever, saints are seeing the spiritual gifts operate in their lives, along with a completely new boldness to witness about Jesus. As a result, many people are being saved and the Gospel is having a far greater effect on our society than it has for a long time.

We are grateful to God for the opportunity to play a part in all He is doing in Sweden and the world, today. We take the storms, attacks and criticisms as a sign of the enemy's uneasiness as he sees believers becoming aware of their advantages over him, acting in faith on the Word of God and going forth in their new found liberty.

7

The Fields are Ripe for Harvest

If you hold to my teaching, you are really my disciples. Then you will know the truth and the truth will set you free (John 8:31,32).

God wants His children to be free, but there are no shortcuts to liberty. I cannot be set free simply by **listening** to the Word. I must hear the Word and take it to myself, just as though every promise was to me, personally. The experience of the children of Israel should be an example for us. They heard the Word, but never really received it with faith into their hearts (Heb 4:2), and so the Word did not remain in them.

The Word of God is living, powerful and active. But it can only bring the knowledge of which Jesus speaks, where it is received and allowed to remain. Then, we will know the truth and the truth will set us free. Everywhere, the people of God are being attacked by demonic powers trying to stop the Word from reaching their open hearts. When they do hear it, these same powers hinder them from actually receiving it. But, the Bible declares, He who is in us is greater than he who is in the world! The Helper, the Holy Spirit, lives in us, teaching us "all the truth."

Today, there is a powerful anointing upon the teaching of the Word of God, making it more living and vital than ever. The Holy Spirit, the Teacher, is instructing and anointing those with ministries to teach as never before. People are taking hold of God's Word, coming to an understanding of their inheritance in Christ Jesus and making the decision that the Word, and nothing else, is to form the foundation of their life.

This is why we are seeing many people entering their liberty, being rooted and grounded in the Word of God and having a powerful anointing on their lives and ministries. Ministers who just a few years ago, were living in obscurity, are now traveling from country to country bringing the message and reality of freedom to different nations. Prayer groups and fellowships that were weak are now growing and thriving, and their members are becoming fearless witnesses for Jesus.

Get Ready to be a Reaper

We are living in a momentous time of preparation—an opportunity that will not return. When the harvest is ripe, it is too late to begin sharpening the tools. They must already be prepared. At harvest time, one must know both **what** to do and **how** to do it. A reaper who persists in running around, asking the others what to do, becomes a burden to the work. A soldier who can't use his own weapon but hopes the others can, becomes a greater asset to the enemy than to his commander.

When a spiritual harvest time arrives, it is marked by both activity and resistance. The enemy will not sit twiddling his thumbs while people are being gathered into God's barn. He will retaliate with pelting rains, floods and winds (Matt 7:25). He will attack and put up resistance. But if the workers stand firm in their purpose, like a house built on the rock, they will prevail.

Just as a house will remain standing if the foundation has been carefully laid, so your life will remain steady and stable, if its foundation is sure. Now, is the time to lay that firm foundation in your life, to dig down to the first principles of the doctrine of Christ. Now, is the time to be unashamed of the simplicity that is in Christ and to allow the Holy Spirit to establish us firmly on the Lord and furnish us fully with His Word. Now is the time to be fully equipped and armed so that when we speak, the Word will burst forth from our spirits like a sharp two-edged sword.

When the Holy Spirit draws the Word out of our spirits and we proclaim it in faith, it will devour all satanic resistance like a flaming sword and win life and liberty for men and women. Therefore, we must dwell in the Word so it becomes living and burning in our spirits. Preparation is not a waste of time. Don't let impatience cause you to fret. Many people want to reap before they've sown—and then become frustrated when they don't see the promises fulfilled. God always keeps His Word—if **we** keep the conditions. The time between sowing and reaping is important. If you remain in the Word and let the Word abide in you, the harvest will arrive without fail—and you will reap.

In Sweden, we are living in a time when a ripened harvest is waiting throughout the land. A heat-wave of God's glory is already breaking over us and a great deal of resistance in the spirit realm has already broken. As the Spirit of God is poured out like a flood in your own country, the seed of the Word in you will be watered and grow. But this can only happen if you have taken the time to sow in your heart. The result will be a yield of signs and wonders, of healing and mighty deeds, of deliverance from demons and of people being born again. Many ministries will blossom and become what God intended them to be. The Spirit of glory and of God will rest upon groups and individuals in a new way. People will see that Jesus is alive today as the glory of God fills His temple, the Church.

Black will be as black as ever and white will be whiter and purer. The contrast between death and life, and flesh and spirit, is already becoming clearer, and the flesh is losing ground.

Many man-made opinions are backing off as the Body of Christ rises to its feet like a giant—free from its chains. The army of God is beginning to advance and go on the attack, sure of victory and success in all it undertakes. The reapers also know what to do. They are no longer sitting, discussing the job with one another. They're getting down to it.

The fields are ripe. It's time to prepare for all the Lord has commanded us to do!

8

You Can be an Effective Witness!

Many Christians live with a sense of condemnation and self-reproach about their witnessing. Knowing that they ought to testify, they feel inadequate or almost like traitors because of missed opportunities to share Jesus with their non-Christian friends. Witnessing has become a chore and brings feelings of guilt, or causes them to come up with various excuses like "...not mature enough yet."

God does not want it to be like that, and He has a wonderful way of setting you free to become a bold and joyful witness. First, you must know that you are called to be a witness. The very first thing Jesus said to His disciples was, *Come follow me...and **I will** make you fishers of men* (Matt 4:19). If you confess Jesus as your Lord and want to follow Him wholly and unreservedly, He has **promised** to make you a fisher of men. A fisherman is someone who catches fish. He doesn't just watch while others haul in their catch, without ever getting anything himself. No, he himself nets them continually too. Why? Because he's a fisherman by profession.

It is the same with your calling as a Christian. You are a fisher-of-men, regardless of your background, profession or situation. The Lord wants to change your self-image from one of failure or disobedience to one of success. It is the devil who loves to torment Christians, accusing them of missed opportunities or lack of boldness. But even if you have never yet led one person to the Lord, stand up in your inward man and confess the Word of God with your mouth, saying, "I follow Jesus. He has called me to become a fisher of men. He always does what He has promised, so in the Name of Jesus I am a fisher of men and I will make my catch. People will be saved as I witness to them because the Word of God never returns to Him unfruitful. It never returns without accomplishing all that it was sent out to do."

As the disciples hesitated about their ability, Jesus said to them in Luke 24:48, *You are able to witness about these things* (Swedish Bible of 1917).

Go Out and Share the Good News

So first, Jesus told His disciples that they were to become fishers of men. The last thing He said to them was, *Go into all the world and preach the good new to all creation* (Mark 16:15). The first and the last words of Jesus are crucial. "Go out and pass on the Good News about eternal life, and fish people into my Kingdom." As you do, the Lord will cause the Word to work and be confirmed by signs and wonders. Whenever Jesus asks you to do something, He never leaves you helpless or unable to fulfill your task. In Acts 1:8 He says, *You will receive power when the Holy Spirit comes on you and you will be my witnesses.*

As a believer, you have been born of the Spirit of God and have the spirit of adoption (sonship) dwelling in you. However, you also need to be baptized and filled with the Holy Spirit, just like the disciples, who began to speak in other tongues as the Spirit enabled them (Acts 2:4).

Jesus had already told the disciples that through His Name (or on His behalf), the believers were to preach, cast out devils, speak with new tongues and lay hands on the sick (Mark 16:15-20).

When you were filled with the Holy Spirit, you were given power from heaven to be a supernatural witness. The Holy Spirit will take you to the right "waters." He will give you miraculous wisdom to answer questions and speak straight into the lives of people so that they will see that God is talking directly to them. The Holy Spirit will be manifested through signs and wonders that will confirm the Word as you witness. Of course, the devil knows all this and he will try to hold you back from witnessing—but you can go forward anyway. The greater One lives in you!

"Now," you may say, "I am filled with the Spirit already, but I don't feel any power to witness." You must know that the Spirit of God is not primarily a feeling. The Word says you have the power within you. When you act on that in faith, and go out to meet the world and open your mouth and talk about Jesus, you will unleash the power of God and the Holy Spirit will become your "Helper" (John 14:16, Swedish Bible). However, He will remain unable to help you until you make the first move! A helper assists someone else to accomplish what he is already doing. You must be doing something, so the Helper can be manifested in your life.

How Are You to Witness?

How then, do you begin?

1. Start by confessing that you are a witness and expect God to use you. Resist every thought of inability. You may feel that your knowledge of the Bible is poor, but you know much more than non-Christians, and the little you know is enough.

2. Remember, you are a witness, not the counsel for the defence. God did not ask you to try and defend the whole Bible, or to explain all the so-called contradictions, nor to defend the behavior of every Christian throughout the course of history! You are to witness about Jesus.

3. Pray for opportunities that fit naturally into your everyday life, and when they come—take them.

4. Share what Jesus has done in your own life, and how He has changed you, rather than things that you have read in books. Don't defend religious organizations or take up controversial religious issues.

5. If you are witnessing in your job, remember that you were employed to work, not to witness. Let your working life be a testimony. The joy, honesty and diligence in your life will witness for you. If you are new at the job, try to be quick in sharing that you are a Christian. Later, when they notice what you are like, they will remember and relate it to God. It will make them curious and sooner or later, they will begin to ask questions. Then you can tell them about God's power, peace and joy in your life.

6. Remember that the power of God is available to the world and is the solution to all its problems. Be bold in praying with non-Christians about their problems. Usually they are tremendously appreciative that someone is willing to concern themselves with their worries.

7. Learn **how** to lead someone to the Lord. Do it as simply as possible. When they have prayed and received Jesus, be quick to follow them up. See them within twenty-four hours and give them some scriptures to stand on from the beginning (scriptures such as, 2 Cor 5:17, 1 John 1:9, 1 John 5:11-13, John 5:24, 1 Cor 10:13, John 16:24). Give them a Bible or a Bible portion, read with them and help them learn to pray in the Name of Jesus. Encourage them to begin sharing with others what Jesus has done in their life.

It is a tremendous joy to see a person receive Jesus Christ as his or her personal Savior and to see their lives changed! God wants to reach many people through you, but you can't reach many until you have reached one. Here, at Word of Life Church, we are seeing people saved each week, and recently there has been a remarkable increase. Why? Because the believers themselves go out and win others, often one by one. Let the power of God flow through you to win one soul, and another, and then another. "But I'm so insignificant," you may say. God says in Isaiah 60:22, *The least of you will become a thousand, the smallest a mighty nation.* Take hold of that promise and start at your own "Jerusalem" by leading **one** person to the Lord.

When someone is willing to receive Jesus, you can pray with him or her as follows: *"Father, I confess Jesus as my Savior and Lord. I believe that He died for my sins, and that He was raised from the dead that I may receive eternal life. Jesus, come into my heart now. Thank you, Father, for the Holy Spirit who now makes me a new creation. Thank you making me your born-again child. All the promises in your Word now belong to me. Thank you for Jesus who is my Savior, my Lord, my Shepherd and my Healer. In the name of Jesus I will go on with Him. Amen."*

Right now you are a witness. You have the power of God and God wants you to testify. Jesus has "fish" waiting for you, so go out to the waters and start to catch them!

9

Go Out With the Word of Faith!

There is nothing more satisfying in a person's life than doing what the Lord has told him to do. When he is obedient and sees the Lord bring results, he will praise the Living God.

We are living in times when the Body of Christ is beginning to rise up, like a sleeping giant. The Church is taking its rightful place here on earth and powerfully spreading the Gospel. However, a body without functioning members is sick, just as an army without trained soldiers is useless. A house cannot be built without materials and a vine cannot bear fruit without branches. So, although the Lord is raising up individual believers in a mighty way today and setting them on their feet, one person should never, and can never, do everything himself. Of course, the opposite is equally true—if each individual believer does nothing, then nothing will be done.

When you and I, as individual believers, begin to take our place and walk by faith, there are no limits to what the Lord can do, through us. Boundaries exist only because others have taught us that we are limited, that we can do little and that we must always have others' approval before we dare to do anything at all. Today, however, the Lord is changing things!

Believer, you are not insignificant! Jesus lives in **you**. **You** can hear God's voice. The Lord speaks directly to **you**. His Spirit leads **you** personally. **You** are precious to the Lord and **you** can be used by Him. The anointing of the Holy Spirit is for **you**! The unsaved can be won to the Lord through **you**. The sick are waiting for their healing through **you**. **You** can bring liberty to the captives.

God has so much in store for you because you are His dear child, His heir. So rise up and walk worthy of your calling. You do have a calling—even if you don't see the fullness of it yet.

Dream God's Dreams

God's freedom is for you, not just for others. You are not alone. Together, you and God are an unbeatable team. See yourself as God sees you and **do** what He tells you. Together you can win! A hundred previous defeats cannot stop God from winning through you today if you will only believe it.

God has put dreams, desires, visions and thoughts within you. Think about them. Dream them into existence! Many think that the good things they're longing for are too good to be from God, but they are from God! God is a good God. He is planning wonderfully for you. He's longing for you to believe what He is personally saying to you so it can become a reality in your daily life.

God gives people plans and ideas. You may long to lead a prayer group, witness to your neighbors or lay hands on the sick. You may have a longing to preach the Word of God, be a missionary or a Bible teacher. God has put that in you. Accept it and believe it because with God, you can do anything and go anywhere. He's longing to do the impossible through you.

Many people have talked openly about their visions. Don't talk about them. Cherish them, nurture and develop them. Prepare yourself to receive them. Develop your faith and fellowship with God so that you can fulfill them together. Be a doer of the Word!

When you align your life with these goals, you'll find that the level of anointing increases in your life and ministry so you can do what you're called to do. Perhaps you think you're too young, but that doesn't matter—so was Jeremiah. Nor does it matter whether you're known or not. Several of the prophets in the Old Testament are not even mentioned by name. What matters is that you are faithful to the visions and dreams God has given you. Then the anointing will carry you through.

Stand up! You are worthy to walk with God because of Jesus. Go out! God has given you the Word of faith. He is with you. The whole world is waiting for individual, liberated Christians, led by the Holy Spirit, who are doing what God has told them to do.

As you go out to do God's will, fellowship with others will no longer be a problem. You will be one in the Spirit and of one mind in the battle for the Gospel. You are like a grain of wheat sown in the earth and producing a hundredfold. When you leave the barn for the field, the power of God will accompany you and work increasingly through you. His life in you longs to flow out and inspire **multitudes** of others. The Holy Spirit in you is full of vitality and pulsating with life. His power breaks the paralysis, lethargy, fear and narrow-mindedness that has hindered the body of Christ from becoming a spiritual giant on the earth.

When you begin to walk by faith and take initiatives together with the Lord, to achieve the desire He has placed within you, then you'll know what "from faith to faith" means. Your whole body will spring to life. A sense of condemnation, apathy and domination from other people will not be able to suppress the living tide rising inside you. It will brim over! Believe that God's Word applies to you! Go out to others with the Word of faith and be a part of their restoration. Release them, so they can go out and receive God's highest and best for their lives, as well.

Nothing is more satisfying than seeing fruit, a vision fulfilled and God's goodness and glory made manifest in the lives of men and women.

10

You Can Cast Out Evil Spirits

Our struggle is not against flesh and blood, but against the rulers, against the authorities, against the powers of this dark world and against the spiritual forces of evil in the heavenly realms (Eph 6:12).

In 2 Corinthians 2:11, Paul says that we are not to be unaware of Satan's schemes. We must not be ignorant and thus allow him and to outwit us. God does not want us unaware of what is going on around us in the spirit world. He wants us to know who our enemy is and how we can defeat him.

In many Christian circles, people have avoided mentioning the devil. His existence has been toned down so much that, in some cases, Christians deny that he exists. If he is mentioned at all, it is as a warning not to overemphasize him, because they claim that he gets glory by being referred to. This is a grave mistake.

How can you fight the good fight of faith (1 Tim 6:12) if you do not know who your enemy is? You must be informed about him and understand how he works. You must realize what your position is in relation to him. If you are ignorant, he can outwit you (2 Cor 2:11).

Jesus calls the devil: the enemy (Matt 13:39), the evil one (Matt 13:19), the liar and murderer (John 8:44), the thief (John 10:10), the prince of this world (John 12:31), and Beelzebub (Matt 10:25). He was not ignorant of His enemy, and you can't afford to be either. However, don't be afraid of him, because Jesus has overcome him, stripped him of his weapons and put him to shame (Col 2:15). This defeat, though, does not mean that he has stopped counterattacking, tempting, lying, stealing and destroying. He launches concentrated offensives against believers in an attempt to steal their victory, and to stop them from reaching out to the world with the glory of God. Even so, the Scriptures declare that if we resist him, he will flee from us! (Jas 4:7).

One of the names Jesus used when referring to Satan is Beelzebub (Matt 10:25), which means "lord of the flies." In Matthew 12:24, Jesus more specifically calls him *Beelzebub, prince of the demons*. In other words, Satan is a prince over evil spirits who are subject to him. If we believe the Bible and understand that Satan exists, we must also believe in the existence of evil spirits. Jesus did, and confronted them and cast them out.

Two Kingdoms in Conflict

The Bible says that two kingdoms are at war with one another. One is "the kingdom of the Son God loves," whose Lord and King is Jesus Christ, and the other is "the dominion of darkness" (Col 1:13) where Satan, who is also called "the ruler of the kingdom of the air," is lord (Eph 2:2).

These two kingdoms are not equal in size. God and Satan are not two well-balanced, opposing powers. God is an omnipotent and omniscient God while Satan is a rebellious former angel who, it is generally believed, drew a third of the angelic host with him in his fall (Rev 12:4).

By His death and resurrection, Jesus received the keys of death and Hades. He has all power in heaven and on earth. He is the head of the Church, His body, and this gives us as believers, a tremendous advantage over Satan—if we will use it.

Although the final showdown took place on the cross, the victory Jesus won must still be proclaimed and enforced, and the ground must be held. Whenever the Church does that, it comes against all kinds of resistance, counterattacks and persecutions. Then, we must realize that we have a battle to fight. However, our warfare is not with people. Our struggle is against *spiritual forces of evil in the heavenly realms* (Eph 6:12).

The devil and his host are structured like an army. Evil spirits of differing rank are his rulers, authorities, world powers and demon forces. There are spirit rulers set over certain regions and lands (Dan 10:13,20), as well as over cities (Rev 2:12,13). There are powers that are specialized in different kinds of sin. This also applies to demons on the lowest ranks of the hierarchy of evil.

Some examples are a "spirit of infirmity" (Luke 13:11, NKJ), a "deaf and mute spirit" (Mark 9:25), an "unclean spirit" (Matt 12:43, NKJ), a "deceiving spirit" (1 Tim 4:1), the "spirit of this world" (1 Cor 2:12) and a "spirit of divination" (Acts 16:16, NKJ).

There are numerous other demons whose job is to possess, hinder, spoil, steal, and even take the lives of men and women. When Jesus gave the Great Commission in Mark 16:17-18, He made it plain that those who believe in Him would cast out demons. Just as Jesus Himself expelled evil spirits, He has authorized, commanded and empowered us believers to do the same:

Jesus declares, *I have given you authority to trample on snakes and scorpions and to overcome* **all** *the power of the enemy; nothing will harm you* (Luke 10:19). We have a mandate from Jesus Himself to cast out evil spirits.

Sadly, we have been unaware of the authority He has given us and of the necessity of routing the enemy from his strongholds, so that men and women can be set free. Any talk of evil spirits has seemed medieval and frightening. Fear of man has made us compromise. We have refused to take up one of our most powerful weapons, and have by that hindered the liberation of thousands of people.

Demons exist and you make it easier for them if you deny it. However, they are defeated through Jesus' victory over Satan and in His Name, you are commanded to use your authority to cast them out and set people free.

Jesus spent about a third of His time expelling evil spirits. The works that He did, we must do also (John 14:12).

The Root Cause of all Sickness

Usually, when evil spirits and sickness are mentioned, two questions arise: 1) Are evil spirits behind all sickness? and 2) Can a Christian have evil spirits?

Concerning the first question I do not believe that everything that afflicts us is caused by evil spirits. However, this is usually not the main problem. People have called all sorts of ailments, evil spirits. The problem has been that one hasn't dared to see that certain troubles are, in fact, due to the influence of evil spirits.

The Bible speaks of both the flesh and evil spirits. When Jesus ministered to men and women, He both healed and delivered them. All was not deliverance and neither was all healing, but it is remarkable how often these two went together. In Matthew 4:24, Jesus healed both the sick and the possessed. In chapter 12 verse 22, He healed a man who was possessed, blind and dumb. In chapter 17 verse 18, he drove out evil spirits from a boy, and He cured him. So the words "healed" and "cured" are used when Jesus delivered people from evil spirits, though not all the healing Jesus performed was deliverance from demons.

The ultimate cause of sickness is Satan, not God. Sickness entered the world at The Fall and ever since, sin, ailments, loneliness, hate, war, poverty and the like have consequently afflicted mankind.

However, just because Satan lay behind Adam and Eve's sin and fall does not mean that everyone who is sick is so because of personal sin.

On the contrary, Jesus refutes the idea when answering His disciples' query about why a man was blind. The disciples asked, *"Rabbi, who sinned, this man or his parents, that he was born blind?"* Jesus responded by saying, *"Neither this man nor his parents sinned...but this happened so that the work of God might be displayed in his life"* (John 9:2-3).

Sickness plagues the world because mankind allowed itself to be led astray by Satan at the onset of history and so fell into sin. As long as we live here, we will experience attacks, but Jesus came to show us the way out of every form of bondage and imprisonment. That's why in Acts 10:38 it says, *God anointed Jesus of Nazareth with the Holy Spirit and power, and...he went around doing good and healing all who were under the power* (oppression and bondage) *of the devil, because God was with him.*

The enemy oppresses people in many different ways, including sickness; but in Jesus, there is healing, deliverance and restoration. That's why He came. As mentioned earlier, all sickness is not caused by evil spirits or possession. However, it is a form of oppression from the enemy, and not something God puts on us for our discipline or advancement in holiness.

Deliverance is the Children's Bread

The other question that often arises is: Can a Christian be possessed? The answer depends on what one means by the word "possessed." If it means a person's spirit, soul and body are totally occupied by demonic powers, then I do not believe that a Christian can be possessed. But if it means that the soul of a believer (that is, his will, emotions and intellect), can be attacked, influenced, oppressed, bound or occupied by demons, then I believe it. A Christian can have demons in the same way that he can be sick.

When you were born again, you received a new spirit. The spirit of the world left, and the Spirit of God took up His home in your spirit. You became a new creature in Christ Jesus, but your mind wasn't automatically renewed or your body necessarily healed. However, on the grounds of Jesus' redeeming work, you came into a position where you could claim and receive liberty as a covenant blessing in every area of your life.

Luke 13:10-16 describes a woman who was possessed by a spirit of sickness and Jesus freed her. We have often been taught from this text that healing is part of Abraham's covenant.

In Mark 7:25-30, we read the account of a Syrophoenician woman asking deliverance for her daughter. Again, we have frequently been taught that "healing is the children's bread", that healing is a blessing only for the covenant people, and that this woman, by faith, laid claim to it. This is correct, but when we read these two narratives, we find they both deal, not with sickness, but with deliverance.

The woman in Luke 13, was bound by a spirit of sickness and Jesus said of her in verse 16, *Should not this woman, a daughter of Abraham, whom Satan has kept bound for eighteen long years, be set free on the Sabbath day from what bound her?* What does He mean? He means that healing and deliverance belonged to her as a partner in the covenant. After all, she was a daughter of Abraham!

Today, you and I **as believers**, are sons and daughters of Abraham. Galatians 3:29 says, *If you belong to Christ, then you are Abraham's seed, and heirs according to the promise.* The blessings of the covenant, (in this case, deliverance,) not only belonged to that woman, but through faith in Christ, to us also who have become beneficiaries of that same covenant.

Deliverance is available to believers today. The Syrophoenician woman discovered that deliverance is "the children's bread." We are God's children, and so deliverance is our bread, too. If we say that deliverance is not meant for believers then neither is healing.

"But," you may counter, "it doesn't say in the Epistles that believers will be delivered from evil spirits." It doesn't say they won't be either! Nor does it say anywhere in the Epistles that we are to go out and evangelize! Yet we know we must! Why? Because Jesus said we should. We've heard many sermons on it and there are results when we do.

Jesus also said we will cast out evil spirits. He did not say, "Cast evil spirits out of unbelievers." He said, "Those who believe will drive out demons" (Mark 16:17). Out of whom? Out of whoever has need of it, and wherever we may meet them!

Jesus has given us authority over **all** the power of the enemy (Luke 10:19) so that men and women can experience the wonderful freedom for which Jesus died and meant us all to have. That is why it would be disloyal to Him to deny or compromise on a truth which means so much for people's lives.

When a person comes into freedom, former hindrances are rolled aside and the glory of God flows through him and out to others. Then, they will see more clearly than ever, that Jesus is alive and that He is the answer to mankind's every problem.

CONSECRATION

*As the deer pants for streams of water, so
my soul pants for you, O God.*

Psalm 42:1

11

Identification with Christ

There are three things you need to know to be able to function effectively in faith. The first is: **Who God is**. Included in this are two major areas—what God has and what God can do. The second is: **Who you are**—what you have and what you can do, Finally, you need to know: Who your enemy is—what he has and what he can do, and more importantly, what he can't do when you stand on God's Word. If you have these three facts clearly established in your life, you will be able to walk as a victorious Christian and withstand Satan's attacks.

In this chapter, we will concentrate on the second point: Who you are in Jesus Christ.

> Neither circumcision nor uncircumcision means anything; what counts is a new creation (Gal 6:15).

Everything in the Christian life stands or falls depending on whether or not you are a new creation. It is absolutely vital that you identify yourself with the new man so he can take form within you and express himself through you. **What is in the new creation** will then become a reality in your life and you will serve God in the way He desires.

The Scripture speaks of a **new** man because there is an old one. When Adam sinned and fell, he died spiritually. At that moment, poverty, sickness and sin were released and death came into existence, both physically and spiritually. Man became separated from God and remained in that position until Jesus appeared, as the last Adam, to reconcile mankind with God. Jesus was the first example of the new man, or the new creation. He is our example of what a man should be and how he should conduct himself in every situation. Jesus was not only our Redeemer but He was also God's Pattern for us to follow. *In this world we are like him* (1 John 4:17). Man, who was inwardly dead and at enmity with God, received both forgiveness for sins and a new man formed within him, through the Holy Spirit, as a result of Jesus' death and resurrection.

I am not an old "sinner" saved by grace. I was once a sinner who is now saved by grace, but I have become a new creature. God has set up His home in me. This fact is so revolutionizing that if you really see what it means, you'll praise God from dawn to dusk, daily! He has recreated you! You are now in the image of God!

God has not only forgiven your sins, He has raised up **a person within you who never previously existed.** It makes no difference what your background is, what disappointments you've had or how many defeats and awful experiences of "Christian" traditions may lie behind you. Those things have nothing to do with who you are now. If you are a new creation, then everything is new. *The old has gone* (2 Cor 5:17), and something completely new has taken its place. This means you have a nuclear bomb inside you, with all the energy that God Himself possesses! It has been placed within you. God Himself lives in you and you have access to all the power He has, as well as all the wisdom, strength and love He can give. God wants to help you, so that what you have been given can be realized inside you and launched out through you!

Supernatural Life

Your identity is no longer in the old man, your flesh, your failures or your past behavior, but in what God has put within you by his Holy Spirit. Once this really dawns on you, a new way of living will begin. God has not called us to a religious life but to a supernatural one!

Your starting point is tremendous! It is absolutely crucial that you realize this or you will never have a chance to do what God wants. Your identity must be completely clear to you. You can never be led by God's Spirit, if you're always digging in the rubbish of your past life. You will only invite the devil to rob you of your power and weaken you. You must identify with who you are in Jesus Christ and what you can do through Him.

We are told in Acts 10:38, *how God anointed Jesus of Nazareth with the Holy Spirit and power, and how he went around doing good and healing all who were under the power of the devil.* This is the Jesus who lives in you! All that Jesus did here on earth, He wants to do through you. Everything He said then, He wants to say through you, today. All that He was, He is in you, today.

"But," you may say, "I've never felt anything of what you're talking about." That is irrelevant. We are not talking about "how" you are, but "who" you are. You may, of course, be living far beneath your privileges, like a prince existing as a beggar in a foreign country. But when you begin to accept and confess who you really are, life will become what you've longed for.

The first time I saw God heal people through my praying for them was two or three weeks after I'd spoken with an unbelieving lecturer at a university. I had written a paper on healing. Later, he approached me somewhat sarcastically and quipped, "Well, how about it then? Have you healed anyone lately?" I felt a holy wrath rise within me over the unbelief coming out of him. I answered, "When I lay my hands on the sick, they recover. Mark 16 says that believers will lay their hands on the sick—and I'm a believer—and they will recover! So when I lay my hands on them, they get healed". And I'd never laid hands on a sick person in my life! What happened was that faith was released. Instead of saying, "Er, ahem...you never know what may happen," I stepped right out and said, "This is what the Word of God says!"

When I affirmed His Word, I got what I said. About two weeks later, we held a service and God healed the sick. It was fantastic to see it. It was the first time I was used in that way. God stands by His Word!

Confess what God Says about You

If this seems strange, then you need to know that it is not a question of just rattling off Bible verses, but a case of answering "Yes" to what God has said about you. If God has said you are a new creation, then you are a new creation. If God calls you an overcomer, then you are an overcomer. If He calls you His friend, His servant and His steward, then that's what you are. No matter what others may say about you and regardless of what your flesh says, you are what God says you are. God wants to use you and is fully able to do so.

See yourself in that light. The Jesus we preach is not a Jesus just sitting cuddling a lamb on His knee. It is Jesus, the Lion of the tribe of Judah! It is the Jesus who is the same yesterday, today and forever—who went about healing everyone. That is the Jesus who is working through you. **He does the work!** That means you can relax because it's not you who is going to do it anyway.

God has not said we're to **try**. He has told us to **do** it. The attitude that says, "All right, we'll try this idea of confessing God's Word for a couple of weeks" will never work. Let it be a deep conviction within you, that when the Word of God fills your inner man, it will do the work. When it is spoken out of your mouth there will be repercussions in your life and surroundings. If instead of praying for one sick person and then giving up, you continue to pray for the next one, and then the next, you will see how the Holy Spirit responds.

Suddenly, you'll see signs and wonders as God confirms His Word in your ministry. This applies whether you have one of the five-fold ministry gifts or are just an ordinary witness for Jesus.

The revival we are going to see will be spread by "ordinary" believers who know they are new creations—and that when they lay hands on the sick, they will recover.

Jesus Christ lives in you! When you were born again, you became a participant in His divine nature. This means that God Himself imparted His own nature to you. 2 Peter 1:4 says that He actually gave of His own being and qualities to you. It is this nature that is to influence and characterize your life.

When God gave you life, He gave you all He is and has. He gave you His health—deposited in your inner man. God gave His riches to you and they are also deposited within you. God gave His wisdom and anointing to you and they are implanted in you. Therefore, when you enter any situation, it is really God Himself stepping in there with you. According to Philippians 2:15, you are a light shining in the world. You are a blessing in whatever situation you find yourself.

The "humility" that says, "I'm nothing, I can't do anything," is only inverted pride. True humility is to submit your thoughts to God's thoughts. I bow the knee to God and acknowledge Him to be right when He says that I have sinned. I reply "Yes and amen" to everything else He says, as well.

Pride says, "It's not really that simple. We can't take the Bible that literally, can we?" That kind of attitude seems humble, but God wants to deliver you from it.

You must answer "Yes" to the fact that the promises are "Yes" in Jesus Christ: "Yes" that you suffer no lack, "Yes" that God is taking care of all your needs, "Yes" that your prayers are answered and "Yes" that you have the power to do what you're called to do. Many weights will fall from your shoulders and lie dead at your feet when you do so.

When you allow God to establish the fact of the new creation within you, your eyes will be opened and you will see Him as He really is. You'll see what will happen when you take the message of the Living God and Jesus Christ to the world—and that is exactly what He has called us to do. When we do it, God will perform miracles in and through our lives.

12

The Spiritual Man

The difference between believers and other people is the Holy Spirit. Without Him we are nothing. When God received you to Himself and saved you, He did not patch you up. He didn't take on an old house and renovate it. He built a totally new house.

We humans usually look on the outward appearance and because of this, we miss what's happening in the spiritual realm. When God does something, He doesn't begin with the exterior. He begins on the inside, in the invisible. Therefore, we must have our eyes firmly fixed on what is unseen instead of what we can see (2 Cor 4:18).

When you were born again, God created something completely new within you. He created an inner man who had never previously existed. It was, and is, an entirely new creation (2 Cor 5:17).

How did God create our inner man? Through the Holy Spirit! Romans 8:16 says, *The Spirit himself testifies with our spirit* (our inner man) *that we are God's children.*

The Bible uses many illustrations of the Christian. We are the temple of God: *Do you not know that your body is a temple of the Holy Spirit, who is in you, whom you have received from God? You are not your own* (1 Cor 6:19).

In other words, our body is a temple, and the Holy Spirit in His glorious presence, the "shekinah", fills the holiest of all in our temple. The holiest of all in your life is your inner man, and there, the Holy Spirit has set up His home.

Walk in the Spirit and Live in Victory

Every born again believer has the Holy Spirit within him. The new birth, came through the Holy Spirit. He is in Christ Jesus today, because he was brought into the body of Christ, through the Holy Spirit. Having been born of the Spirit, we are now to walk in the Spirit. This means that the abundant life implanted within us will now begin to issue out from us.

Romans 8:2 says, *Through Christ Jesus the law of the Spirit of life set me free from the law of sin and death.* The Spirit of God gives me life, and by walking in the Spirit, I walk in that life and blessing. I escape corruption and live in victory over sin.

God's Spirit supplies me with life from heaven. That is why Jesus said to Nicodemus in John 3:3, that he had to be born again, or "born from above," as the Greek says.

The Bible speaks of three categories of **life**: The first is *"bios,"* or physical life—that which makes your body live and function. The second is *"psyche,"* or the soul life, expressing itself through the mind, will and emotions. Finally, there is *"zoe,"* or spiritual life—the overflowing life, the life that is from God.

1 Corinthians 2:14 speaks of "the natural man." Other translations term it the "soulish man" or "the man without the Spirit." This is the unregenerate person who has *"bios"* and *"psyche"* but who does not have *"zoe."* The Bible says that kind of person, *does not accept the things that come from the Spirit of God, for they are foolishness to him, and he cannot understand them, because they are spiritually discerned* (1 Cor 2:14). What does this mean? It means that the life that comes from God is so different, that the normal soul life is not capable of understanding it or living it. That is why we must be born again!

An unregenerate person cannot live the Christian life. Many have tried and totally failed. It is not enough to try living up to the ethics of the sermon on the mount. Nor is it sufficient to be a man of fixed principle or to safeguard traditional values. It is possible to have opinions in line with Biblical teaching and still be lost and go to hell.

Conversion to the Core

A man or woman must be born again and receive the life of God into themselves. It is not enough to embrace Biblical doctrines with one's soul. Many have made this mistake. If preachers do not preach conversion and new birth, they only cover a wolf nature with a sheepskin. When crises and problems arise, the skin slides off and that old, unregenerate, adamic nature is revealed. It rebels against God, it refuses to follow Him and it does not understand spiritual things at all.

No wonder revival has a tough time in some established circles. Those in leadership and positions of authority in churches are not born again themselves! These are soulish people who adopt a generally conservative, moral position. They may be a little more well-manicured and cultivated than the man in the pub and therefore see themselves to be superior, but they still have the same unregenerate and depraved nature that the Bible calls "the old man."

When revival comes at last, and people begin to be saved and healed, it is strange and foreign to them. They no longer feel at home in their old churches. When clapping, dancing and singing in the Spirit occur, and when people are "slain" in the Spirit, or laugh or cry, they react violently. They don't understand because it is *foolishness to him, and he cannot understand them, because they are spiritually discerned* (1 Cor 2:14).

No wonder there are problems. Spiritual things cannot be received on a mental and soulish level. First, the soulish life must be annihilated and die. You must make a complete turnaround and realize your need of the cross and blood bought salvation in Jesus Christ. You have nothing to offer God, but He has something wonderful to offer all mankind—a completely new life in Christ, the life of the Spirit.

Some people try to jump on the bandwagon of God's activities, but on their own conditions and with their own personal ambitions or other ulterior motives in mind. These motives are always rooted in the ego. One wants to be great, another wants prestige and position, and yet another wants to be a know-it-all. God accepts no such motives and can never use such persons to the full.

It is interesting to see how soulish, unregenerate or carnal Christians respond in crises when things don't go their way. They often react strongly. If their soulish ambitions are unmasked by the Spirit of God, repercussions are usually quick in coming. They are like a spoiled child. All is well as long as they get their own way—but if anyone confronts them, what is really in their heart comes out. Self-pity, self-righteousness, anger, slander and all kinds of bitter talk begin to spread. Why? Because the soulish, fleshly self-life had been camouflaged beneath fashionable, religious and pious talk.

When a person is born again, he is not immediately made perfect. He is still in his flesh. However, Romans 8:12 says that we have no obligation to the flesh. We are to live and be led by the Spirit.

A newly born believer needs to renew his mind. The old mental ruts where he has tramped back and forth still furrow his mind, as God's Spirit begins to present new thoughts to him and lifts him out of the old ways and up to another level. That's why there are always teething problems in infant believers and in new situations where God is at work.

God Looks on the Will and the Motives

It is always important to look on the heart. If a person's heart is right, God's pleasure is there, even if carnality is present.

God deals with fleshiness as a man grows in Him and begins to recognize what is fleshly, worldly or demonic influence and rejects it immediately.

"But," you may say, "is there a key about how to do it?" Yes! Resist your adversary, the devil, and stand **steadfast in the faith**. The key word for putting him to flight is **faith**. Therefore, it is no wonder that he hates the word **faith** and does everything in his power to obstruct the believer from growing and walking in it!

God looks on the heart. He looks on the person's willingness to humble himself under Jesus and flow with the life issuing from his regenerated spirit. The *"psyche"* (soul life) must submit itself to the *"zoe"* (spiritual life) so that the spiritual life can flow out with God's love, presence, wisdom and power. Jesus must be Lord of the will and of the intellect as well as of the spiritual life. If Jesus really is my Lord, His Word will work in my life because I have given up all my soulish, egotistical and other personal ambitions of being in the limelight. This is where the battle line is really drawn in a believer's life.

Galatians 5:17 (NKJV) says, ***The flesh lusts against the spirit, and the spirit against the flesh;*** *and these are contrary* (at war) *to one another, so that you do not do* (are hindered from doing) *the things that you wish.* In this battle, it is possible for the soul and mental life to deceive people. If my thoughts, emotions and will are not truly submitted to Jesus, then, like Ananias and Sapphira in Acts 5, I will retain things for myself. I will have ulterior motives and I will be steered by rebellion, a soulish life and my ego instead of the Spirit of Jesus.

What does that mean? It means that there are areas in my life where I nurse selfish ambitions which I am not willing to give up. I camouflage them instead with religious phrases, so that my soulish life won't be discovered by those around me. People like this can sound so nice and pious and even quote lots of Bible verses, but behind it all, the ego is ruling everything. They've never really surrendered everything or paid the necessary price to receive what God is offering and they're not willing to go where God wants. They want the blessing without obeying Him from the depths of their lives, or without acknowledging His way of doing things. This is a constant danger, even in new churches where God is working.

Whenever God does anything new, people who have hungry hearts but who are not perfect, join in. Jesus loves it. He has always been a master at dealing with imperfect people. However, at the same time, people who have somewhat doubtful motives and others with completely wrong ones, also begin to arrive. When Paul warns in 1 Timothy 6:5 against using godliness as a means for personal gain, he is not referring only to money, but also to soulish ambitions and lust for position.

God works through imperfect people who are devoted to Him and accept His conditions. Devotion means that I totally surrender myself so that God's life, not my own, can shine through me. God must be allowed to do **what** He wants, **in the way** He wants, **when** He wants, **how** He wants and **through whom** He wants. He decides, because He is Lord, not me.

This kind of attitude will make it impossible for me to act like Naaman the leper who wanted his healing **in his own way**. When it didn't turn out as he'd thought it should, he became angry and wanted to go home. However, when he humbled himself, he was made well. He was blessed only when his underlying pride and wrong motives were revealed and he humbled himself.

God's Word Divides Between Soul and Spirit

Consecration of this kind paves the way for the Spirit of God to lead men and women into all that He has for them. Opposition, disappointments and backbiting will then no longer give rise to fleshly reactions of bitterness and self-pity. Instead, life in the Spirit will continue to flow and God can then accomplish His will. Although the spiritual person is not yet perfect, he or she is pure. Motives and intentions are purged from egotistical cravings to be the center of attention and purified from jealousy and self-will.

Today, this is more important than ever because God is raising up leaders everywhere, who must possess these qualities. Many people have had problems with the role of leadership. They have considered it distasteful and wrong to take initiatives or a leading role. They've been afraid of appearing dominating or power hungry. The enemy has taken advantage of this to sow fear, doubt and uncertainty in leaders, to prevent them from doing what God has called them to do. As a result, many preachers are troubled by a bad conscience, hesitancy and an unsound dependence on others.

God has no intention of wiping out leadership. He wants rather, to ennoble it. Therefore our motives must be pure. We must no longer listen to Satan's religious reproaches which are aimed at producing a guilty conscience. He wants us to overthrow our God-given initiatives and abdicate our spiritual authority. If our motives are right, and we wholeheartedly long to please God and serve Him with a clean heart, then He will bless us. We have presented an acceptable sacrifice to God and His fire will fall from heaven. However, if our motives are mixed or aimed at self-gratification, they are egocentric, and God's fullest blessing cannot come. People's words may sound alike and they may have similar ideas; but one has a revelation, a word from God, while the other has a religious idea, a thought which in itself may be reasonable and correct, but it has underlying, hidden motives.

How can we discern between soul and spirit? Hebrews 4:12 says that the Word of God divides between them and *judges the thoughts and attitudes of the heart.* Hebrews 5:14 tells us that through the Word of righteousness, we should have our senses *trained...to distinguish good from evil,* and 1 Corinthians 2:15 says, *The spiritual man makes judgments about* (discerns) *all things.*

The Holy Spirit gives us the key to victory over the flesh. He will work with the Word of God to enable you to discern your underlying motives, if you really **want** to follow Jesus on His terms. In this way, you can be rightly guided and understand things that previously confused you. You will also discern between your mind, or soul, and your spirit. God's Spirit will then be able to lift you to a higher level where you can begin to act as a spiritual man or woman!

13

Your Gold in the Dust!

Accept instruction from his mouth and lay up his words in your heart. If you return to the Almighty, you will be restored; If you remove wickedness far from your tent and assign your nuggets to the dust, your gold of Ophir to the rocks in the ravines, then the Almighty will be your gold, and the choicest silver for you (Job 22:22-25).

God wants to remove everything that hinders you from following Jesus. This means that you must **settle in your heart who is going to be your Lord**. For example, those who suffer from the fear of man have other people as their Lord. People can have their church, their denomination, religious leaders—all kinds of things as their lord. God is saying that you are to lay aside anything and everything, even if it appears as precious and beautiful to you as gold. You must remove it, if it comes between you and Jesus, otherwise, you cannot do what He wants you to do. So, *assign your nuggets to the dust...and the Almighty will be your gold.*

Then, verse 26 says that you will delight in the Almighty and lift up your face to God. By aligning your life in this way you make the declaration, "I am going to follow Jesus, no one and nothing else. I'm going to do what He wants, not what others think I should do. I am simply going to follow Him. He is my Lord and Savior. I consecrate myself with all my heart to Him."

The Scriptures say that the eyes of the Lord search throughout the earth to strengthen those whose hearts are fully committed to Him. Nowhere in the Word of God does it say that because you happen to visit church on Sundays, and read your Bible once in a while, that God will hear you, answer your prayers and do just what you want! Never! It says that when you consecrate yourself to Him, follow Him and let Him purge your life of everything that would prevent you from being His disciple then *You will pray to him, and he will hear you* (Job 22:27).

A Living Sacrifice

Consequently, *What you decide on will be done* (Job 22:28), because you will have come into line with God's will. Your life will then be purged and purified, and, as it says in Romans 12:1, you will have presented your body a living, holy sacrifice to God. You will then be able to say, "I will not permit my knowledge (which is often reckoned as gold) to stand between me and God. I will not allow my experiences, feelings, education, friends, successes, and most important, my failures, to come between me and Him. I'll let nothing come there. I consecrate myself to Him. I accept no prestige from what I'm doing and I make myself available to Him. If He wants me to go and stand for hours on the square and play an accordion to His glory, I'll do it. I am willing to do anything for Jesus!"

Pride then disappears and any religious spirits that may be around, become very nervous, because they have no hold left with which to manipulate your life. The devil then knows that you will go to any lengths to do exactly what God wants, whenever and however He tells you to do it—regardless of what people may think. It has nothing to do with what others think or feel—because you've let the Almighty be your gold. Your joy is in Him. You delight in Him. He is your Shepherd and you do not want. He satisfies you. Even when you walk through the valley of the shadow of death, He's with you, supporting you, His rod and staff are there, keeping you. He prepares a bountiful table in the presence of your enemies and He makes your cup overflow.

When the Holy Spirit has helped and trained you to become what the Scriptures call "poor in Spirit" (Matt 5:3) you will become simple, whole hearted and only *one* thing will be important. Then, He will hear you and you will become sensitive in your spirit to pray those prayers that the Holy Spirit puts within you.

What you decide on will be done, and light will shine on your ways. When men are brought low and you say 'Lift them up!' then he will save the downcast (Job 22:28-29). The real intercession follows in verse 30, *He will deliver even one who is not innocent, who will be delivered through the cleanness of your hands.*

Abraham's experience was precisely this. Lot was not innocent when he lived in Sodom, but because of Abraham's prayers, he was saved. When you are led into intercession by the Spirit and travail until the birth of the answer, you will see Him deliver many who are not innocent. When you cry "Lift them up!" He will rescue those who are on their way down to the abyss and take them to Himself. Something happens in their lives so that they receive Jesus Christ. It happens because of the cleanness of your hands, your righteousness, and because of the prayers that the Holy Spirit put into you to pray.

Someone Must Pray the Harvest into Being

Take your stand, Christian! Rise up, daughter of Zion! Rise up and be who you really are! We can be in the very midst of an event without really being aware of it. So keep praying, and believe like Daniel, when he noticed in the Scriptures that the seventy years of Israel's captivity were nearly at an end. Nothing indicated either change or improvement. Everyone continued to preach as they always had, but Daniel saw what the Scriptures said and he began to pray. The prayers of one righteous man avail much, according to James 5:16. If the prayer of one righteous man gets a lot done, what will the prayers of three, one hundred, or ten thousand do! According to Jesus, we should discern the signs of the times and be aware of what's going on in the days in which we live (Matt 24:32,33), so we know what to pray.

When Abraham met the Lord who said "I am on my way to judge Sodom," he did not reply, "Just a moment, Lord, I'm having a little trouble with my flocks. Can you come over here and lay hands on them and heal them? I've had such problems with foot and mouth disease recently." He was not so taken up with his own circumstances that he couldn't hear what God was saying about something more important. He was sensitive and began to pray for Sodom.

When the Word says, *Ask the Lord for rain in the springtime* (Zech 10:1), start praying! God will send the rain. The time of the spring rains is approaching and we are in the end times, near the return of Jesus. Scripture tells us that before he comes, there will be a fully ripened harvest all over the world, so someone **must pray it into existence**. We must also begin to pray for workers who can go out to the fields and reap.

When rain starts to fall, the ground becomes softened and the seed begins to sprout. The seed is the living Word, filled with power. However, if the ground of your life has a crust on it, the power of the Word cannot be manifested in you, no matter how much you've heard it.

In the past, God has overlooked such ignorance but the nearer we come to the end, He will begin to work more rapidly, not only through miracles out on our streets, but also through signs such as happened to Ananias and Sapphira in the midst of the church. The sword is going to be wielded in judgment!

We must submit ourselves to the Word. There are some who have a show of submission, but who deny its power in their lives saying, "Of course I believe it all, but don't ask me to put it into practice." Such an attitude will automatically put a distance between us and God and we will not experience the full manifested presence of the Holy Spirit.

When Jesus rose again, the disciples' initial reaction was one of fear. However, when He began to expound to them from the Scriptures, showing them that events had taken place exactly as He had said, they began to put their faith in Him. It will be just the same when the Holy Spirit begins to do things that far exceed what we are used to. He will begin gently with you, taking good time. You will have plenty of opportunity to see things in the Scriptures, before being presented with the choice to either accept or reject them.

As the rains begin to fall you'll be among the first to say, "I'm going to be a part of this, I'm going to be a blessing to people around me." Why? Because you've been involved in its birth through prayer. Those people whom God is going to use in the revival that lies before us, are those who have travailed in its birth and prayed and prayed and prayed and prayed it into being! These are the ones who have come into line with the Word of God and know "the signs of the times." These are the people who are best equipped to carry it out in the way God has intended.

14

Be Eager to Know God

In Philippians 3:10-14, Paul makes a number of important statements. His heart and mind are after only one thing: *I want to know Christ and the power of his resurrection.* From the first day on the Damascus road to the day he finished his course, Paul had only one desire—to know Christ better. The whole of his life was one consuming hunger for the Living God and one great thirst for more of Jesus' resurrection power. In Acts 20:24 he says, *I consider my life worth nothing to me, if only I may finish the race and complete the task the Lord Jesus has given me—the task of testifying to the gospel of God's grace.* Paul had one single aim, one purpose only: to fulfill the commission God had given him and, as fully as possible, come to know His power.

The life Paul lived was no mundane, dreary, aimless existence. On the contrary! His life left a mark in history, not only in his own generation, but even in ours. When he entered a town it was said of him and his companions: *These men who have caused trouble all over the world have now come here* (Acts 17:6).

Through his life, the world has been changed. Why? Because **he** had been changed by Jesus. When we read of Jesus, Peter, Paul or other men of God throughout history, we think, "How wonderful that God chose them and used them! What a privilege! It would be terrific to be used like one of them." And we stop there, for we are sure that it was only for them and could never happen to us. For a second or two, we raise our spiritual sights to the example given us in the Scriptures, only to let our gaze fall again and get entangled again with the cares of this world, which like thorns and thistles, choke the Word within us.

For years, I read John 14:12 where Jesus says, *"Anyone who has faith in me will do what I have been doing. He will do even greater things than these."* Almost every time I read this verse I thought, "Yes, but I'm not like that and I can't ever be like it either." So the devil succeeded in rooting up what God had sown, and my sights were lowered again to the circumstances, lack and defeat in my life. But praise the Lord for revelation that is flowing from the Holy Spirit at this time! Praise Him that we can receive knowledge of who we are in the Lord and what we can do through Him. Praise the Name of the Lord that the contents of the Gospel are available for us, here and now—not just for them, then and there!

Your Works will not Frustrate God's Grace

You will not frustrate the grace of God by becoming active. After Paul was saved, Jesus revealed a mystery to him that had been hidden from the beginning of the world. That mystery was the Gospel of Jesus. Colossians 1:27 says that the mystery is; *Christ in you, the hope of glory*. Jesus in us is God's power. It is not a long way off, like something inaccessible or mystical. It is available and present within you through the Holy Spirit.

Even though God's power is within us and available to all of us, it is evidently more effective and flowing in some than in others. Why? The answer lies in what Paul says in Philippians 3:10-14. We know that **by the grace of God**, Jesus, with His power and presence, is made available to us all. Grace is what God has done for us.

We may be afraid of frustrating God's grace by doing things ourselves. We know that we can do nothing to earn our salvation, for Jesus has bought it for us. But that does not mean that we are to be inactive. Not at all! Because we are saved by grace, we become more active. The more you understand God's grace and what He has done for you, the more you do, not to win His favor or be accepted, but because you **are** accepted. You want to give the whole of your life to Him who gave His life for you. You deeply desire to know Him who has won you. When you begin to perceive the depths of what Jesus did for you on the cross, you will say as Paul did, "My life is nothing in itself. I just want to run my race and do all God has called me to do."

In Philippians 3:10, Paul says that *I **want** to know Christ and the power of his resurrection*. That is something more than a general desire. It is an active determination of the will—a quality decision that one has thought through and for which one is prepared to take the consequences. It is a final, immutable choice from which there is no turning back. You do not back down in the face of opposition. All opposition seems flimsy in the face of the strong desire to break through into the flow of His resurrection power. What else does Paul say? He continues, *I press on to take hold...straining toward what is ahead. I press on toward the goal* (v. 12-14). What does all this mean? It means that, with the whole of his being, he pressed toward obtaining what he knew was rightly his.

The devil will do everything in his power to withhold knowledge from you. If you do not know what is yours in Christ, you will neither expect it nor seek after it, When you do receive knowledge through the Word, he will try everything to stop it from being put into practice in your life and becoming a manifested reality to you.

One of the devil's methods is to get you to mentally learn and accept certain doctrines which you observe to be true. You are happy to hear them preached, but you never wholeheartedly seek the reality behind them. They never leave the level of head knowledge for the deeper, burning passion of your spirit to know Him and the power of His resurrection.

God Strengthens Those
Who are Fully Committed to Him

When you call to mind the answers to prayer you have received you'll often find a connection between them and times when you became desperate and stood on the Word. Why? Because you were wholehearted and laid aside everything that hindered you. You began to reach forward, totally determined to achieve your goal. Then, it became a reality in your life.

In 2 Chronicles 16:9, it says, *For the eyes of the Lord range throughout the earth to strengthen those whose hearts are fully committed to him.* Who are the ones He strengthens, or strongly supports? To whom is the power of His resurrection revealed? To those whose hearts are fully committed to Him! Those who reach out and press toward Him! They conduct themselves in a manner quite puzzling to the world and its adherents of religion. They do not hold just their intellect for God, but give themselves wholly to their Lord. Just as David danced before God, they dance before Him. When the mind says "Don't dance now, don't speak in tongues openly, don't clap, don't sing quite so loud, don't rejoice publicly over the devil's defeat..." their spirit presses on all the more passionately to know Him more and more! No one frightens the devil as much as an uninhibited believer who will not be intimidated by empty words and threats and who refuses to be robbed of his freedom and consecration. These are the ones with whom God will stand and whom He has promised to strengthen.

Why was Paul so earnest in pressing on to know Jesus? It was because he had seen Him! When you really **see** who Jesus is, what He has for you and what He's done for you, then you will **strain forward to know Him.** We must learn from what the Lord said to Abram. He told him, *Lift up your eyes from where you are and look north and south, east and* *west. All the land that you see I will give to you and your offspring forever* (Gen 13:14,15).

In Ephesians 1:18-19, Paul, led by the Holy Spirit, prays that the eyes of your heart may be enlightened and see your inheritance in Christ. It is only when you see what belongs to you, and take your eyes off yourself, to focus on what God has for you in Jesus, that you seriously begin to press on to know Him. When you discover that it is possible for you to live in victory, and that healing is really for you; when you realize that you can be free from the thing that binds you, then and only then, will you really begin to seek it.

Press on Toward the Goal—Don't Give Up!

You may receive information or even revelation about your rights of inheritance in Christ that have been bought by the precious blood of Jesus, but this is not enough. You must act upon what you know. A prisoner who receives notice of his reprieve and sees the prison gate open but who does not walk out, will never be free—no matter how much knowledge of his pardon he may have. That is why Paul said, "I press on." He had made up his mind. He involved his will. He engaged all his powers. He resolutely acted on his decision, pressing on toward the goal. He never gave up.

Some people will say, "I've tried all that teaching about faith and victory, but it didn't work." It will not help to just "try" it. It doesn't help to dip your little toe in the water. You must throw yourself in and swim. God wants to see you make a wholehearted decision to go with Him and then refuse to back down from it, regardless of the circumstances.

Every choice you make and every step you take toward God, will be challenged by the devil who, if he can, will keep you bound by your circumstance so you don't gain the victory. Tests, attacks and trials will be aimed like flaming arrows at stopping your walk in triumph. Therefore, God encourages you to *Fight the good fight of faith* (1 Tim 6:12). That's why He has given you an armor and *a shield of faith, with which you can extinguish all the flaming arrows of the evil one* (Eph 6:16).

"The three men in the flaming furnace" (Dan 3) had their faith tried, but they would not bow to difficult outward circumstances. When they refused to bow, they didn't have to burn. Why? Because a fourth person joined them, *and the form of the fourth is like the Son of God* (Dan 3:25, NKJV). Your decisions will be challenged, tried and tested. The devil will throw all he has at you to try and move you from the spiritual and supernatural into the soul realm and the flesh.

Once you are there, you are trapped and easily defeated. Don't let him dupe you with fine words. You are too important to the Kingdom of God to be held prisoner by the devil's lies. Make up your mind to let priorities be priorities. Get to know Jesus and the power of His resurrection.

God wants us to be well acquainted with His power. The power of God, attended by supernatural signs and wonders, has been rare and unfamiliar to many—but praise God, that is already a thing of the past. Throughout the world, believers are rising up and beginning to see *the riches of his glorious inheritance in the saints, and his incomparably great power for us who believe* (Eph 1:18-19). We are discovering what it is to flow in the supernatural. We are beginning to see how the power of God flows through a believer to meet a world in need. We are finding out who Jesus really is and seeing for ourselves that He is *the same yesterday and today and forever* (Heb 13:8).

To guard against this being only a mountain top experience in your life, you must decide that you "want to know Christ and the power of His resurrection." What Jesus has won for you is yours now. It belongs to you, so reach out for it, strain toward it and press on. Nothing is more important to you. You are not living for yourself. You need what God has for you so you can say like Peter in Acts 3:6, *What I have I give you. In the name of Jesus Christ of Nazareth, walk.*

15

Do You Know Your Father?

God is love. For the majority of Christians, this is already abundantly clear, but the question is, do we really understand this? The revelation that God is love, that He acts lovingly and that He shows His love to me, personally, is of immense importance. We need to be deeply convinced of this truth by a revelation in our hearts, so that it constantly guides our lives. When we begin to know God our Father in this way and see His love for us, our lives will change.

Fear, anxiety, loneliness, rejection, hardness, pride and indifference find no room where the love of God has been revealed. For this reason, it is not enough for us just to mentally assent that "God is love." We need the insight of this truth planted deep within us as our motivating and driving force. What we need is a revelation of who our Father really is.

Who is God? Let's refer to some things the Bible says about Him:

1. **God is almighty!** What does that mean? When we hear such words we often think in vague terms like "almighty" means that He created heaven and earth. This is true, but it means much more than that. It signifies that He is almighty toward you. It means that nothing is too hard for Him (Jer 32:17). Nothing is impossible for God. No hindrance, problem or circumstance in **your** life is so difficult that God cannot do something about it. That is what God's omnipotence means to you.

2. **God is love.** This means that God who **can** do anything is also **willing** to do anything. One definition of God's love is His willingness to use His almighty power. It is often no great problem to believe that God can—but that He will, and for me, is more difficult to accept and believe. We actually doubt God's love more than we doubt His power. That is why it is so wonderful when the leper in Matthew 8:2 cries, *Lord, if you are willing, you can make me clean,* to hear Jesus answer, "I am **willing**, be clean." The love of God expressed itself in His willingness to use His power and heal the leper.

God is love. That means that He loves everyone. He is no respecter of persons and has no special favorites. However, we often have the idea that He does have certain favorites whom He sanctifies more than others and equips with more gifts and graces. But this is wrong. If we think like that, we become guilty of causing personality cults and exalting men and women in a wrong way. This will either create idolization of the person, or conversely, discouragement, self-pity and envy in the one who doesn't consider himself as well-equipped, used, sanctified or loved. This attitude and thinking must be totally eradicated from our lives—even from the very depths of our hearts.

Identify with Who You Are

An incorrect attitude concerning the love of God, for example, thinking that God has favorites, can be extremely destructive. It can cause secret bitterness toward God in the belief that "He has abandoned me in favor of someone else." It can cause envy and gossip about someone whom God is using, tempting us to criticize rather than encourage him. It also causes us to forget that **we have our identity in who we are**, not in what we do. I **am** God's child, thoroughly loved and accepted. What I do or don't do is of secondary importance. When I know I'm loved, I can easily take second place. I don't need to always stand in the limelight. I don't have to exhibit my spiritual prowess, or prove that I hold the right theological views. My identity is no longer derived from these things. I can praise others and esteem them more highly than myself and let other Christians overtake me in their race. We're not competing with one another. Everyone has his own course to run.

When I see that God is love and that I am loved by Him, things become so very different. I no longer have to frantically seek people's appreciation and acceptance. The love of God is enough, and knowing that, I come into rest.

As He prayed to the Father, Jesus said: *"You...have loved them even as you have loved me"* (John 17:23). God does not discriminate between people. He doesn't even love Jesus more than He loves me! He loves me **as much** as He loves Jesus. What a truth! It's wonderful! The Father has such great love toward me.

When the truth of this revelation dawns on your heart it is revolutionary. You begin to realize that you don't stand in a "courtroom" relationship with the Father, but in a "family" relationship, This means you never need to have a guilty conscience when you come to Him.

Hebrews 10:22 says, *Let us draw near to God with a sincere heart in full assurance of faith, having our **hearts sprinkled*** *to cleanse us from a guilty conscience*. We have a great high priest, an advocate, making intercession for us. Our hearts are sprinkled with the pure blood of Jesus and purified from a guilty conscience. When you live in forgiveness and accept the fact that God lovingly forgives your sins, you can come boldly to your Father, conscious of righteousness and free from any sense of shame or shortcoming, because you are justified. You have been washed clean and God is now your heavenly Father in whom you trust, and from whom you expect every good thing.

The revelation of the love of God removes all feelings of guilt and self-allegation which the devil, the accuser, loves to throw at you. You can stand tall with a natural confidence and firm assurance, while having fellowship with your Father, just as a son or daughter has contact with his or her father. You are no longer apprehensive or afraid of God.

God Stands by His Word

Many people are afraid of God, wondering if He is going to hit or punish them or take all the joy out of their lives. That image of the Father vanishes when God's love is revealed to us. It's easy, then, to give ourselves to Him from the depths of our hearts and to let go of our fears and the need of safeguarding our life. We dare to release our grasp and "lose" our own life so God's life can manifest itself through us.

3. **God is faithful**. This is tremendously important. It means, for example, that He always stands by His Word and fulfills what He has promised (Num 23:19). This means that the Father, who has spoken to you through His Word, will stand with all His power to fulfill everything He has promised. God's promises are true, and they apply to you personally. What He has said, He has said to you.

God likes us to take Him at His Word and believe Him, and this often involves a struggle for a Christian. The world, the flesh and the devil will do everything to divert us and induce us to believe our feelings, negative experiences, circumstances and other people, rather than believe what God tells us in His Word.

At this point, the accuser will try to creep in and spoil your image of God as a loving father. "This can't include you, of course," he'll say. "You've made so many blunders, you're so sinful, and so on." But the opposite is true! It does mean you, and it is precisely because you have sinned so much that you need the promises of God. Genuine humility means trusting in God's word, more than one's own emotions, imaginations and feelings. Genuine humility is daring and bold, happy and willing to accept all that God has promised—just because He has promised it! It gives glory to God when we believe His Word and take His promises seriously. This is what Abraham did. He *did not waver through unbelief regarding the promise of God, but was strengthened in his faith and* **gave glory to God**, *being fully persuaded that God had power to do what he had promised* (Rom 4:20-21).

God is faithful. He wants you to believe and rest assured that He will give you everything He has promised you. His Word is true! Find out for yourself what His Word contains so you can stand on a promise, and not on the shifting sands of feelings. What God has said will be fulfilled. He is not against you, He is for you. He wants the best for you, and has already given you so much. A revelation of the love of God will make His promises a reality in your life so that your walk with Him will be real, living and powerful!

16

You Can Know God's Will

People often stand perplexed and irresolute in the face of life's decisions. In vital decisions and day to day choices, deep-seated uncertainty can often be found, together with an underlying fear. How can I know I'm about to do the right thing? How can I know that this is the right verdict? Apprehension and misgivings often render us inert and so hinder our progress.

Fear of making the wrong move cripples more plans than anything else. Can we be sure what is right or wrong? Can we find the will of God? Is God interested in the details of my daily life? Does He have a plan for my future? What really lies ahead for me?

God wants you to discover His good and perfect will, become familiar with it and have the confidence to walk in it. Then you'll be able to live the most exciting and satisfying life possible on this earth!

Romans 12:2 says that we will be able to test and approve what God's will is, His good, pleasing and perfect will, by the renewing of our minds. Paul prays in Colossians 1:9 for the believers to be filled with the knowledge of God's will through all spiritual wisdom and understanding. God is anxious for you to know His will. Only then will you know inner assurance, and be able to take the steps He wants you to take.

Many Christians have strange ideas about discovering God's will. One pictures it as almost impossible to know what He wants. Another feels that he is outside God's will and can only come into it by means of feverish activity. Some feel that remaining in God's will is like walking a tightrope—just one tiny error and everything will end in disaster. A sense of hesitancy, confusion and condemnation oppresses others. God does not want it to be like that. He does not keep us in suspense. He's not playing hide-and-seek with us to tease us, and most important of all, we are **not** outside God's will, blindly fumbling for the keyhole! We are God's children. We belong to His family. Just as your earthly father has no intention of keeping you guessing about which family you belong to and what your privileges and responsibilities are at home, so your heavenly Father will never keep you doubting either.

You were Born Again into the Will of God

It is not difficult to know the Father's will! When you were born again, you were born into it. Jesus became your Lord and you began to follow Him. The Spirit of God came into your spirit, and you became a new creation. In Romans 8:14-16, we read that we have received the Spirit of sonship which testifies with our spirit that we are the children of God. The Holy Spirit, whom Jesus calls the Comforter, Helper, Teacher and Counselor, is the one who confirms to you from within the irrefutability of your childhood to God. You don't need to doubt your salvation. In 1 John 5:13, we read, *I write these things to you who believe in the name of the Son of God so that you may know that you have eternal life.*

The same Spirit who confirms your sonship to God will also testify and confirm God's will for your life. The Holy Spirit's task is to lead you (Rom 8:14) and guide you rightly so that you come into God's good, pleasing and perfect will.

When you were born again, you were born into the will of God. Your starting point as His child was in His will, not outside it. A newborn baby is in the family's will. It is encompassed with the family's love and care, and usually, the family's full attention. The same is true of someone who is newborn, spiritually. God does not expect one of His babies to immediately take the world by storm. As a father, He feeds it so it grows, and gradually, the child is given more responsibility and bigger tasks. If jobs are given and the child doesn't obey, it begins to leave the father's will. However, in every born again believer there is a Helper, in covenant with God, assisting the child to follow the Father and obey His will, by following the Holy Spirit.

Many Christians begin to daydream of things they can do for the Lord. They may even be goals inspired by the Spirit for some time ahead, but we must know that nothing God wants happens automatically. Everything must have its proper foundation. The time of preparation may not always be especially inspiring but it is nonetheless important. To enter God's specific will, you must first come into His general will. What is God's general will? It is what applies to every believer. His specific will may be that you are to travel to Hong Kong and testify, but this isn't for everyone. However, we are all called to be witnesses. If you are not willing to be a witness where you are, then God can never say, "Go to Hong Kong and testify there."

It is the general will of God that I make Jesus my Lord in **every** area of my life. My work, studies, family, time, money and interests must be given, without reservation to

Him. It does not mean that I am deprived of them but that I have turned them over to the Lord. God is not inhumane. If you have a family, He does not demand eight hours of prayer on your knees, daily. He knows you don't have time because He has given you responsibility for your family. It is no more spiritual to pray than to take the practical responsibility is yours. In such a case, prayer can actually be an escape from responsibility and become superspirituality. However, when the Lord says, "In this special instance I want you to give me eight hours of prayer," you must immediately be willing and available, for it is Jesus who is Lord, not work or family. God is looking for your readiness and availability.

Don't Neglect the
Foundations of your Christian Life

Having now become your Lord, Jesus will begin to develop **four areas** in your life. Two of them are concerned with your relationship to Him, and two with your relationship with others.

The **first** area is your relationship to your Father, through the **Word**. If God's Word is not given priority and allowed to influence your life; if you do not dwell in and abide by His Word, you will not know the truth and be set free. The Spirit of God can only hear and act upon the Word, rather than discuss religious theories. God's Spirit will never lead you contrary to His Word, but through it and in line with it. Your mind will be renewed through God's Word and you will begin to think His thoughts instead of the world's. You will then hear the Shepherd's voice and follow Him.

The **second** area is **prayer**. Many people talk **about** God but nurse their own religious thoughts and ideas, at the same time. However, God wants you to talk **to** Him. There isn't anything too ordinary or trivial for Him. A housewife's prayer that her washing machine will work is just as important to Him as anything else. When Jesus says, *"Whatever you ask for in prayer..."* (Mark 11:24), He means, whatever! When you realize that prayer is neither dead formulae nor hysterics but conversation with your heavenly Father, you can pray for hours without getting tired. Prayer puts demons to flight and clears the atmosphere for revelation and the knowledge of God to flow freely. Confusion and wrong ideas, mostly founded on fear, are then demolished and God's will comes into view.

The **third** area is **fellowship** with other believers. No one is an island, separated from everyone else. If you are born again, you have something to give other believers. Don't let the devil fool you through feelings of condemnation so that you think you have nothing to give. You can share God's Word with them, pray and lay hands on them and bless them financially and practically.

One trick of the devil is to make you believe that you must be a full-time worker or have a special calling in order to build up other believers. When you become involved in other people's lives, God's power will be so unleashed through you that you won't have time to be self-centered, thinking only of yourself and your own personal problems. Deep, unfathomed reservoirs of potential lie in every believer. But you cannot expect God to use you in greater ways until you begin to help those around you.

The **fourth** area is **witnessing**. Every believer has been called to witness and everyone who has been filled with the Holy Spirit, has received the power to do so (Acts 1:8). Jesus has promised to make every disciple a fisher of men (Matt 4:19). Around every Christian there are people who are longing for God and who will be saved when they share the good news of what Jesus has done for them. Jesus wants you to begin at your "Jerusalem." If you are faithful there He will lead you to the ends of the earth. However, you will never be led to the ends of the world until you have first testified in your present surroundings. God does not want you to live in a world of make-believe, depression and failure. He wants you to be a witness right where you are.

When you say, "I can't witness," Jesus replies as He did in Luke 8:39, "Return home and tell how much God has done for you." You can talk about what changed your life. You can talk about a miracle that has happened to you. God doesn't demand that you be His counsel for defense, defending every detail in the Bible. God wants you to speak out about what you have seen and heard. Set yourself to win one person to the Lord. Do not just pray for the masses and for continents—pray for individuals as well. Ask God to lead you to someone, and you will see how He takes you from His general will into His specific will for your life. When you run into problems, go back to the basics! Check yourself. How is your relationship with the Father? When was the last time you blessed a believer? Are you still reaching out to people? What is your prayer life like? If these foundational areas are not working in your life, neither will anything else. Go back to the point where you missed it and pick up the trail there. Don't be so superspiritual that you miss the essentials. Begin where you are and God will increasingly reveal His good will for you.

FAITH

Now faith is being sure of what we hope for and certain of what we do not see.

Hebrews 11:1

17

Faith is Knowing God

In Mark 11:23 Jesus says, *If anyone says to this mountain, 'Go throw yourself into the sea,' and **does not doubt in his heart but believes** that what he says will happen, it will be done for him.*

Jesus told the woman who had been subject to bleeding, Daughter, your faith has healed you. Go in peace and be freed from your suffering (Mark 5:34).

In Mark 10:52, Jesus says to the blind beggar Bartimaeus *Go...your faith has healed you* and in Mark 9:23 He says to the father of the boy with the dumb spirit, *Everything is possible for him who believes.*

In these and other places in the Gospels, Jesus tells us what faith can do. Faith can move mountains, receive healing—it can do anything!

Time and again, Jesus returns to the fact that a man's own faith can produce supernatural results. He clearly says that faith can move mountains; it can turn hopeless situations around and create miracles. There is an enormous potential in a man's faith. 1 John 5:4,5, says that our faith overcomes the world. What's in the world? Jesus said there is trouble in the world, but, praise God, faith can overcome any and every trouble.

Jesus spoke the truth when He said that faith could move mountains and that everything was possible to him who believes. Faith overcomes the world so no wonder your faith comes under attack! The devil is the prince of this world and the god of this age. He does not want you to be victorious and free, or to have your prayers answered. On the contrary, he will do anything to oppose you and present God's power from being made available to you and becoming active in your life.

Romans 1:16 says that the Gospel is *the power of God for the salvation of everyone who believes*. When you believe the promises of God His power is released. The devil hates this, which is why he will do anything to prevent, paralyze and overthrow your faith.

Satan uses various methods of attack. For example, he tells you that you don't need any faith, maybe God will work anyway. It sounds good, but it is not true. Ephesians 2:8 says, *By grace you have been saved, **through faith***. Romans 4:16 states, *Therefore, the promise comes by faith, so that it may be by grace*. Grace is God's gifts, promises and power offered to you. And faith is your response to this. When you receive by faith what God has promised, it becomes valid for you personally. Then grace, the power of God, becomes real and active and the miracle takes place.

Another tactic the devil uses is to malign faith and make you believe that it is something different from what the Bible says. Jesus often talked about faith. He says we all need it and that it can move mountains. If that is what Jesus says, it is true. No one can say we don't need faith, because then we would deny miracles, power and freedom to people.

Jesus doesn't want us to be hesitant about possessing faith. If He says we can have it, then we can. Romans 12:3 says that God has given to everyone a measure of faith, so if you are a believer, then you have faith. God has given you a measure of faith that He wants you to use. When you turn that faith loose, it will work miracles because it can do anything.

Faith is not a Formula

If you have a distorted picture of faith, you will not use what God has given you because of lack of knowledge or fear. But we cannot pretend to help by changing the rules to supposedly make it easier for people. That would be like lowering the bar in the high jump so everyone could get over! Everyone would clear it all right, but there would be no worthwhile results. But this is precisely what many people are doing today. They lower the standard and don't dare talk about faith for fear of offending someone. They "lower the bar" and everyone feels better, but the signs, wonders and supernatural, the things that Jesus spoke about, are not there.

Jesus does not want us to be like this. He has put **ability** inside those who jump (to use this illustration again) to rise up and make it. He has given you the power and the measure of faith that He wants you to use. The faith you have will do the seemingly impossible. Our God is both good and true. What He says works. When He says something it is always for our good. He holds nothing back from us. He wants to give us everything that's good, and if we follow His instructions, we will have it.

There always seems to be someone, however, who says; "You're making faith a formula or a feat of strength." No, not at all. Faith is neither desperate effort nor shallow, repetitive formulae. Faith is knowing our Father and doing what He says.

The eleventh chapter of Hebrews speaks about the heroes of faith in the Old Testament. They were people who accomplished tremendous things through faith. They are our examples. They were not theorizing academics with stilted ideas to defend their unbelief. They were men and women who acted on God's Word and attained enormous heights.

How did they succeed? How did Noah build an ark? How could Moses lead a whole nation out of captivity from Egypt? How did Joshua take the promised land? How could the three men survive in the flaming furnace? How could Daniel stop the mouth of a lion? How could the weak become strong and powerful in battle and put foreign armies to flight? Because they knew their God!

When you walk with God and seek His face, you begin to know Him. You come to know His power, recognize His presence, His footsteps and His voice! You see His character. You know His ability. You begin to really trust Him. This is faith!

Faith is to Walk with God

When you know who God is and what He can and wants to do, you begin to obey Him. You walk and talk with Him, and He becomes your wonderful Counselor who is so kind to you. Obedience is easy with such a relationship and that very obedience is faith. It is not a superficial formula and the hope that a snap of the fingers will produce the desired result. No, faith is obedience to God's Word. Faith consist of returning to God and constantly abiding in His presence so that He Himself, His Will and His power are manifest. Faith is allowing God's presence and holiness to change your life and make you more like the Son. Faith is seeking God's face, not just for the sake of our prayers being answered, but for God Himself. Faith is to worship, honor and praise God continually for who He is.

When you do this you enter the rest of faith. You know who God is and you experience His love and His nature. Suddenly, you realize that He never lies, that He always keeps His promises and that there are certain things He will never do. You realize that sickness, poverty, depression and sin don't come from Him. They are not gifts from your heavenly Father, but attacks from a hateful enemy who begrudges any believer getting to know the Father's glory and receiving His wonderful gifts.

Faith is no longer a desperate performance but it comes naturally from this relationship with your heavenly Father. It is a natural confidence that God is who He says He is, and that He will do all He has said He will do. This trust pleases God.

"Without faith it is impossible to please God, because anyone who comes to him must believe that he exists and that he rewards those who earnestly seek him" (Heb 11:6).

God will reward you when you seek Him, and it pleases Him that you expect it. The champions of faith in Hebrews 11 were not idle, hairsplitting theorists. They were active, and their faith produced tremendous results. Faith is not a theoretical statement of belief. Faith comes from the heart; it is a power, placed there by God, and when it is released, it will accomplish enormous things. It has an energy that moves mountains and reverses circumstances. It liberates God's power for salvation, deliverance and healing.

When faith fills your heart, you will become busy. You will see possibilities where others see nothing but difficulties. You will see miracles when others see only impossibilities. You will see the power of God working when others see nothing but problems. You will see the fulfillment of the promises when others are apologizing for what Jesus said.

The devil is terrified of you realizing the faith you have as a believer. He is frightened that you may see how simple it is to walk in faith with God. He is afraid that you might begin to stand on God's Word and His promises, so that His heavenly power is unleashed here on earth.

Jesus said, *Everything is possible for him who believes* (Mark 9:23). You are a believer, and everything is possible for you. God wants to release His power and work His miracles both in you and through you, so don't let anything intimidate you! God is who He says He is, and He will do what He has promised.

18

Why the Devil Detests Faith

Nothing threatens the devil more than the teaching of faith. He fears it and opposes it with all he has. He knows that **the day the believer really believes, it will spell the end of his influence in his or her life**. The Word of God is a mighty effective weapon against him, but without faith, the Word will be powerless. Hebrews 11:6 tells us why: *Without faith it is impossible to please God.* The devil knows that if we do not walk in faith then we cannot please God—and that is exactly what he is after. He would like to produce a multitude of Christians who do not please God. In this way he can impede God's work and then accuse Him, by pointing to these unbelieving Christians and their inconsistency.

Faith is God's gift to us (Rom 12:3). Every Christian has personally received a measure of faith, although not every believer uses his faith. Some are not walking by faith. In many Christians, faith is lying sleeping and inactive and fear reigns in its place. In others, the mind has usurped the place of faith and head knowledge—what is seen heard, felt, thought and known by experience—then determines actions rather than God's promises in His Word.

The devil has limited and bound believers by lying and threatening, and by taking advantage of their ignorance and dependance on circumstances. In this way, he prevents them from carrying out the works of God. When Paul wrote to Philemon he prayed that, *"You may be active in sharing your faith, so that you will have a full understanding of every good thing we have in Christ"* (Philem 6). God wants your faith to be active and this will happen as you speak the Word, acknowledging every good thing that is in you, through Christ Jesus. Therefore, the devil wants to thwart your faith by making you passive and ignorant of what really belongs to you.

Faith Puts the Devil to Flight

The devil is the god of this world and despite his defeat by Jesus on the cross, he still has the right to exercise an influence on earth. We, however, are not **of** this world. 1 John

5:4-5, says that **your faith overcomes, that is, defeats the world.** The devil knows this, but he is not thinking of lying down. He has no intention of releasing his grip on men and women that easily. He does not want them to enjoy freedom, peace and an abundant life. So what does he do? He shoots at **faith** because is it the only thing that can overthrow him!

1 Peter 5:8-9, tells us the devil *prowls around like a roaring lion, looking for someone to devour. Resist him, we are told, standing firm in faith.* James 4:7 adds that when we resist the devil, **he will flee from us**. We can resist him and according to God's Word, he must flee. You can chase the devil away from your life and circumstances, your prayer group, church, job and family.

How? By resisting him and **standing firm** in the faith. The key to his removal is **faith**. No wonder that he detests the very word and does all he can to obstruct the believer from walking and growing in it?

No Christian on this earth can live in a dream world, exempt from attacks, problems or difficulties. Walking by faith does not mean burying one's head in the sand like an ostrich, or floating through life on a bed of roses. In the world we come under attack and suffer trouble. The devil does not like it when you go around his "territory" shining like a light from heaven, advertising a better kingdom than his. He is going to shoot at you. But Ephesians 6:16 says that if you take the **shield of faith, you** will be able to extinguish the flaming arrows of the evil one. Your faith is the shield that will extinguish and repel every attack against you. Faith does not prevent attacks from coming, even when you are able to use faith to bind up resistance in advance and claim victory, long before the arrows reach their target. Faith, first of all, furnishes you with the power you need to prevail when the onslaught comes. Satan will then immediately attack your faith that allows you to win and overcome his flaming arrows. It annoys him intensely when you win—and your faith is the key to that victory.

The devil does everything he can to make the saints weak and inactive. However, if you are born again, God's power resides in you and is available to you. You can accomplish things with it that you would never have dreamed possible. Mark 9:23 states, *Everything is possible for him who believes.* The devil knows that if you realize what Jesus says is true, you will rise up in the power of God and accomplish the impossible. Until now you may have believed the devil's portrait of how weak you are, how impossible everything is, what little you can do and how little you are worth. But when you acknowledge every good thing that is in you in Christ, your faith will become active. The words in Hebrews 11:34 will then apply to you—they *whose weakness was turned to strength; and who became powerful in battle and routed foreign armies.* Your enemy does not want you to rise up in the power of God or put any of his armies to flight, and so he always attacks your faith.

Let the Word Increase Your Faith

God wants the works of Jesus to be visible here on earth to display His great power and to break man's spiritual death, bondage, poverty and loneliness. The Gospel is *the power of God for the salvation of everyone who believes.* Jesus states in John 14:12-13, that anyone who has faith in Him will do what He had been doing. He wants His work to be done here on earth today through His body, the Church. However, if we do not believe what Jesus says, the power of God that imparts new birth, healing and liberty for mankind, will not spread into all the world. This is, of course, exactly what the devil wants, and he has done his worst to block the channel of God's power to men. He has sold his lies to the Church and stolen her weapons. He has divested her of her authority, of her supernatural wisdom and power and tried to render her impotent, insipid and without "salt" in the world.

You may wonder how Satan has managed to achieve this. He has done it by causing the saints to doubt God's promises and the commands of Jesus, and by getting the Church entangled in questions of doctrine and allowing herself to succumb to fear of man.

But Jesus is changing all this! The Holy Spirit is bringing revelation to the Scriptures and the eyes of believers hearts are being enlightened. We are seeing the *riches of his glorious inheritance in the saints, and his **incomparably great power for us who believe*** (Eph 1:18-19). As we perceive this, we begin to obey Jesus' commands. The **saints** are beginning to drive out demons, speak in new tongues and place their hands on the sick. The full Gospel is being preached and God is confirming His Word with accompanying signs and wonders (Mark 16:15-20).

No wonder the enemy hates faith. Faith casts him out, breaks his influence over men and women and replaces it with the Kingdom of God and His glory. Jesus said in John 11:40, *Did I not tell you that if you **believed**, you would see the glory of God?*

Through faith, we will see the glory of God manifested in our midst. Prepare yourself for it now. Set aside all the time you can to study God's Word so that your faith will increase and grow. Use every available minute to seek Him. Talk to Him. Use all the Bible teaching within your reach so you can become a disciple well able to impart the power of God to others. The devil will not like it, but God will rejoice, and men and women will be set free!

19

Hindrances to Faith

The Bible says that *the righteous will live by faith* and that the shield of faith extinguishes *all the flaming arrows of the evil one*. Jesus tells us in Mark 9:23, *Everything is possible for him who believes.* These are remarkable statements, far beyond our wildest imaginations, but what Jesus says and does is nearly always above us—and He is no less accurate for it. What He says and does always works!

Faith in Jesus and His Work releases God's power and enables Him to set up His Kingdom and establish His glory on the earth. When God entered a covenant with us, through Jesus Christ, He placed all that He has at our disposal. It becomes ours when we surrender our lives to Him. God Himself is the initiator of this covenant relationship. He has voluntarily placed all that He has and is, at our disposal. When we believe Him and accept the conditions and promises of the covenant, it gives God the moral right to establish it here on earth, through us. **Faith releases God's power**. Faith acts as a **runway where Gods's promises from heaven can land**. That's why faith comes under such attack. Satan wants to destroy that runway and he will do everything in his power to stop your faith from growing. Some of the methods he uses are as follows:

1. Lack of Awareness that you Possess Faith

Romans 12:3 says that we have received a measure of faith. No believer should say "I have no faith." **Every believer has faith**, though not every believer's faith is active and productive. In Philemon v 6 *your faith* is mentioned. When we realize we have faith, we will not succumb so easily to the devil's accusations. The teaching of faith is not aimed at putting you down or accusing you of lack. Rather, with the Word of God, it should help you release the faith you already have, and enable it to grow stronger. Then like Abraham, you too can believe for and receive the impossible.

2. Ignorance of God's Promises

In Hosea 4:6 we read, *my people are destroyed from lack of knowledge.* Paul prays in Ephesians 1:17 that *the glorious Father may give you* (the saints) *the Spirit of wisdom and revelation, so that you may know him better.*

Faith rises when God's will is known. You must know what the Word of God has to say about your needs and problems. You must know what Jesus has done for you and understand your Father's readiness to answer your prayers.

Hebrews 11:1 states that faith is "certainty." When you are certain of what God has said, faith is not difficult to attain. The more you know someone, the more you can rely on that person; and the same is true of your relationship with the Father. The more you know God and His promises, the more your faith will grow.

3. Unwillingness to Obey God's Word

When the Word of God becomes clear to you, mental reservations and objections based on worldly wisdom may rise up against it. Often, we search frantically for excuses to avoid obeying, because our mind and experiences don't want to accept God's Word at face value. Nevertheless, the Word is true whether you understand and have experienced it, or not. God has not asked you to have a mental grasp of everything He says: He has asked you to obey Him. When you obey, you will understand it! (Heb 11:3).

4. Neglect in Confessing God's Word

Many of us enjoy sitting alone at home, happily reading our Bibles and agreeing with every word. But, what happens when we close the book? We get up, walk away and immediately begin to talk in a way that is contrary to everything we have first read. Even though God's Word tells us not to be anxious about anything, we start worrying immediately about all kinds of things. Not only that, we think it is fine to talk all about our problems—despite the fact that God's Word says we are to hold fast to the good confession—especially when circumstances seem to point in the opposite direction.

We often quote our circumstances instead of God's Word. However, we must realize that the Word of God is creative. When we confess and declare it, circumstances change, first in the spirit realm and then as a manifest reality in the physical. The devil wants to implant doubt in your mind before you see the results. Then you begin to speak negatively, contrary to what God has said in His Word, and thus cripple the Word's creative ability in your situation.

Jesus tells us that we will receive what we say (Mark 11:22-24), and this works both ways. If the devil can get you to speak contrary to God's promises, he can delay their fulfillment in your life. That's why it is so important to keep to what God has said. *If anyone speaks, he should do it as one speaking the very words of God* (1 Pet 4:11). Speak the Word, and the mountain must move! Hebrews 10:23 says, *Let us hold unswervingly to the hope we profess, for he who promised is faithful.*

5. Neglect in Doing God's Word

James 1:22 tells us not to merely listen to the Word and so deceive ourselves, but to do what it says. In other words, it is possible to be self-deceived—even in a situation where the Lord is active and the Word is being faithfully preached. Merely hearing the Word is not enough. You must apply it to yourself immediately. Do not allow it to lie dormant. For years, many people have been instructed to wait until they're mature, and been cautioned that they must be careful not to act in the flesh and so forth. This has succeeded in hindering them or even stopping them completely. But God's Word is true, His **power** is available to us and it is **released when we act on the Word**. When you boldly act on God's Word you show the Lord that you trust Him. He honors such behavior and you will see the results. If you want to exalt and follow God and be a blessing to those around you, then God will confirm His Word as you obey it.

6. Lack of Patience and Endurance

Some have said, "Well, I'll give the Word a try and see if it will work." No! God does not respond if we "give it a try." He responds if we believe and if we are convinced. When a farmer sows his seed, he doesn't haphazardly "give it a go." He knows the capacity of his ground and he expects results. He doesn't become impatient, ill-tempered or sorry for himself if he doesn't see ripe grain the following day. However, we often respond in just that way. We accuse ourselves of having made mistakes and complain about our circumstances, or even blame God when we don't see immediate results. But we must not do this. Jesus says in Mark 4:26-27, *This is what the kingdom of God is like. A man scatters seed on the ground. Night and day, whether he sleeps or gets up, the seed sprouts and grows, though he does not know how.* Notice He says that 'nights and days' pass. Every farmer knows it takes time for the seed to produce. The seed that is sown into our lives is the Word of God. Just as it takes time for the seed to spring up in the natural and ripen for harvest, the same is true in our lives. But as time passes and we don't see results, many of us are tempted to give up and begin to dig in the ground to see if there's anything sprouting there. Don't do that! The Word itself contains the power of life and growth. If it is only allowed to rest in the earth, the harvest will arrive. Not all answers to prayer come immediately, but that doesn't mean they are not on the way. Don't allow the devil to stop or hinder your faith through impatience.

7. Lack of Love

Galatians 5:6 says that **faith expresses itself through love.** You will not be able to believe for anything or expect any result, if you do not walk in love. The Bible says that three things are eternal: faith, hope and love. Each of these qualities should have a place in your life. Hope is often the forerunner of faith. If people have difficulty believing, the Holy Spirit begins by awakening their hope. Hope is forward looking, whereas faith is a conviction that we have what we're praying for **now**, even if we can't see it. But remember, faith will not work where love is absent.

Where there is little faith, there is usually not much love either. Faith and love go together. Faith is of the heart and produces unity in the Spirit. Faith is not an intellectual assent to certain facts, even though it is based on facts. Faith produces a unity that goes deeper than the natural soul unity that the world experiences when people are of the same mind. Oneness of opinion will slap its fellows on the back, but mock and despise those who think differently. Faith doesn't do that. Faith expresses itself through love. It is patient and kind, and can take contradiction; it is objective, full of hope and enduring. Faith believes the best and doesn't go around gossiping or slandering. It checks the facts and always sees the positive side where others only see the negative. Faith blesses, and never curses.

When a believer learns to control his tongue and walk in love, an incredible power is released in his life. As bitterness or hatred and misguided zeal die away, the flow of God's strength takes hold. Rather than trusting in people and then being disappointed in them, he learns to trust in God, who never fails. His joy does not diminish during times of temptation. Instead, it releases the power of God so that His Word can be confirmed by signs and wonders.

Jesus says in Mark 11:25, *When you stand praying, if you hold anything against anyone, forgive him, so that your Father in heaven may forgive you your sins.* Unforgiveness and refusal to forsake known sin will always stop faith from receiving the power of God.

The voice of our inner man, our conscience, enlightened by the Holy Spirit convicts us of sin. Be swift to confess and quick to forgive. Keep no record of personal injustice and don't be bitter against those who've injured you. Whether they were right or wrong, you cannot afford to hold grudges or be bitter. Let them go. Don't demand apologies. Go on with the Lord yourself.

Be sensitive toward any appearance of sin in your life. Correct yourself where necessary—without being oversensitive. Don't allow Satan to plant accusations or vague, unspecified feelings of condemnation in your mind. If they are not clear and specific and don't include a way out, they are not from God. If you've done wrong, you will know it. God will tell you. Then, put the matter right and go forward again. If you are unaware of any sin, do not open yourself for accusations. Defend yourself with the breastplate of righteousness and the shield of faith instead, and they will extinguish Satan's flaming arrows. When all the hindrances to faith are pushed aside, you'll see Jesus' resurrection power work in you!

20

Eternal Faith

And now these three remain: faith, hope and love. But the greatest of these is love (1 Cor 13:13).

When we read this verse, we usually think only about love as being eternal, but what we commonly forget is that faith and hope are also eternal. This means that not only will love be with us forever, but that we will also have the use of faith in heaven. Faith is of eternal substance. Those things that you take with you into eternity have to be developed here on earth! God wants your faith to grow—and He has not set any limits!

2 Corinthians 4:16 states, *We do not lose heart. Though outwardly we are wasting away, yet inwardly we are being renewed day by day.*

What is in your inner man? God's Spirit, His life and the faith He has placed within you. When you were born again, God gave you a measure of faith (Rom 12:3). He did not put it in your physical body or your mind, but by the Holy Spirit He deposited it in your **spirit**. **Every** believer has a measure of faith in his heart.

For this reason, it is easy for your inner man to believe in God. The new creature within you loves God, trusts in Him and wants to obey Him. If you're born again, you will want to follow Him. You will want to renew your inner man daily not by eating ordinary food or enjoying happy, physical circumstances, but by "every word that comes from the mouth of God" (Matt 4:4), that is, from God's Word.

The Word of God is the seed sown in the ground of a person's heart that produces fruit, or results, in his life. His inner man is developed through God's Word and the Holy Spirit. Ever increasing faith on the inside is proof that a believer is obeying Jesus, that he's living from the Word and being renewed daily. It shows that God's Word takes first place in his life. Circumstances, feelings, and the mind have no say in the matter. Even if your situation is the opposite of what God has said and our outer man feels as though he's going under, our inner man is being steadily renewed and our faith is growing day by day.

Faith has an Inner Ability to Overcome

Faith is of an eternal nature and produces eternal results. Romans 10:17 says that *Faith comes from hearing the message, and the message is heard through the word of Christ.* God's Word is "the imperishable seed" (1 Pet 1:23) producing everlasting results in the life of any person who believes and receives it.

We are responsible for using and increasing the measure of faith God has given us. It will not grow automatically. God wants our faith, though, to keep on increasing and reaching out for new challenges. Paul says in 2 Thessalonians 1:3, *We ought always to thank God for you, brothers, and rightly so, because your faith is growing more and more, and the love every one of you has for each other is increasing.*

While God is overjoyed with our growing faith, Satan is upset. He hates the Word of God being planted in men's hearts and bearing fruit there. He does not want people living in victory and in line with the laws of the Kingdom of God. He knows only too well that every believer has the inherent capacity to overcome his kingdom, and it disturbs him greatly.

Although Satan was defeated and disarmed by Jesus' victory on Calvary, he was not banished from earth. He is still able to assault people and to steal, kill and destroy. This is why James 4:7 exhorts us to *Resist the devil, and he will flee.* We have to actively resist his aggression and fight him off in the power of Jesus' victory on Calvary.

1 John 5:4-5, says that *everyone born of God overcomes the world. This is the victory that has overcome the world, even **our faith**. Who is it that overcomes the world? Only he who believes that Jesus is the Son of God.* Through the faith God gave us at our new birth, we have the ability to overcome this world and its influences upon us. The god of this world is vanquished. Receive the truth of his defeat by faith and do not allow him any influence over you. When you don't give him a chance (Eph 4:27), he will be forced to run from you, as the power of faith in your heart overcomes him.

Doubly Effective Faith

Your faith works in two ways: First, it resists the enemy and quells his attacks in your life. Ephesians 6:16 speaks of *the shield of faith, with which you can extinguish all the flaming arrows of the evil one.* Second, faith conquers new ground. Faith of the heart receives what God says and believes it, even if circumstances seem to point in quite the opposite direction and even refute it. Faith of the heart knows God and finds it easy to rely on His Word. From 2 Corinthians 5:7 it is evident that when we arrive in heaven, our faith will be changed into sight. This means that what we believed and embraced here, even though we didn't see it, will become visible there. 1 Peter 1:8 says, *Though you have not seen him, you love him; and even though you do not see him now, you believe in him and are filled with an inexpressible and glorious joy.* In heaven, our faith will be replaced by sight and we will see Jesus. He will become visible and tangible to us, but that does not mean we will stop believing Him. *Faith is being sure of what we hope for and certain of what we do not see* (Heb 11:1); and it is also to rely on, have confidence in and expect everything good from God and to obey Him. All these things will continue in heaven because of the eternal nature of faith.

With God's faith in your heart, you will never be passive. By nature, faith wants to conquer new ground. It firmly embraces the promises of God and keeps reaching forward to new territory. The champions of faith in Hebrews 11, were not a score of passive, introverted souls. They were enterprising men and women. Instead of contemplating their own inabilities, they looked on the ability of God and achieved their goals.

When David was King of Israel, its borders continually expanded. He was always conquering new ground, tirelessly putting the enemy to flight and constantly increasing his territory. Faith knows no bounds because God is boundless!

A certain king in Old Testament times once visited a prophet who told him to strike several times on the ground with a bunch of arrows he held in his hand. The king struck only three times and the prophet became angry and told him that if he'd struck five or six times, he would have defeated the enemy and completely wiped it out. The king limited his achievements through his own unbelief.

A father asked Jesus if He could heal his son. Jesus replied, *If you can? ...* **Everything** *is possible for him who believes* (Mark 9:23).

There are no boundaries to faith. There is no limit to what faith can achieve. At the creation, God told man to increase in number and subdue the earth. This principle is written in the heart of everyone who is a new creation. Within every believer there is a desire to initiate, increase, expand and conquer. It is not something negative but a principle of faith, implanted by God Himself. He wants us to move forward, to grow mighty in faith, to conquer and take new ground.

Faith Knows No Bounds

In 1980, God led me to visit Tulsa, Oklahoma in the USA. The whole trip was a faith project from beginning to end! It was wonderful to see how God led and blessed my colleagues and I during our three week trip. At a certain point we visited *Oral Roberts University* and viewed the whole fantastic campus with its faculties and multiplicity of buildings. Suddenly, the Lord began to speak to me in my spirit, "Go aside and look to the north, east, west and south." I did so and saw the prayer tower in the north, the university buildings and sports arena to the east and the *Mabee Center* with 10,000 seats and the TV studios to the west. Then I turned and could see the whole hospital, *City of Faith*, which was still under construction at the time. The Lord then said, "All that you see here, I can do through one person who will trust me."

As I heard the Lord say those words, something broke inside me. A whole battery of objections, negative and critical thoughts and human protests about what, how and when God should do things, dissolved. My soul was filled with a tremendous expectancy and conviction that **nothing** is impossible and that the only restraints are those we impose on ourselves. There are no limits in God or in the faith He has given us. This is why faith is so significant. It draws on the invisible resources of heaven and makes them visible on earth.

Heaven is brimming over with deliverance, health and salvation. It is full of guidance, protection and blessing. Miracles and mighty deeds are available there. In heaven there are new churches, new projects and new missions for the whole world. Everything mankind can possibly need is found in heaven. Faith sees these invisible things and embraces them.

Romans 1:17 says, *The righteous will live by faith,* this means no limits have been set for us. Whatever Satan does to frustrate us or to get in the way and cause things to stagnate, faith still urges us on, to burst through every barrier and expand into new territory.

God is with you and He does not want you to stay on the same level. He wants you to continue believing for expansion in Him, so that new "gardens of the Lord" will spring up everywhere, each one like a paradise, filled with the perfume and glory of His presence.

Don't give up. Never let disappointments or lethargy stop you. Don't allow fear to enter. Remember Jesus' words to Jairus when everything looked hopeless, ***Don't be afraid; just believe*** (Mark 5:36).

21

Aggressive Faith

Who through faith conquered kingdoms, administered justice, and gained what was promised; who shut the mouth of lions, quenched the fury of the flames, and escaped the edge of the sword; whose weakness was turned to strength; and who became powerful in battle and routed foreign armies (Heb 11:33,34).

Faith is by nature and origin, aggressive. It attacks and conquers; it confronts and penetrates. It continually marches forward toward new territory, to conquer and overcome.

At the same time, faith involves rest and peace, trust and patience. Many believers have discovered a particular aspect of faith and then wrongly assumed that they knew all there was to know about it. This attitude creates confrontation when the Holy Spirit emphasizes an aspect of faith they are not accustomed to or refuse to accept. In Scandinavia and Europe, the Holy Spirit is especially emphasizing a side of faith that tends to cause many to react—the aggressive nature of faith. Our present spiritual climate is a result of several decades of insidious dechristianization by the enemy. What used to be taken for granted twenty years ago, cannot be take for granted today.

For many people, the picture of Jesus has become vague and any contours that may still remain have become blurred. The content of sermons and religious broadcasting on television and radio has been virtually emptied of any Gospel ingredient. The activities and services of many churches have almost completely departed from New Testament Christianity. Prayers have been formalized, theology has been liberalized and the Christian life has been secularized. In many cases, love for Jesus has grown cold, as believers have been rocked to sleep by the secular enticements of sin and worldliness. They have been dulled by a religious form of consideration that says, "Don't disturb me, don't exhort me, don't tell me to stop sinning, don't be hard on my flesh." All of these things have crept up on Christianity and produced lethargy and hard-hearted indifference.

"My people have committed two sins: They have forsaken me, the spring of living water, and have dug their own cisterns, broken cisterns that cannot hold water" (Jer 2:13).

These are the sort of cisterns in which worldliness disguises itself. The wells contain no water so the sheep do not come to drink but are left to wander thirsty, in search of life, peace and restoration. When Christianity reaches such a state, God always does a new thing. He comes with grace, mercy and goodness. He brings the Good News sharing the true nature of Jesus and the wonderful victory He has won for us. This message, the full Gospel, is a message of power.

This is the Gospel: that faith in the completed work of Jesus at Calvary includes the forgiveness of sins, physical healing, deliverance from evil spirits, victory over sin and worldliness and a new life in the supernatural power of God. The Gospel declares that the goodness of God is so great, that He is able and willing to grant victory in every area of life to those who come to Him. This is the Good News! Jesus died to give us abundant life. He was made a curse on the cross so we could be blessed. He took our sin and unrighteousness so that, by His grace, we might be clothed with the gift of His own righteousness. Jesus took our sickness and our anguish so that through Him we might be both physically and mentally whole. By His wounds we have been healed.

This is the Good News: Jesus has defeated Satan so we can receive deliverance from the influence of evil spirits. The Good News is: that Jesus became poor, so that in Him we could receive financial blessings and be able to finance evangelism and the preaching of the Gospel throughout the world. The Gospel is: that God has a good plan for everyone. He wants us to be Jesus' disciples, following Him, walking by faith and watching Him perform miracles in every area of our lives. This full Gospel is the answer to backslidden religion and the hopelessness of this world. This Gospel is the power of God for salvation for all those who believe.

Aggressive Faith Brings Change

Just as Jesus met with opposition when He preached these truths, so we are bound to experience the same thing today. In fact, Jesus said we would, so it should come as no surprise to us. The same Gospel that produces life in one person can produce death in another (2 Cor 2:14-16). What may mean great joy for many, can mean hatred and bitterness for others. The same thing that can cause some to step into the light of truth, be exposed and then delivered, will cause others to draw back using fleshy excuses only to end in deceit and darkness. No one can remain neutral toward the Gospel; he is either for it or against it. This is why backsliding eventually becomes active opposition when the Gospel is preached in power during times of revival.

There have always been Christians who have tried to avoid talking about resistance and opposition because of the negative connotations of these words. However, far from being negative; these things are Biblical. God has never promised us times of peace and quiet for our pleasure and enjoyment. All revival and preparation for revival are periods of transition, opposition, attack and counterattack. They are times of conflict, struggle and conquest. This is why the Bible is full of pictures that liken the believer to a soldier of Christ with spiritual weapons engaged in a spiritual battle. His battle is waged not from beneath but from above; from the victory of Jesus on the cross.

Some say that we do not need to fight because Jesus has already fought for us. It is true that Jesus has fought the battle for us. As believers, we have a position of tremendous victory with Christ, far above every spiritual authority and power (Eph 6:12). Biblical references to warfare always act as a stumbling block to lethargic, worldly and carnally minded Christians.

Any teaching can be taken to extremes. The nature of teaching is such that it often emphasizes one thing, for the purpose of education. If the gifts of the Spirit are being taught, it is difficult to teach about the tabernacle, the end-times, the Trinity and water baptism at the same time. However, just because someone goes into detail regarding the gifts of the Spirit does not mean they discard belief in all the other areas, merely because they fail to mention them in the same sermon. The same is true for the teaching of aggressive faith and spiritual warfare. Teaching on these subjects does not imply that healing, soul winning and the Name of Jesus have been forgotten. However, there is an obvious need today to awaken believers so they see the weapons they have been given and learn how to use them. An unwillingness to discuss the spiritual battle that is currently raging, indicates an unwillingness to take part in something that demands one's full life and attention and which will put to death one's flesh.

Aggressive Faith Creates Unity

The Lord is mobilizing His army for the last days. These will be days of mass evangelization and harvest from every nation, but they will also be days of strong confrontation. Satan is not going to sit on the sidelines, applauding as the army of

God advances. Although he is already defeated, this does not mean that he is imprisoned and silenced. Instead, the Bible says that he goes about like a roaring lion, seeking whom he may devour, and that we are to stand against him and watch him flee from us in fear and terror (1 Pet 5:8-9; Jas 4:7). The enemy would like nothing more than for believers to throw away their weapons, relax and concentrate only on themselves. Instead, we must do exactly the opposite. The Spirit of God urges us into battle, not with other people, but against the strongholds of Satan that need to be torn down. Intercessors and evangelists must work hand-in-hand rather than against each other.

Events in Jerusalem on the Day of Pentecost, were the result of several years of preparation through the ministry of Jesus, with much of the preparation being done through His strong prayer life. Throughout history, every revival has been preceded by powerful, victorious prayer. This has broken resistance in the spiritual realm and allowed evangelists to go out and win the lost, empowered by the Holy Spirit. It is not a question of choosing between one thing or the other, both are needed!

This is why the Spirit of God has a side called the Spirit of War. It is the same as the Spirit of Might described in Isaiah 11:2. When this Spirit came on Samson, he picked up the jawbone of an ass and slew 1,000 Philistines (Judg 15:14-15). The Spirit of God, manifesting Himself through aggressive faith, produced the breakthrough. This same Spirit was on Caleb, Joshua, Gideon, Jephthah, David, Samuel, Elijah...; a spirit of aggressive faith. This is the church which, as a militant, aggressive body of believers, is rising up out of weakness, confusion, timidity and denial and becoming "valiant in battle and routing foreign armies" (Heb 11:34).

Why is this particular aspect of the Spirit of God so necessary? Because the Lord is a warrior (Ex 15:3) and the enemy remains an active opponent. The Church has been called to advance and she needs the strength to stand and continue going forward under external pressure and opposition. A breakthrough in the spirit world changes the spiritual climate and creates the necessary conditions for revival. A spirit of war confronts and removes resistance to the Gospel. Aggressive faith brings freedom in people's lives, as the power of God's Spirit is manifested in healing, restoration and deliverance.

You must get to know this aspect of the Holy Spirit. It will help you out of weakness and enable you to drive away the works of the enemy from around you. You will become the soldier of the Lord you are called to be. You will be able to run the race set before you, with joy and victory as you fight the good fight of faith (1 Tim 6:12).

Nothing will bring more satisfaction than knowing that you fought and won, that you struggled and triumphed, that you attacked and got the breakthrough, that you went on the offensive and saw the enemy flee (Rev 2:7,11,17,26; 3:5,12,21). *The Lord is with you, mighty warrior!* (Judg 6:12). Keep going! Don't back down! Don't be afraid! Refresh yourself in the Word of God! Remember your position of victory, but don't fall asleep or be deceived. Advance in joy and power and in the knowledge that the Lord has given you the victory!

22

The Good Confession

The Bible speaks of several different kinds of confession. We are familiar with some, such as the confession of sin, but the type that needs to be more evident in our everyday lives is the confession of faith, or *the faith we profess,* as Hebrews 4:14 calls it. A confession is something one declares with one's mouth. It is an outward expression of an inward heart attitude. *Out of the abundance of the heart the mouth speaks,* Matthew 12:34 (NKJV) declares. We are told in Romans 10:10 that *it is with your heart that you believe and are justified, and it is with your mouth that you confess and are saved.* We can see from these scriptures that what we say is very important!

To understand the significance of words we must remember that we are created in God's image. The ability of speech dearly distinguishes man from animals. It is one of the signs of our creation in the image of God.

God speaks, and when He does, He creates. *And God said, 'Let there be light,' and there was light.* These words recur throughout the entire creation process (Gen 1:3,6,9,11,14, 20,24,26). God creates with words—and He has given that same ability to man. We too create with words. Just consider how negative and venomous talk breaks down and destroys, while the right words at the right time comfort and encourage.

In Matthew 12:36, Jesus says we will have to give account for every careless word we have spoken. God looks seriously at our words. James 3:1-12 explains in depth the role of the tongue, showing it to be like a small rudder that is able to turn a large ship, or a little fire that is able to set a whole forest ablaze. Proverbs 18:21 tells us, *The tongue has the power of life and death and those who love it* (or use it) *will eat its fruit.* We can see that the tongue and its language are extremely important to God. This is true for both the positive and negative use of our words. The confession of our faith must be applied practically to our lives.

If we make a quick analysis of our daily conversation, we could easily be discouraged, because much of it consists of negative statements, criticism, dismissals and unbelief like, "This will never work," "Not me," "I can't" and so forth. In the middle of this kind of talk, the confession of our faith comes in and teaches us to declare and confess what God says instead.

"To confess." ('confession' in Greek), means to "say the same thing as." When God urges us to hold unswervingly to the good confession, He means that He wants us to say the same things about ourselves, our lives and our circumstances as He says in His Word.

When the Holy Spirit convicts us of sin and unbelief we should confess our sins; we should say **the same thing** as God is saying to us about that situation. We affirm what He says, confess the sin and receive forgiveness.

Faith Speaks Creative Words

It is not just our sins, however, that God wants us to confess. He has many other good things to say about us in His Word, and by the confession of faith, we are able to say the same as he does in these areas also. But how many of us fall short here? We are so used to confessing our sins and shortcomings that we tend to continue quite generally confessing all kinds of negative things about ourselves. When we do, we act like non-Christians; like those without the Spirit of God and without hope, whose speech is negative, critical and self-destructive. We are to confess the same things that God says about us—regardless of our circumstances.

Abraham presents us with a fine example of the right reaction. *He did not waver through unbelief regarding the promise of God, but was strengthened in his faith and gave glory to God...being fully persuaded that God had power to do what he had promised* (Rom 4:20-21). Abraham had received the promise, "You are going to have a son." He knew it was physically impossible. Circumstances were against him—as were common sense and feelings. Not only that, but a long time passed without God appearing to fulfill His promise. Still, Abraham held fast. He didn't confess his weakness, impotency or doubts, but God's ability on the basis of what He had promised him. He was totally convinced that God would do what He had said. *Now faith is being sure of what we hope for and certain of what we do not see* (Heb 11:1). *We live by faith, not by sight* (2 Cor 5:7).

We are not to act based only on what we hear, see or feel at the moment. We stand on God's promises. Like Abraham, we confess what God has told us, even if we do not see it at the time and circumstances seem to point in another direction.

By the **confession of the mouth** we hold fast to what God has said to us and invite it to become a physical reality in our lives. **Faith comes on hearing the Word** (Rom 10:17)

and is confirmed by the confession of the mouth. 2 Corinthians 4:13 says, *It is written: "I believed; therefore I have spoken." With that same spirit of faith we also believe and therefore speak.* This means that our words are much more important than we may ever have imagined. The Scripture repeatedly warns of the vain use or misuse of the tongue and strongly encourages us to speak out the words of faith. When we proclaim God's promised Word in a given situation, we become procreators with Him, bringing about His will in those circumstances. Our words are "containers," either for garbage or for God's will and power, and we are His co-workers.

What, then, are we to confess?

1. What God has accomplished for us in Christ, through the redemption.

2. What God has accomplished in us by His Word and Spirit at our new birth and infilling with the Holy Spirit.

3. Who we are in Christ.

4. What Jesus is doing for us now at the right hand of the Father, where He is living to make continuous intercession for us.

5. What God can do **through** us and what His word on our lips is going to achieve.

This is the content of the confession of your faith. Go to the Word of God and find the promises you can base it on.

Make a list of Bible references that you read and confess every morning. It will revolutionize your attitude toward many things, because you will begin the day by looking on the world and yourself through God's eyes. God wants you to do this—and you can—because you are seated with Christ in heaven (Eph 2:6) and therefore enjoy a completely different position and perspective than the flesh would admit to or allow.

Take hold of God's Word in a given situation and confess what is yours in Christ Jesus, instead of what you observe or feel at the moment. Then you will see how it changes situations, allowing God's will to be done and His Kingdom to increase in your life.

A Testimony to God's Faithfulness

Now let's look at how the "good confession" can work in practice: I had long prepared for a period of study in the USA and had laid money aside for my stay there. The ticket was already paid.

During the days immediately prior to my departure, several large unexpected bills arrived that had to be paid without delay. After paying them there was nothing left for the trip.

Humanly speaking there was little possibility of obtaining more money quickly enough. I felt that to borrow would be wrong, so I sat down and prayed, putting the matter into the Lord's hands. I was certain He wanted me to go. I quoted the promises in Philippians 4:19 and 4:6-7, thanked God that they were true in my case and mentioned my needs.

The needs were plain to see, but I confessed my faith in God's resources and promise that "according to His glorious riches in Christ He would meet all my needs." Therefore my needs were already taken care of and I didn't need to be anxious about anything.

Some hours later, a person who had absolutely no knowledge of my predicament, came and handed me a number of bills, feeling that I might need them. I could hardly believe my eyes. The answer to my prayer came the same day I'd prayed so I could be assured that God would take care of the rest of the needs. How wonderful it is to see that God's promises are more than beautiful words! What a joy it is to say "Yes!" and "Amen!" to them. This is the good confession!

23

The Power of the Spoken Word

From the lips of children and infants you have ordained praise because of your enemies, to silence the foe and the avenger (Ps 8:2).

The Lord has ordained that we should have power over our enemy through the words of our mouth. Our words are more significant and have greater effect than we think. That is why they are so very important. Often we undervalue the effect of words saying, "Oh, it was only something I said, I didn't really mean it." Disappointments, exaggerations, a barrage of information from every side, television, daily newspapers and the like have all played their part in reducing the value, of our words. However, God looks on our words in an entirely different way.

Jesus says in Matthew 12:36 that we will be held accountable for *every careless word*. Every word is important to Jesus. Why? Because the whole universe sprang into being and is sustained, by words. When God created the world, He did it through faith-filled words. He had a vision, a plan, in His heart to create a universe and make man in His image. Man was to rule creation, be God's co-worker and reflect His glory.

The dream and plan He had for His family materialized when God spoke them into existence. By His words He created the heavens and the earth. Psalm 33:9 tells us, *He spoke, and it came to be; he commanded, and it stood firm.* Verse 6 continues, *By the word of the Lord were the heavens made.* God's words are spirit and life, and when He pronounces them, life springs into being.

God's words are the bearers of His power. Hebrews 1:3 says that Jesus, the Son, sustains *all things by his powerful word.* The Bible says God created man in His own image, in His likeness. As He rules and reigns over creation, man is also to reign as His regent, subordinated to Him. How does God rule? By His words! How is man to reign? By words! For this reason, our words are tremendously important—more important, than we often think.

2 Corinthians 4:13 says, *It is written: "I believed; therefore I have spoken." With that same spirit of faith we also believe and therefore speak.* Your speech has more to do with your faith than you realized. Here on earth, we receive answers to prayer, miracles, changed circumstances and victory over attacks, by faith (Rom 12:3). But faith is not always active. When faith comes into action, it releases the power of God and miracles take place.

The Continuing Role of Our Confession

God's power is released as you confess with your mouth, by faith and total heart conviction, what God says about any subject, while it is still unseen. When God's Word fills your heart concerning any need, problem or special circumstance, a conviction arises within that it is going to turn out just as God has said.

Abraham had this kind of conviction. Even though his body, his circumstances, his friends and his wife all spoke to him, saying it was impossible for him to have a son, he knew he was going to have one. He was convinced that it would turn out exactly as God had said, even though the circumstances pointed in the opposite direction. *Yet he did not waver through unbelief regarding the promise of God, but was strengthened in his faith and gave glory to God, being **fully persuaded** that God had power to do what he had promised* (Rom 4:20-21).

When God speaks, faith in His promises grows. Faith in the heart becomes convinced that it will be just as God has said. The mouth will speak our of the fullness of the heart. That is why Paul says in 2 Corinthians 4:13, *I believed; therefore I have spoken.* What do we speak about? 1 Peter 4:11 tells us—*If anyone speaks, he should do it as one speaking the very words of God. We speak what God's Word says and when we do, God's promise concerning the situation is released in power. When the Word of God is on our tongue, His unbridled power works miracles.*

Romans 10:10 says, *For it is with your heart that you believe and are justified, and it is with your mouth you confess and are saved.* **The way you entered God's kingdom, is the way you will go on in it.** The confession of the lips releases God's power for salvation, and this includes deliverance, protection, preservation, healing and a sound mind. This is what salvation means.

Each of us has problems or difficulties in our lives. The devil's flaming missiles are aimed at everyone. When difficulties arise, it is usually because the devil has lured us into saying what he says about the problem, instead of what God says, which, of course, is the solution.

The devil knows that we are called to reign as kings here in life and that we can reign over circumstances by our words. That is why he wants to fill your mouth with words of unbelief, doubt, discouragement, fear, sickness, hatred, envy and criticism. If you continually utter these things, the power of God will be bound in your life and you will give Satan occasion and permission to manufacture them in and around you. He knows the creative power of your words, and he would like to use them to spread his kingdom and multiply its wicked fruits.

Words Change Circumstances

The tongue has the power of life and death, and those who love (or use) it will eat its fruit (Prov 18:21).

Words are "containers" of life or death and we are the ones who decide what will pass our lips. God wants your mouth, to be filled with His words so they can become a force to be reckoned with *to silence the foe and the avenger* (Ps 8:2). As God's words proceed out of your mouth they change the prevailing circumstances. Many people react against this, saying, "How can only words change my difficult situation? It can't be done, can it?" Yes it can, because it isn't "only words" coming out of your mouth. God's own mighty Words proceed out of your mouth as you speak by faith, in Him. They are invested with exactly the same creative power as His words when He Himself is speaking.

In Mark 11:23, Jesus speaks about the power of the spoken word. If you have a "mountain" in your life—if you have seemingly insurmountable problems, Jesus says to you, *I tell you the truth, if anyone* (that means any person, not just some special group of people) *says to this mountain* (notice that Jesus says **to** not **about**. We are often guilty of speaking about problems rather than straight **to** them.) *"Go throw yourself into the sea," and does not doubt in his heart but believes that what he says will happen, it will be done for him.* (Some translations say, "he shall have whatever he says.")

In the parallel passage found in Luke 17:6, Jesus talks about a mulberry tree instead of a mountain, but He uses the same principle, saying that we should **tell** the tree to be planted in the sea *and it will obey us*. What is Jesus saying? He's telling us that real things, mountains and trees—unfavorable circumstances barring the way—will *obey us* when we speak to them. In other words, circumstances must change when we speak the Word of God to the "mountain" in our life. The power of God is released to perform miracles when you declare His promises over every difficult situation.

We are used to our circumstances "speaking" to us about how impossible the situation is. We have obediently listened and adapted ourselves accordingly. But Jesus invites you to begin speaking God's words to your surroundings and assures you that they will obey you. Why? Because the universe is created and sustained by the Word of God and His Word contains power to transform any situation.

Guide Your Life by Words

As a quick review, the Bible calls upon us to hold unswervingly to the faith and hope we profess—"the good confession" (Heb 10:23,4:14; 1 Tim 6:13). To **confess** means to **"say the same thing as."** We are to say the same things God says about situations, no matter how they may appear. As we do, we pronounce the solution to the problem and God can do the miracle. When we confess what God says about any problem instead of what the devil says, and hold unwaveringly to it, knowing that He who has given us the promise is faithful, the Word of God in our mouth will silence our foe. The power of God will be released and our "mountain" will disappear.

Therefore, every Christian must control his tongue and preserve its purity. James 3:2 says, *If anyone is never at fault in* **what he says**, *he is a perfect man, able to keep his whole body in check*. Verse 4 describes ships which *are so large and are driven by strong winds...are steered by a very small rudder wherever the pilot wants to go*. You are the pilot and your tongue, that small part of your body, acts as a rudder, guiding you wherever you want to go.

Your words exert a far greater influence on both yourself and others than you think. For this reason, watch your language! Never speak disparagingly of anyone. Keep yourself from backbiting, jealousy, gossip and the like which will drag you and others down and give the devil ground to steal and spoil in your life. Speak the Word of God in faith and love, and His power will be liberated in your life and surroundings and you will be a blessing wherever you go.

"Faith comes from hearing the message." This means that faith will arise even when you listen to yourself speak the Word of God aloud. At first, Satan will try to make you feel it is laborious, mechanical and unspiritual. However, as you continue to faithfully confess the Word of God, faith will arise in your heart until you know it is going to **be** as God and you have said. **You first speak "to faith," and then it will** become **"by faith."** The eternal truth of the Word of God will flow from your spirit and produce supernatural results. God's Word will form a conviction in your heart of who you are in Christ, what you have in Him and what you can do in Him. Your inner man will rise up, the Greater One within will take over and he that is in the world will flee!

PRAYER

For our struggle is not against flesh and blood, but against the rulers, against the authorities, against the powers of this dark world.

Ephesians 6:12

24

Authority in the Name of Jesus

When Jesus was on earth people were amazed at His teaching because He taught *as one who had authority, not as the teachers of the law* (Mark 1:22).

The word used here for authority is the Greek word *exousia*. Jesus came with authority and spoke authoritatively. With what authority was He invested? Delegated authority! He had been authorized by His Father to speak and act in the Father's name, and on His behalf.

The Father revealed Himself in the Son and everything Jesus said and did was exactly what The Father wanted (Heb 10:7). Just as an ambassador is authorized to speak on behalf of his country, so Jesus had authority to speak for the Kingdom of God.

However, He did not just speak with authority; He also acted with authority as well. On one occasion, when He entered a synagogue He met demonic resistance. A man possessed with an unclean spirit cried out, *"What do you want with us, Jesus of Nazareth? Have you come to destroy us? I know who you are—the Holy One of God!" "Be quiet!" said Jesus sternly, "Come out of him!" The evil spirit shook the man violently and came out of him with a shriek* (Mark 1:24-26).

This powerful display of demonic activity and of God's deliverance took place right in the "church," and *The people were all so amazed that they asked each other, "What is this? A new teaching—and with authority! He even gives orders to evil spirits and they obey him"* (Mark 1:27).

Words with Authority

In Matthew 8:5-10, Jesus met a military officer whose servant was sick. The Centurion asked Jesus to heal his servant by just **saying a word**. The officer was in the army and was therefore familiar with the effect of words spoken in authority. Such words were orders, and orders were to be obeyed. He knew that when Jesus spoke the command, the illness would simply obey. Jesus called that *great faith* (Matt 8:10).

Later in the evening, as Jesus was praying for demon-possessed people, *he drove out the spirits with a word* (Matt 8:16). There was authority in His word because His words were God's words. Sickness and demons had to obey Him when He ordered them to stop their activities, because He had come with delegated authority from heaven.

The Kingdom of God had come and was witnessed by the people as they saw the demons flee. The Pharisees were unwilling to acknowledge that Jesus had been sent with authority from the Father. They argued that it was by Beelzebub, the prince of demons, that He was driving out the evil spirits. At this, Jesus answered: *But if I drive out demons by the finger of God, then the kingdom of God has come to you* (Luke 11:20). Where the Kingdom of God is present you will find power and authority—and all other powers, evil powers and evil spirits must give up their ground.

As Jesus went about teaching and openly demonstrating the presence of the Kingdom of God, He simultaneously trained and commissioned His disciples to do the same things He Himself was doing. He called them to Him and *gave them authority to drive out evil spirits and to heal every disease and sickness* (Matt 10:1).

Jesus authorized His disciples to do exactly what He was doing. He sent them out not only to proclaim the wonderful things their master could do, and not only to gather crowds to Himself; but He also sent them out with the authority and power to do the same things themselves.

In Luke 10, Jesus sent not only the twelve disciples out but seventy others as well. As they returned full of joy, they said, *Lord, even the demons submit to us in your name* (Luke 10:17). They had discovered that when they went out, authorized by Jesus to act in His Name, the same things happened as if Jesus Himself had been there. When Jesus ordered the demons out with just a word, they retreated. When the disciples commanded the spirits to come out in **the Name of** Jesus, they submitted. They were forced into submission and obedience at the presence of a greater power. The disciples did not have this authority in themselves, or of themselves. It had been delegated to them by Jesus, because He had given them the right to use His Name.

Just as you may receive a letter of authorization or power of attorney from a person (for example to deal with his bank), so the disciples received authorization from Jesus. Your authority is a signed document giving you, the bearer, all the power of the signatory. It is as though the person who had signed was there in person. His presence, and all that he is and has, is represented by his name.

The Name of Jesus Means Salvation

In the Old Testament there is an abundance of teaching on the meaning of God's names. His names stand for His abilities. For example, when He revealed Himself as the Lord your healer, it means He is able and willing to heal you. His nature and will are revealed in His names. All the different Old Testament names for God have been summarized in the New Testament in one single name, **the Name of Jesus**.

The name Jesus (Jeshua) means in Hebrew, "Salvation." This salvation includes all that God has revealed in His covenant names. It also contains all that Jesus said and did. It is a total salvation embracing every part of life. This salvation is anchored in the Name of Jesus, and therefore, every one who calls on the Name of the Lord will be saved (Rom 10:13). The Name of Jesus represents God's presence; it is God Himself who stands behind that Name enforcing its power. When you use it, you are acting on behalf of Jesus, who is always present and working through His own Name with you.

As the disciples returned filled with joy, Jesus said to them, *I have given you authority (exousia=authority) to trample on snakes and scorpions and to overcome all the **power** (dynamis=ability) of the enemy; nothing will harm you* (Luke 10:19). Jesus delegated to the disciples the right and authority to overcome **all** the power of the enemy. The Greek word *dynamis*, power or ability, is the same word that is used in Acts 1:8 where Jesus says, *But you will receive power* (dynamis) *when the Holy Spirit comes on you; and you will be my witnesses.*

In other words, Jesus is saying, "I grant you authority over all the power and ability that Satan has. However much power he deploys in his attacks against you, you still have the delegated authority and the command to annihilate it." We have received unprecedented authority from Jesus, giving us tremendous advantage over the enemy—but we must use the authority in His Name.

If we do not make use of the Name of Jesus, Satan will get the upper hand, as Paul says in 2 Corinthians 2:11 (NKJV), *Lest Satan should take **advantage** of us.* God does not want Satan to take advantage of you or to outwit you so he can steal from you and cause carnage in your life.

This truth of our authority in the Name of Jesus is something Satan has tried to hide from the saints, so he can overcome them and impede the work of God here on earth. This is why, when the disciples returned to report the results of having used His Name, Luke 10:21 says, *At that time Jesus, full of joy through the Holy Spirit, said, "I praise you, Father, Lord of heaven and earth, because you have hidden these things from the wise and learned, and revealed them to little children. Yes, Father, for this was your good pleasure."*

What does this mean? **It means that it gives Jesus great joy when we understand our authority in His name and use it to destroy Satan's kingdom and overcome his power.** This is a tremendous truth and it is essential that all disciples understand and live in it. Only those who are childlike can do so, Only those who give themselves wholeheartedly, humbly and solely to follow Jesus can take this authority to themselves. The quibblers, critics and those who are wise in their own eyes cannot receive it. They become like the scribes and Pharisees who can quote, dispute and speak whole commentaries, but who have no power, authority or real help for the people.

Authority for Every Believer

Before He returned to heaven, Jesus imparted His authority and power to every believer. It wasn't just for a chosen few disciples, but for every one of them. In Mark 16:17-18, He says, *And these signs **will** accompany those who **believe:** In my name they will drive out demons; they will speak in new tongues; they will pick up snakes with their hands; and when they drink deadly poison, it will not hurt them at all; they will place their hands on sick people, and they will get well.*

These were Jesus' last words to the disciples before He left them and so it was extremely important. This was the Great Commission that all believers need to obey.

In this commission Jesus has furnished us with the weapon we need to spread the Gospel and lead people into the Kingdom of God: His Name, the Name of Jesus, has been given to every believer. We must realize that the Name of Jesus is more than some good luck charm tagged to the end of a prayer. It is precious currency with the Father in heaven and the Name at which all authorities and powers in the spiritual realms tremble. It is the Name that indicates God's presence. It is the Name that reminds Satan of what happened on Calvary; how Jesus, by His death and resurrection defeated him and stripped him of his weapons. It is the Name above every other; the only Name to which the Father responds and in which your prayers are answered. In this Name, demonic activity in your life is forced to give way, circumstances are put right and victories are won.

Make use of the authority Jesus has given you. Put the enemy to flight! When you see what the Name of Jesus will do for you, your faith will rise to use it boldly in every situation. No wonder John challenges us with the words, *this is his command: to believe in the **name** of his Son, Jesus Christ, and to love one another* (1 John 3:23).

25

The Prayer of Faith

And without faith it is impossible to please God, because anyone who comes to him must believe that he exists and that he rewards those who earnestly seek him (Heb 11:6).

Faith is the **foundation** of the Christian life and so every believer must be taught about it. God says that faith pleases Him. He wants your prayers to be answered. He doesn't want you just to pray and keep on praying, but to pray in such a way that enables Him to answer your prayers. This is why the prayer in itself is not the central issue. When you pray, your attitude is very important. If you look at your own prayers, and those of many others, you can see that many of them go unanswered. You may have heard hundreds of people pray, yet observed few results. Notice again what this verse says; *And without faith it is impossible to please God, because anyone who comes to him must believe that he exists.*

This means more than believing that "there is a God." It means knowing who He is. His name is "I am who I am." When I **know** who God is, I know that He is omnipotent, He is loving and that He is my Father. Because I know His character, I can come to Him in the assurance that He will respond to me. However, if I come to God without the belief that He is going to respond to me, it won't help even if I start praying like a prayer machine, because I am not confident that He will reward me and answer my prayers. This kind of attitude does not please God. Prayer is not based on grinding, legal duty. It is founded on an **attitude** toward God that draws you to Him on the sure grounds of knowing who He is and what He has said. When you come to Him like that, you know He will respond to you. He is pleased because He likes that attitude of trust and so He will answer your prayers.

God never does anything wrong. If anything is wrong anywhere, it is always to do with us. There is nothing wrong with God's "transmitter." If something is not right, it is with the "receiver," and in that case, it needs to be adjusted. Don't get upset or feel down about it. If there's something wrong with your radio you don't ring up the broadcasting company and scold them. You adjust your set. You don't feel in the least convicted that your receiver isn't working, you just tune it.

This is the attitude you must have regarding your relationship with God, if you want a balanced Christian life. You're not to become angry with God for things that happen in your life. Don't ever blame Him. You'll get nowhere doing that. There are two pitfalls you must avoid: One is to accuse God and be bitter toward Him because of things that happen to you. This is not faith and it stops God from giving you what He has for you.

The second obstacle is the feeling of condemnation that says, "If it's lack of faith; then it's all **my** fault. I can't believe. Oh, how miserable I am. I've tried and it doesn't work." You realize that it can't be God's fault and grudgingly admit, "Okay, then it's not God's fault, it's mine, of course. I can't do anything. I'm useless, and I'll never be any better."

This isn't the attitude you have toward your radio when it is out of tune. You simply adjust it until it works. In this way the Holy Spirit wants to help you tune your life to God. If there are things that aren't quite perfect yet, He'd like to help you adjust yourself through the Word and His private instruction so that all will be well. The righteous will live by faith (Rom 1:17).

Don't Give Up!

When you are first born again you become God's little child. What happens when a little child begins to walk? It stumbles, doesn't it? When an infant stumbles, he doesn't start accusing his parents for his inability to walk with words like "It's my parents fault I can't walk." No child does that. Neither when he stumbles and falls does he lie there forever and complain, "I've tried once and it didn't work. I don't want to walk any more." There's not a child like that. We Christians, however, are often guilty of both. Partly we complain at God and partly we say, "Now I've tried faith and I'll never ever try again." What God wants you to say instead is, "All right, I tripped up. It wasn't God's fault. I'm a spiritual baby. I'm learning to walk step by step. I'll try again and if I fall I'll pick myself up again. I don't feel at all down about this. I'll just get up and go on."

We must realize, as we're learning about faith, that the devil always tells believers that they don't have any faith! This is his usual trick. There is a common misconception that only a few people have faith; the lucky ones, those whom God is going to use. But we, the rank and file, don't have any faith, so God can't use us. This is a lie. The Bible says that every believer has faith. Every one of us was given a measure of faith from the moment we were born again. You were born again by faith. From that moment, faith was found in you. You will have it for life, but it must develop and grow. Just as a child learns to walk, so you learn to use your faith. The child walks, stumbles, gets up, goes on and then suddenly discovers that its legs hold. The first steps he attempted were wobbly and unsure but suddenly, he's walking.

You'll begin to see how God answers your prayers and uses you. Mountains will be cast into the sea and things that were once problems are no longer problems at all, because you've walked with your God and become, as the Scripture says, "strong in faith" and "growing in the grace of God." This is how it works, so do not entertain condemnation in any area of your life. It is the same for us all. We all have to go forward step by step.

Pray in Faith—Don't Doubt

> If any of you lacks wisdom, he should ask God, who gives generously to all without finding fault, and it will be given to him. But when he asks, he must believe and not doubt because he who doubts is like a wave of the sea, blown and tossed by the wind (Jas 1:5-6).

If you need wisdom, or anything else in your life, the principle given in these verses holds true. If you need guidance or wisdom concerning the future, for example, the Word of God says you should pray about it. The above verses state that God will give to all who pray, without finding fault. God Himself has given us this promise. If you lack wisdom you should pray and then you will receive. In other words, the key is prayer. But, he says in the sixth verse (and this means there is a condition you must meet if what you pray for is really to become yours), But when he asks, he must believe and not doubt. This is God talking. If He talks like this then that's how it is, regardless of what you or I think, and in spite of any teaching we may have received to the contrary, or even the experiences of other people. What God says is true. You will receive wisdom, or whatever you pray for, as long as you pray in faith and do not doubt, because he who doubts is like a wave of the sea, blown and tossed by the wind. That man should not think he will receive anything from the Lord; he is a double-minded man, unstable in all he does (Jas 1:6-8).

You need to pray in a certain way in order to receive answers to your prayers. Hebrews 11:6 says, *And without faith it is impossible to please God, because anyone comes to him must believe that he exists and that he rewards those who earnestly seek him.* If the person praying does not believe this, then there is no point in praying, James writes, *because he who doubts is like a wave of the sea, blown and tossed by the wind.* Anyone who prays and does not believe but doubts, or says a prayer out of a sense of duty, not expecting to receive what he's praying about, cannot have his prayer answered.

Some faith preacher did not come up with this idea, it is God who says it in His Word. He had it written so you and I could grow in faith and receive all that we pray for. God does not punish anyone! It is religion that condemns and binds people. God makes us free so we can receive what His Son, Jesus, died to give us. We are to follow His instructions in His Word: pray in faith without doubting, and then we will receive our answer.

Don't *Try* to Believe—Live in God's Word!

If you doubt, you are wondering whether God is going to answer you or not. This is not seeing God by faith for who He really is. Take healing as an example. When you learn what the Bible has to say about healing, then you pray for healing if you need it. What happens then? You receive healing. However, the Bible also tells us what will happen, if while you pray, you are thinking, "I wonder if anything happened? I can still feel the pain. It's still there." *That man,* God's Word declares, *should not think he will receive anything from the Lord; he is a double-minded man unstable in all he does.*

Is God miserly for saying, "That man should not think he will receive anything?" "It's because you're not able to believe." The devil would like to tell you. But that is not the point. It's not a matter of being "able" to believe. You don't even need to try to believe. You are to live in God's Word and then you will believe automatically. As you read the Word, faith rises like a crop, from the seed sown within you. God does not withhold His blessings. He attempts to give. He says, "Pray, and you will receive."

We read in Mark 11:22-24, *"Have faith in God,"* Jesus answered. *"I tell you the truth, if anyone says to this mountain, 'Go, throw yourself into the sea,' and does not doubt in his heart but believes that what he says will happen, it will be done for him. Therefore I tell you, whatever you ask for in prayer, believe that you have received it, and it will be yours."* **"Whatever** you ask for in prayer...it will be yours," Jesus says. God knows no bounds. Whatever you pray for, you may receive, but there is a condition attached which is found in verse 24, *Therefore I tell you, whatever you ask for in* **prayer**.

In this case, the word prayer (Greek *aiteo*=call for, crave, desire), is a very strong word. Among other things, it means to claim. Jesus says you can **claim** from God. If He says you can, then it is true, no matter what people think. Jesus speaks the truth. He is the truth. If Jesus has said, "Claim!" then you can **claim**. "But surely we can't claim anything from God," some would say. Why not? If you read the verse, you'll see that this is precisely what Jesus is telling you to do. You are not making a claim because you are anything special. You're claiming what Jesus has done for you. I am justified because of what Jesus has done for me and I have the right to come boldly to my God and find grace to help, at the right time. I have the right to make a claim, and it pleases God when I say "O God, I'm in need of such and such, I ask you for it and claim it as mine."

Unconvinced Prayer will not Bring Results

When you become so wholeheartedly single-minded that you cast yourself on God, you will see how He answers your prayers. However, if you say, "God help me with this," while thinking, "On the other hand, the bank can help me with this too," or "Jesus, help me with that," and at the same time, "But I've got a friend who can help me as well," it will not please God. It pleases Him when you say, "O God, I need you now." For such prayers there are no limits. Whatever you ask for in prayer, Jesus declares, believe that you have received it, and it will be yours. When have you received it? When you pray. When do you believe? When you pray. When do you know you have it? Not when you see it, but when you pray.

How, then, are you to have your prayers answered? We saw in James 1:7, *That man should not think he will receive anything from the Lord.* If I am double-minded in prayer, I cannot expect an answer. If I'm double-minded, I vacillate. I pray expecting nothing. I pray for wisdom, then go and complain that I have none. "That man" should not fool himself by thinking that he is going to receive anything from God.

The attitude that Jesus is speaking about in Mark 11 is totally different. When you ask in prayer, believe that you have received it **as you are praying** and it will be yours. There is no double-mindedness in this prayer. In the natural realm, everything changes constantly—sometimes for the better and sometimes for the worse. Circumstances change. If you look at the circumstances, you'll become like the double-minded man who trusts God a little and circumstances a little. Jesus, however, says that when you pray, you are to believe you have received the answer. But how can a man know that the answer will be given him as he prays? He has to have spent time in the Word of God.

This type of prayer, the prayer of faith, is what James tells us that Elijah prayed. Elijah was a righteous man and *The prayer of a righteous man is powerful and effective* (Jas 5:16). The prayer of faith is based on what God has said to you. *Faith comes from hearing the message, and the message is heard through the word of Christ* (Rom 10:17).

When you know what the Bible has to say about any area of need in your life you can come to God **with conviction**, as described in Hebrews 11:6, and He will be pleased. You believe that He exists and rewards those who earnestly seek Him. So **don't pray so much** if you're not sure about what is written. Go first to the Word of God and learn what it has to say about your prayer **before** you pray it. If you don't, the devil will come, despite your prayer, and through circumstances, he lures you away from the answer. Sometimes when you've prayed, things go contrary to what you prayed. I have experienced times when I've prayed and the opposite has happened. The situation greatly worsened after I'd prayed. But because I knew what God had said in His Word I held firmly to the promise, "Whatever you ask in prayer...it will be yours." The devil attacks us repeatedly on this point; when we haven't spent time in the Word before we've prayed and then, we pray in a panic rather than in the calm assurance of what God's Word has taught us.

When we pray in a panic, it is easy to be rocked by the devil. We pray, and say we believe that we will receive our answer, but add: "Well, I really hope something will come of all this." If we consider the turmoil and deplorable conditions our world is in and to look at the risks and human impossibilities, we can lose all that God has promised to give us. However, this is not because God is holding it back.

Healing can take time. You don't need to go around making the claim, "I don't have any pain." It's a lie to say that if you do have pain. However, you have more than pain. You have the Word of God that has promised you healing. You've received it by faith and it will be yours. You hold firmly to what God has said and not to what you feel at the moment. *Whatever you ask for in prayer, believe that you have received it, and it will be yours* (Mark 11:24).

The Prayer of Faith is Based on Conviction

> This is the confidence we have in approaching God: that if we ask anything according to his will (His will is expressed in His written Word), he hears us. And if we know (are convinced because of what God has said in His Word) that he hears us—whatever we ask—we know that we have what we asked of him (1 John 5:14-15).

How do you **have** it? You have it in the Spirit and you don't necessarily see it with your physical eyes. Jesus said, *Believe that you have received it, and it will be yours.* When I pray about my need, having the Word of God as the basis for my prayer, I receive what He has promised me in His Word **now**. I **have** it. I have prayed according to His will, so I know that I already have what I've prayed for. But, as I leave my prayer closet for the world, a challenge arises. The devil throws everything he's got at me, to hinder the answer from coming and cause me to doubt, to waver and even to give up altogether.

Some people believe we are led by open or closed doors. You are not led by open or closed doors. You are led by the Spirit of God. As you're led by God's Spirit, doors can close everywhere. That is not the time for you to stay at home crying. You are to **go by what God has said.** You know you have what you asked for because Jesus has given a promise that you will have it. You are not one of those people who is "unstable in all he does," because you are basing your prayer on God's Word. You're not blown and tossed by the wind and waves. On the contrary, you thank Jesus like this: "I have the answer to my prayer. Thank you, Jesus, that you've given me what I've prayed for and you'll see to it that the manifestation will come in due time." Suddenly, you will have the wisdom you needed. You will know exactly what you're to do, and those who have much more natural wisdom and experience will be confounded. They'll wonder, "How can he have so much wisdom." "He's only been around a year and I've been here thirty years..." However, it is not a question of how many years you've been around, it is a question of what you have done with what God has given you.

In the book of Job we read that wisdom does not depend on advancing years, but on the spirit in man (Job 32:7-9). The spirit in a man grows if he converses with God, spends time in His Word, drinks it in and believes what God says rather than what people say. He says, "I believe what God says and I receive it by faith. I now have it and I praise you for it, Father." If someone should ask you a little sarcastically how you are feeling, you praise God and thank Him, being fully persuaded that what He has promised He also has the power to fulfill. You're certain of it. You have received it and know that what He has said, He will do. In this way you will overcome the onslaughts of the devil, God will be glorified and you will produce abundant fruit.

26

Draw on Your Inheritance

For several years now the Lord has been doing wonderful things in Sweden. He is laying a firm foundation in the lives of men and women in a way unparalleled in recent history. The word of faith is encouraging many Christians to live in the inheritance we have in Christ Jesus. In the past, many believers were totally unaware of their inheritance. They did not know what their inheritance was or even how they could claim it. We have suffered nationally from a religious inferiority complex. It has hindered us from approaching *the throne of grace with confidence, so that we may receive mercy and find grace to help us in our time of need* (Heb 4:16). The devil has obstructed us from living confidently before our Father and has veiled our spiritual eyes from seeing God's love and care for us.

God has a wonderful inheritance for us in Christ Jesus. We are His heirs and own the full rights of sons (Gal 4:6-7). This inheritance is ours here and now. It is here on earth that we have needs. For this reason Paul prays that the eyes of our heart should be enlightened so we could see *the riches of his glorious inheritance in the saints* (Eph 1:18). Notice that, when he writes about heaven, he uses the present tense, not the future tense. Heaven is waiting with all its glory, but God also has a glorious inheritance for us here, on earth. We **have been** blessed in the heavenly realm with every spiritual blessing in Christ!

When we as believers discover our inheritance and make use of our rights, we glorify our Father. Often, we mentally connect "glory" and heaven together. But "glory" that really means light and radiance, is found wherever God is. His glory is His manifested presence. When you discover the glorious riches of His inheritance and begin to draw on them, God's presence will be manifested. The devil has contested this truth. He has led Christians to believe that they have nothing, are nothing and can do nothing—before they get to heaven. But this is entirely wrong. We have a gloriously rich inheritance **now**. We are blessed **now**. We take part of God's nature **now**. He who is the Greater One, lives in us **now**. **Now** we're overcomers. **Today** we overcome the world.

When we see this and begin to apply it in our lives by drawing on our inheritance, God's glory will be manifested. His presence will be displayed as He makes Himself real to His own. He will become known as the God who answers prayer. He will become my Shepherd who leads me. He will become my Rock in whom I trust. He will be a real person to me, not simply a theory with which I agree. Then, I meet with Him, the one true God of my life, and His presence becomes preciously tangible to me.

God Gave us Everything with Jesus!

The world is attracted by God's presence. The world has never been genuinely attracted by religion. The world needs facts, something that works, but it also has a deep, hunger for the supernatural. If we do not present the world with God's supernatural goodness, Satan will offer them his supernatural wickedness instead. An explosion of demonic phenomena always has its roots in the fact that the Church has failed to live in the supernatural, where God is manifested among the saints.

When people in the world do not see God, they are led astray by wickedness instead. The devil has kept believers in ignorance of their inheritance and their rights in Christ far too long. Romans 8:32 says, *He who did not spare his own Son, but gave him up for us all—how will he not also, along with him, graciously give us **all** things.* God freely gave us **everything** with Jesus. He held nothing back because He wanted His glory, His manifested presence, to be seen among us.

What does our inheritance in Christ contain? Galatians 3:29 says, *If you belong to Christ, then you are Abraham's seed, and **heirs** according to the promise.* We are heirs to the blessing God gave to Abraham. Verses 13 and 14 in the same chapter tell us that Christ became a curse for us so that Abraham's blessing might come to us. The curse that Jesus took for us—in our place—was sin, spiritual death, sickness, poverty, loneliness and eternal separation from God. Jesus took all of this upon Himself. God did not spare Him, but gave Him up for us all (Rom 8:32).

When Jesus took our curse upon Himself, it made it possible for God to graciously give us all things with Him instead. What does "all things" mean? The blessing of Abraham! What does that include? Your inheritance containing everlasting and abundant life, righteousness, peace, healing, economic prosperity and much, much more. God has a name for every need we have, and He has covered it in the inheritance

He has given us in Christ. He want us to take our rights of inheritance seriously—they cost Him the highest possible price. He wants us to claim them and see *the riches of his glorious inheritance in the saints* (Eph 1:18). Then He'll be glorified and His presence manifested among us.

Through the years, the Lord has been proclaiming this news so that believers will see what they have in Christ Jesus. Then, like Peter, they can begin to say to the lame, *What I have I give to you. In the name of Jesus Christ of Nazareth, walk* (Acts 3:6).

In the past we have not seen much evidence of signs and wonders because the devil has tried to deceive and blind us with religious lies. He has told us that we do not have a claim to any inheritance. As a result, we have claimed nothing—and received exactly that in return! Now, however the Holy Spirit is changing things and we are realizing what is ours, believing it, acting on it and discovering *his incomparably great power for us who believe* (Eph 1:19). God's power is being released as a result of the Word that is being sown into people's hearts. As they perceive their heritage, they can expect a widespread demonstration of its power!

The Lord has already begun a visitation in some countries, but we are on the way to still greater things—a harvest of colossal proportions. The power of God is going to sweep over lands like a wave, bringing salvation to the masses. God's Word has been implanted in individuals' hearts and now His work will spring forth with wonderful results. The seed is ripening and there will be widespread manifestations of His power and presence.

The Body of Christ, which has been like a slumbering giant, is going to rise up and stand tall. Expect great things from the Lord!

27

Ask and It Will be Given

If you remain in me and my words remain in you, ask whatever you wish, and it will be given you (John 15:7).

What does it mean to "remain in Jesus"? It is to love Jesus, talk about Jesus and pray to Jesus. It does not mean just coming to Him when you're in need. God doesn't want to answer your requests only. He wants your company too. He wants you to converse with Him so that your character and thoughts become like His. As you develop this kind of relationship with God, do you know what will happen? Every prayer you pray will be answered. God wants every one of your prayers to receive an answer—and they will, if you have fellowship with Him and spend time soaking in His Word, thinking His thoughts and seeking His Kingdom first, instead of constantly busying yourself with your own needs. God doesn't want your thoughts to keep circulating around "me" and "mine." He wants you to pray with all your heart, "May **your** Kingdom come."

Your whole attitude must be one of "your kingdom come." There is a great difference between a nagging, complaining, self-centered attitude and one where you hurry to the Father in prayer with the needs of people around you. God can use such a person anywhere and everywhere. The Holy Spirit is always with you and can tell you what to say, if you remain in Jesus. When you live in this way and keep yourself filled with the Holy Spirit, concerns, burdens and prayer worries will drop from your shoulders. You'll see how things are added to you. God will see to it that they arrive at the right time, simply because you are seeking His Kingdom first.

Give yourself wholeheartedly to the Kingdom of God. This is the first step in the right direction. Do not be ashamed of praising the Living God. Be proud of it—He longs for a people who praise Him, and if you take every opportunity you have to do so, He will respond with, "Amen. That's exactly what I've been waiting for. I love you. I'm delighted with you. I'm rejoicing over you" (Zeph 3:17).

If you have this kind of relationship with your Father, there will be no problems obtaining answers to prayers. Many of us haven't received replies because we have based our prayers on a need, not on a relationship. God is interested in **you**.

Let God's Word Remain in You

If you want to receive an answer to your prayers, the first condition is that you remain in Jesus. Secondly, Jesus tells us, you must let "my words remain in you." It is not sufficient for you only to remain in Jesus. The Word of God must also abide—have its permanent dwelling and home—in you. The Word of the Lord must always remain in you, not pay an occasional visit. It is to reside with you permanently. When anxieties, perplexities and difficulties arise, the Word must rise from its resting place within you, if Jesus' will is to be done and His promises fulfilled. When everything seems to be against you, keep your hold on the Word and your delight in the Lord. This is God's revealed will for you. You will then **know** what to pray and how you are to pray. If His Word abides within you like this, you can request anything.

We are not robots steered here and there by God's remote control. We are created in His image, co-workers with Him in His Kingdom. He asks you questions like, "How would **you** like this or that?" He's created you with a will, a mind, emotions and the five senses, so that you can use them. When His Word is planted in your heart He then gives you moral responsibilities and relies on you to fulfill them. You can't go wrong with His eternal Word in your spirit, because your mind is constantly being renewed. You think the thoughts of God and desire only what He wants. Your prayers are no longer a mere "sighing" to God, but utterances filled with power. Pay no attention to how insignificant or unworthy you may feel when you pray in the Name of Jesus. It is the Name above every other, and the Name either revered or feared in the three realms—heaven, earth and under the earth. Even the spirits must bow their knees to that Name. Everything does not depend on you, but on **the Name** you declare. Everything that rises up in resistance to the will of God must bend before that Name—the Name of Jesus!

Is it God's will for you to live in depression and worry? Not at all. The Word of God says that He will fill you with peace, wisdom and fullness of joy in His presence. Learn what God's Word has to say about every area of your life. The Bible teaches us that people are destroyed for lack of knowledge. In other words, it is not what **we** think that counts, but what **God says in His Word**, and so we must find out what He says and then abide by it.

God stands by what He has said so I don't have to be anxious about billows and storms rolling toward me. He has said in His Word that He hears me, answers me and gives me whatever I ask for, if I abide in Him and His Word abides in me. When I pray, I send out His Word which is so powerful that no one can stop it. It was the Word by which the heavens and the earth were made. The only hindrance the Word can meet is in me—if I am impatient and lacking in endurance, faith and trust or in my knowledge of God. But if I have seen and met Him, if I know Him and His desires, people around me will see that **He is alive** and that He wants to meet their needs. Then the Kingdom of God can spread further, through me.

28

A Developed Prayer Life

Most Christians agree that prayer is important, but for many, that is as far as it goes. However, the Holy Spirit is urging believers to their knees like never before and they are learning to pray in a way they once found difficult, or even impossible.

The prayer of a righteous man is powerful and effective we are told in James 5:16. In the Amplified Bible it reads: "The earnest (heartfelt, continued) prayer of a righteous man makes tremendous power available (dynamic in its working)."

Anointed teaching of faith and righteousness has been powerfully released by the Spirit in recent years, throughout the world. We as believers are being established in our righteousness in Christ, so that former feelings of condemnation have lost their foothold in our lives.

Through the blood that Jesus shed on Calvary, we have entered the new and living way to our Father in heaven. We have realized that He is not against us, but for us. The Holy Spirit has shown us in the Word what God has placed at our disposal—our true inheritance and the privileges incorporated in the New Covenant. We have seen that faith pleases God and that the "just ones," the righteous, are to live by it—moving mountains and seeing God's power released in impossible situations.

All of this has given us a fresh, new relationship with our Father so that when we come to Him, it is with the expectation that He will both hear and answer us. And He does. Hebrews 11:6 says, *Without faith it is impossible to please God, because anyone who comes to him must believe that he exists and that he rewards those who earnestly seek him.* God Himself promises that He will reward us when we seek Him—and He expects us to believe that He will actually do it. If we pray expecting no reward, we give Him no pleasure. Just think how many unpleasant prayers have been prayed to God. Consider the great number of people who have slavishly spoken millions of religious prayers without the slightest conviction or anticipation of an answer.

The Lord has commissioned the teaching of faith to put an end to all of this. When people begin to discover their true identity in Christ, as revealed in the Word, and what they have and can accomplish in Him, their expectations in God begin to rise steeply. They no longer go around under a cloud of condemnation or a general feeling that God is never with them. No, they're established in righteousness, striding forward in faith and perfectly assured that He will always be with them, just as He has said.

Assurance of an Answer Motivates Prayer

You are justified, or made righteous by Jesus Christ. Therefore, James 5:16 says of you, *The prayer of a righteous man is powerful and effective.* The rediscovery of this truth and the resulting anticipation and belief that our prayers really do accomplish much, is sweeping through the Body of Christ worldwide today. When the Holy Spirit impresses our spirit, so that **we begin to believe that God can radically transform situations through our prayers, it is time to pray in earnest.**

As mentioned earlier, one translation reads, "The prayer of a righteous man makes tremendous power available." When we see God's power at work answering our prayers, we're motivated afresh to pray. However, many believers have found it difficult to pray. Why? Because they've been unsure of obtaining an answer. Once, it was deemed almost pious **not** to receive an answer and even rather proud to ask God for anything at all. But, praise the Lord, those days are over! We've begun to see clearly in the Word that God **wants** to answer our prayers. Jesus says in John 15:7, *If you remain in me and my words remain in you, **ask whatever you wish, and it will be given you.*** Further, in John 16:24, *Until now you have not asked for anything in my name. **Ask and you will receive, and your joy will be complete.***

We have seen that it really is the mind of the Father to answer all of our prayers. When the Holy Spirit corrects our mistaken attitudes through the Word, a new longing and desire to pray begins to grow within us and we devote ourselves to prayer in a completely fresh way. Prayer invokes the will of God here on earth, it brings those things that already exist in heaven, down to the earth. It is praying as Matthew 6:10 says, *Your will be done on earth as it is in heaven.* If we don't know what the will of God is, how can we pray for it? God's will is His Word. Only when we know what His Word promises, can we be motivated to pray it down to earth so it becomes evident among us.

When the motivation to pray and the expectation of an answer is planted in our spirit, the Holy Spirit comes to our aid and assists us in our prayer. As quoted earlier, James

5:16 says, *The prayer of a righteous man is powerful and effective.* What is this power? It isn't thunderous volume, pious phrases or ecstatic utterance. **It is the work of the Holy Spirit in your heart, helping you pray what God wants you to pray.**

Spirit-Led Prayer Obtains Results

You have almost certainly noticed in your private prayer life and in your prayer group, how some prayers in themselves are perfectly right and correct, but behind them, there lies no sanction from the Holy Spirit. At other times God's sanction, His authorization and empowering, is plainly saying, "This is what you are to pray about now!" After such prayers, a deep peace and satisfaction confirms that, "this is what the Spirit wanted us to pray about." Romans 8:26 says, *In the same way, the Spirit helps us in our weakness. We do not know what we ought to pray for, but the Spirit himself intercedes for us with groans that words cannot express.*

The indwelling Holy Spirit knows what we are to pray for, so when we let Him lead us, He will show us what to pray for and also empower us as we pray. Then He'll go into action concerning what we've prayed about and assure us of the answer. We should always pray in this empowering. Such Spirit-led and inspired prayers are "powerful and effective." These prayers do not have their origin in our heads. They are not hatched out in our mind, but petitions born in our heart. They come from our spirit, in fellowship with God. They are conceived in our inner man and prayed out in the words of our mouth.

In John 4:23 Jesus says, *A time is coming and has now come when the true worshipers will worship the Father in spirit and truth, for they are the kind of worshipers the Father seeks.* The Father has longed for true worshipers. He's hungered for a people who don't just rattle off empty words (Matt 6:5-7) or whose prayers aren't such religious phrases filled with unbelief that He can't respond to them (Jas 1:6-8). He's waited for a people who will pray according to His will, who will pray from their hearts, and in their spirits, be led by the Holy Spirit. These are the worshipers who will draw the power of heaven down to earth, all over the world.

Throughout the world, God is preparing and training such worshipers. This is why the Spirit is drawing believers into their prayer closets the world over. When we have learned to pray by ourselves, God will allow us to pray with others. When we've learned to pray with others in our prayer groups, He'll teach us to pray together in the church. When the local church has learned to gather and pray and seek God, the powers of darkness that have bound the areas around them will lose their hold. Then the unbridled power of God will be made available to man in a degree we've never yet witnessed—and revival will break out.

Nation Winning Prayer

Allow me to pass on a personal testimony here about my own country, Sweden. I share it in the hope that it will be an inspiration and a challenge to you for your country. It is a tremendous challenge for us to take up our nation—but God **has** said that Sweden will be saved. He has promised us that we can take this country and we are going to do it. First and foremost it will be done through **prayer**. When we believe what God has said and devote ourselves to Him in prevailing prayer, His power will be made available, signs and wonders will take place and men and women will be saved. Sweden is going to be shaken by the power of God.

2 Chronicles 16:9 tells us that *The eyes of the Lord range throughout the earth to strengthen those who hearts are fully committed to him.*

If we commit ourselves to God, believe what He has said and pray accordingly, **He will assist and strengthen us** with His power which will be released in the land as never before. Darkness will be forced to retreat in every town where the church has learned to seek God, be led by the Spirit in prevailing prayer and bind the powers of wickedness there.

God is raising up intercessors and churches that are growing mighty in prayer throughout the land. No revival can make a decisive breakthrough. People everywhere are devoting themselves to God in bold, overcoming prayer that God's power will shake the devil's strongholds and set his captives free.

In 2 Chronicles 7:14 it says, *If my people, who are called by my name, will **humble** themselves and **pray** and **seek my face and turn** from their wicked ways, then will I hear from heaven and will forgive their sin and will heal their land.*

Listen to what the Spirit of God is saying and begin to set time aside more regularly. then you will become a vital link in the chain of those dedicated to the healing of the land, the restoration of what has been broken down and the salvation of what is lost.

Don't let the devil lead you to believe that you cannot pray, that you don't have time to pray, or that you don't get answers if you do pray. These are his lies to hinder you from using the most powerful weapon you have—**the Name of Jesus.** You are a believer. You have the Name of

Jesus. You can pray. God hears your prayers and is going to answer you "immeasurably more than you can ask or imagine" (Eph 3:20). Don't let the devil fool you into thinking you don't have the time to pray. The truth is that you cannot afford the time it will cost you, if you neglect to pray. God will abundantly compensate you for the time you give Him in personal prayer. Not only that, but He will also make you stronger than ever in the Lord. It is time for us to pray. Go into your closet, pray as never before, and you will see signs and wonders in answer to your prayers.

29

The Lord is a Warrior

When you get to know a person closely, you get to know his character. His personality comes clearly into view and you become acquainted with his different qualities. To experience, and appreciate a person's distinctive features and unique personality is one of the greatest benefits of fellowship. In this same way, God, your Father, wants you to get to know the different sides of His personality. Then you can understand Him better and appreciate Him all the more.

God's characteristics are fantastic! 1 John 4:8 says that God is love. Romans 3:26 says that God is just. Isaiah 6:3 tells us that God is holy. Genesis 17:1 says that God is all present, or omnipresent. He is also omniscient, or all powerful. Our God is wonderful and has many different characteristics with which we need to become acquainted.

Not only does the Bible state that God is loving, just and holy, it also says that God is a warrior. Exodus 15:3 declares, *The Lord is a warrior; the Lord is his name.* God who is love, is also a warrior, that is, a soldier. God is a God who fights; this characteristic is part of His very being. A warrior is one who fights more than just now and then. A warrior is someone who is a trained professional. He lives with it day and night.

Ephesians 6:12 says, *For our struggle is not against flesh and blood, but against the rulers, against the authorities, against the powers of this dark world and against the spiritual forces of evil in the heavenly realms.* When God's Word talks about war, weapons, authority and victory, people who are unversed in the Bible tend to react negatively. They believe such vocabulary should not be used among Christians because God is love. But those who talk in this manner have not understood the Gospel.

The Battle is in the Spirit

The Gospel is the love message telling us that God so loved the world that He sent His Son (John 3:16). What did the Son do? Jesus Himself tells us in Luke 11:22, *when someone stronger* (Jesus) *attacks and **overpowers** him* (the devil), *he takes away the armor in which the man trusted and divides* *up the spoils.* Jesus attacked, overpowered and disarmed the devil and demolished his works. **Urged on by love, God sent His Son to fight and win.**

Ephesians 6:12 says that we have to fight a battle, but it is not a physical, carnal fight. The Scripture does not literally talk about a physical war where flesh goes against flesh. It is not a battle against flesh and blood, but **against the spiritual forces of evil in the heavenly realms.**

Therefore, Paul says in 2 Corinthians 10:3, *Though we live in the world, we do not wage war as the world does.* We are on earth as physical beings, but we do not fight as people usually do, although **we certainly do fight!**

Throughout the Bible we read about wars and battles. Every Christian is at war and as long as we live, we will be in it. There is a tremendous war going on in the spiritual realm and we are involved. It is useless to practice "ostrich theology" by putting your head in the sand and pretending the trouble will pass by. It will not pass by until the final victory is won.

Paul states in 2 Corinthians 10:4, *The weapons we fight with are not the weapons of the world.* (We don't fight in a human way with bloodshed, economic warfare, terror, persecutions, hate campaigns, propaganda, lies, slander and so on.) *On the contrary, they* (our weapons) *have divine power to demolish strongholds.* These are spiritual weapons powerful enough to demolish arguments and every pretension that rises up against the knowledge of God (2 Cor 10:5).

If these weapons are not used they become useless. Then the enemy, who is the devil, and not people, will take over and hinder the power of the Gospel from setting people free.

No Victory Without Combat

A person who is in a spiritual war and possesses weapons but does not use them is like a deserter; he's an advantage to the enemy. Therefore the devil has worked overtime to infiltrate the believers with spiritual pacifism. He has deceived them into believing they do not have spiritual weapons or the ability to use them. But those days are over! The Holy Spirit is now saying very distinctly to the Church that it must use its spiritual weapons and fight as never before.

In the book of Nehemiah, the Israelites became weary as they were restoring the walls of Jerusalem. They were constantly harassed by their adversaries (Neh 4:10). They were surrounded by doubters and sceptics who exhorted them to stop building (Neh. 4:12). Nehemiah saw how the people's morale declined. He realized that the resistance they were meeting caused them to look at their own circumstances and because of it, the flesh wanted to give up and capitulate.

Many believers are in a similar situation today. They are willing to desire blessing, but are unwilling to pay the price. They are willing to have the victory only if they can avoid the fight. **However, there is no victory without combat.** There is no glory without sacrifice and cost. You must break through the resistance and battle to reach the other side victoriously. Jesus has won the decisive battle over the enemy at Calvary, and by virtue of His victory, you can win your battles. He is your strength.

Nehemiah helped the Israelites realize this when he said to them, *Don't be afraid of them. Remember the Lord, who is great and awesome, and fight for your brothers, your sons and your daughters, your wives and your homes* (Neh 4:14).

The Warrior Lives Within You

When the people wanted to give up and flee; when they began to listen to the lies of the enemy about how impossible it was to restore the walls and that they never would get their freedom back, Nehemiah exhorted them, to *remember the Lord who is great and awesome.* Who is that? It is the Lord our Warrior. He who fights for us. Exodus 14:14 says, *The Lord will fight for you.* Nehemiah told the people, *fight for your brothers.* When you decide to fight, taking up the spiritual weapons God has given you, and refuse to flee or surrender, you benefit your brothers. **The victory you win, will be enjoyed by many.** What you do can affect thousands of people.

Consider the Lord! He is a warrior. In Isaiah 42:13 it says, *The Lord will march out like a mighty man, like a warrior he will stir up his zeal; with a shout he will raise the battle cry and will triumph over his enemies.* God does not passively sit by, while His enemy makes headway, plunders and destroys. No! He shows His might against His enemies. This is what He is doing all over the world today. He is demonstrating that He can do whatever He wants, whenever He wants, however He wants and with whoever He wants. He has the necessary power to turn your country in the right direction— and He will do it!

The Lord is a warrior. He is the Commander-in-chief of His army. When Goliath abused Israel, David said in 1 Samuel 17:36 that he was defying the armies of the Living God. God does not appreciate being blasphemed and He doesn't like it when His army, the Church, is abused. When believers are railed on and scorned, it is easy to react in a fleshly way, for instance, with self-righteousness or with fear, like the soldiers who were afraid to take on Goliath. However, as a believer you have the nature of Jesus, and His love is in you, so you don't need to defend yourself in a fleshly way, although you can turn the other cheek. When they abused Jesus, He didn't open His mouth. When you refuse to wrestle with carnal weapons, the Lord Himself will be your champion and fight for you.

Isaiah 31:4 says, *This is what the Lord says to me: as a lion growls, a great lion over his prey—and though a whole band of shepherds is called together against him, he is not frightened by their shouts or disturbed by their clamor—so the Lord Almighty will come down to do battle on Mount Zion and on its heights.*

The Lord is like a lion. Jesus is the Lion of the Tribe of Judah. He is not just a lamb; He is also a lion. When you were born again, the Lion of Judah came into you. The Lion hunts and flings itself upon its prey. Jesus is the Commander-in-chief of the army of the Lord. He leads the forces, but it's the army that does the fighting. God wants to fight together with you and through you!

It's Time for Battle—Take up your Weapons!

The Lord is the Warrior who lives inside you and He wants you to cooperate with Him in the battle. You are a soldier in the army of the Lord. Don't sheathe your weapons; take them up and let God use you to conquer for Him.

In Judges 6, Gideon considered himself the least and most insignificant in the tribe of Manasseh. He thought he was nothing; a nobody, having nothing, knowing nothing and never to become anything. Maybe you think you don't have much either and that the enemy is superior everywhere, but God does not look on you in that way. He says to you as He said to Gideon, *The Lord is with you, mighty warrior...I will be with you, and you will strike down all the Midianites together* (Judg 6:12,16).

God changed Gideon's image of himself from an insignificant nobody, to a brave warrior—and He is doing the same thing in His people today. He calls you His valiant warrior, even though you do not feel like one and have known hundreds of defeats. He lights the fire inside you that causes you to love righteousness and hate iniquity (Heb 1:9). You rise up, refuse to accept the attacks of the devil and use the weapons of the Lord to fight for yourself and your brothers.

Ephesians 5:1 says that we "are to be imitators of God as dearly loved children." If the Lord is a warrior, we also should follow and imitate Him as warriors.

It is not time now to relax, It is not time to flee. It is not time to give up or compromise. When you are under fiercer attack than you've experienced previously, it's time to stand more firmly, fight back harder and go on the offensive more than ever.

The world needs the Gospel. Without it there is no salvation. If you run away, who will give them life? Don't lose your boldness. The Lord is with you, mighty man of valor!

We will witness great victories with God and the Lion of Judah will leap upon its prey! The devil is terrified and on the run. That's why he is howling. He is losing his grip over your country. So, use your weapons and conquer!

HEALING

He took up our infirmities and carried our diseases.

Matthew 8:17

30

Seven Reasons Why Healing Is Yours

1. Everything that God Created was Good

When God created the earth and "the fullness thereof" He was satisfied with everything He had made. From the depths of His own nature, His goodness, glory and fullness, He created an abundance of animals, plants, minerals, etc, on the earth. Finally, He created man to govern and administrate creation. When all was ready the Bible says, *God saw all that he had made, and it was **very good*** (Gen 1:31).

There was no deficiency, no defect, no mistake and nothing was overlooked in all of God's creation. Man had been created in His own image, to be like Him (Gen 1:26-27). There was no sin, sickness, lack, poverty or death in man.

God wants us to respect His creation. When, for instance, you consider your own body, you should never look down on it or despise it. Do the opposite. Your body is the temple of the Holy Spirit (1 Cor 6:19) and therefore of great importance. It is to be highly valued and esteemed—a noble vessel in which God wants to glorify Himself (1 Cor 6:20). The body has built-in defence systems against sickness and fights them with everything it has. It never accepts diseases or counts them as assets or blessings, but mobilizes every available resource to repel each attack.

2. Sickness Entered the World at The Fall

Sin entered the world through one man, and *death through sin,* and in this way death came to all men, because all sinned (Rom 5:12).

As a result of Adam's transgression, the gate was opened to sin and all its wanton consequences in creation. The spirit in man died and his relationship with his Father was broken. His soul was gradually filled with fear, pride, hatred and bitterness. Man's body was yielding to weakness and sickness;

a destructive process which, if allowed to continue unchecked, always leads to death. From the day of The Fall until now, the presence of sin, sickness and death has been felt in the earth. Everyone has been afflicted by these things that come from one and the same source and have the same father—the devil, These things are not from our heavenly Father. Jesus says in John 10:10, *The thief comes **only** to steal and kill and destroy; I have come that they may have life, and have it to the full.*

Some people react negatively at the thought of the devil being the ultimate source of all sickness, although this is the unequivocal teaching of the Bible. This truth, however, is sometimes wrongly taken to mean that anyone having even a cold is either possessed or extremely wicked. Unbelievers may be confused or maliciously accuse people but as believers, we should be so familiar with the Scriptures that we do not fall into the same trap they do and blame God for the devil's doings. To deny the devil's existence or his deeds, for fear of what people may think, only increases the scope for his ugly intrusions into God's creation.

To recognize the devil as the ultimate cause of all sickness is not the same as declaring that every sick person is a vile sinner or demon-possessed. *Some things...are hard to understand, which ignorant and unstable people distort, as they do the other Scriptures, to their own destruction* (2 Pet 3:16). We see clearly that *Jesus went around doing good and healing all who were under the power of the devil, because God was with him* (Acts 10:38). Sickness is a form of attack from the enemy (and he aims those attacks at all of us), but praise the Lord, there is victory over it. Jesus healed the sick.

In Luke 13:10-17, Jesus healed a woman who had been crippled for eighteen years with the words, *Should not this woman, a daughter of Abraham, whom **Satan has kept bound** for eighteen long years, be set free on the Sabbath day from what bound her?* Jesus did not call her condition a blessing, He called it a **bondage.** He did not say either, that it had come from God. He declared that it came from **Satan.** He did not maintain that she should be left in the same state, but that she should be **set free** from it. In this particular case, the woman was bound by a spirit of sickness (Luke 13:11) and Jesus loosed her. Some sicknesses are caused by a spirit of sickness, but by no means all of them. However, the devil is the ultimate cause of them all.

Some people react to the truth of God's Word and are then on the defensive and exclaim, "Oh yes! Does it prove I'm guilty of sin then, because I'm sick?" They look accusingly at you, expecting an apology, because you supposedly made such a fearful insinuation that they had committed some awful crime. Nevertheless, the fact is—and this upsets the unbeliever—that everyone is a sinner and in need of grace, forgiveness and salvation.

However, a particular sickness is not always the result of a certain sin. The situation can be similar to the case of the blind man recorded in John 9:3 where Jesus declared, *Neither this man nor his parents sinned...but this happened so that the work of God might be displayed in his life.* In Jesus' time, a tower in Siloam fell, killing eighteen people, and He remarked in Luke 13:4 that they were not guiltier than anyone else, adding in verse 5, *I tell you, no! But unless you repent, you too will all perish.*

Sickness and similar ailments are found in this world, and if anyone is a child of the world, he has little protection against the devil's onslaughts, which tragically plague even the apparently innocent. However, it is more tragic when people will not admit they have sinned before the Almighty, and refuse to receive forgiveness and salvation and so put everything right with Him.

3. Healing was Included in the Old Covenant

When the Lord made Himself known to His people Israel, He revealed Himself to be *The Lord, who heals you,* and promised to keep sickness away from them (Ex 15:26). In Exodus 23:25, He adds *Worship the Lord your God, and his blessing will be on your food and water. **I will take away sickness from among you.***

Protection from sickness was included in the blood covenant which "the Lord our Healer" made with His people. When they lived in obedience to Him, believing His Word, He set up a "safety net" of protection around them, keeping them from the curse of sickness that had come as a result of sin. In Deuteronomy 28, the Lord blessed the people and promised them protection from disease as a part of that blessing.

4. Jesus Healed Everyone Who Came to Him

Jesus came to earth as *the radiance of God's glory and the exact representation of his being* (Heb 1:3). **Everything** Jesus said and **all** that He did, was, and still is, the Father's will. He came to earth with the express purpose of doing the will of God (Heb. 10:7). *My food,* Jesus said in John 4:34, *is to do the will of him who sent me and to finish **his work**.* In John 5:19 He tells us, *The Son can do nothing by himself;*

he can do only what he sees his Father doing because whatever the Father does the Son also does.

This means that when Jesus healed anyone, it was the Father's will to heal that person. The next question is "Did Jesus heal everyone?" Yes, He did. He healed **all who came to Him.** He did not empty the hospital in Israel, but when the sick came to Him for healing, He healed them.

A large crowd gathered around Him, *who had come to hear him and to be healed of their diseases. Those troubled by evil spirits were cured, and the people all tried to touch him, because power was coming from him and healing them all* (Luke 6:18-19).

In Luke 9:11 we read, *He welcomed them and spoke to them about the kingdom of God, and* **healed those who need healing.** When anyone was in **need** of healing, Jesus healed them! Again and again the Bible records that He healed all who came to Him. (Read Matt 8:16-17, 9:35, 12:15, 14:14,35-36, 15:30-31 and Mark 6:56.)

Jesus turned no one away. He never said, "I can't," "I don't want to," or "I don't have the time." Never! When someone once asked Him He replied, *I am willing... Be clean!* (Matt 8:3). No one ever went home disappointed after having met Jesus.

5. Jesus Carried our Sickness on the Cross

Jesus did not just come to heal those who lived at the same time and place as Himself. He is the "Lord who heals us" in every generation. He is our Lord and Savior today, just as He was for the people of His own time. He offers salvation now as much as He did then, because He died for our generation too. He paid the ultimate price for mankind's eternal salvation on the cross. He died, once for all, that we might live forever. He Himself bore our sin and debt in His body on the cross and then carried it away into death. He paid the final price for our transgressions.

The Scriptures also establish the fact that **in the same way** that He bore our sins on the cross, He also took our sicknesses. Isaiah 53:4-5, states plainly, *Surely he took up our infirmities and carried our sorrows, yet we considered him stricken by God, smitten by him, and afflicted. But he was pierced for out transgressions, he was crushed for our iniquities; the punishment that brought us peace was upon him, and by his wounds we are healed.*

What a wonderful truth this is! Jesus paid the utmost price for the whole of your humanity—including your body. He ransomed you wholly, and by His wounds you are healed!

Some attempt to dismiss Isaiah 53, calling it poetry or defining the infirmities as spiritual only—despite the clear Biblical evidence in Matthew 8:16-17, which shows that it was physical illness Jesus carried on the cross. This is a grave form of denial and a conceited rebuttal of the total redemption that Jesus won on the cross of Calvary, for us all.

6. Jesus Sent the Disciples out to Heal

Jesus did not reserve the right to heal the sick only for Himself. He commissioned His disciples to do the same and to heal as He did. He first sent out the twelve, instructing them in Matthew 10:1-8 and Luke 9:1-6 to preach the Kingdom of God, giving them authority over unclean spirits and a command to heal **every** disease and sickness (Matt 10:1), He told them to both preach and heal (Matt 10:7-8; Luke 9:2).

The disciples *set out and went from village to village preaching the gospel and healing people everywhere* (Luke 9:6). Everywhere they went, the sick were healed. Subsequently Jesus sent out the seventy—not just the twelve apostles—and told them, *When you enter a town and are welcomed, eat what is set before you. Heal the sick who are there and tell them, The kingdom of God is near you* (Luke 10:8-9).

After the resurrection, Jesus reappeared to the disciples and told them that all those who believed in Him were to go into the world and preach the Good News to all creation. Jesus said the believers were to drive out demons, speak in new tongues, and when they placed their hands on sick people, they would recover (Mark 16:17-20). You and I are believers, the disciples of Jesus who are commanded to go out and to preach and heal. Why? Because Jesus still wants to save and heal people. He is the same *yesterday and today and forever* (Heb 13:8). He wants to show people He is alive today; He loves them and He is able and willing to do wonders in their lives.

7. Jesus has Commanded and Empowered the Church to Heal the Sick

The command to heal the sick is included in the Great Commission (Mark 16:17-20). Jesus has handed the keys of the Kingdom of Heaven to the Church (Matt 16:16-19) for us to unlock its blessings to the nations. He does not ask us to do anything we cannot do. He has given us authority to heal the sick.

When the Holy Spirit came on the disciples, they received power to be Jesus' witnesses (Acts 1:8). Everything that is necessary to heal the sick has been deposited in that power of the Holy Spirit, in the Name of Jesus and in His Word. Jesus has not left us without resources to impart His healing. It is to flow out from His Body to men and women in need. God has provided many ways for this healing power to flow. Healing comes through the laying on of hands (Mark 16:18), through the prayer of faith (James 5:15-18) and through taking the Lord's Supper (1 Cor 11:29-30). It can come through the gifts of the Spirit (1 Cor 12:8-10) or through a word from God, as in Matthew 8:8, *Just say the word, and my servant will be healed*. Healing comes through the Name of Jesus (Acts 3:16, 4:10) and through prayer cloths, handkerchiefs and aprons (Acts 19:12).

God has an abundance of ways to impart healing to you. He is eager to meet you and is full of love and compassion. He is for you, not against you. He let Jesus die so healing could be yours. He sent His Holy Spirit and His Word to bring His miraculous power and healing to you. He loves you and wants to heal any need you may have. He also desires to make you a channel for His Gospel, His healing and His restoring power to men and women so that through you, they can see that Jesus is Lord.

God wants His Church to rise up, shake off its doubt and fear of His Word, use the weapons He has given it and go out to set the captives free. Today, thousands are taking Him at His word, standing to their feet and beginning to march in step together with their Lord!

31

Healing in the Redemption

Our God is a good God! His love for us is eternally sure. He does not change, He is steadfast. His revealed will is established and valid forever. *God is not a man, that he should lie, nor a son of man, that he should change his mind* (Num 23:19). Our God is neither erratic nor fickle. He is what He says He is and does what He promises. He has revealed His mind to us through Jesus and the Scriptures, and it is there that we can see what God's express will is.

Here I am—it is written about me in the scroll—I have come to do your will, O God (Heb 10:7). Jesus came, the Bible tells us, to do God's will. When you look at Him you can see exactly what the will of God is because everything Jesus said and did was God's will. He only did what He saw the Father doing (John 5:19), and spoke what He heard the Father saying (John 8:26,28).

This is the firm ground you must tread when you walk with your Lord. You must know that His mind is revealed and that His promise is His pledge. God has no other will than what He has expressed in His promises. He means exactly what He says.

God's promises are His covenant agreements and are for **everyone** in covenant with Him. He does not discriminate. If you are born again, confess Jesus as your Savior and Lord, and want to follow Him, all His promises are for you. You are embraced by the New Covenant on the grounds of Jesus' redemptive death. God's promise includes you and it is available to you. He has arranged and completed everything. When you see it, you can come freely and joyfully with gratitude to Him, and receive by faith all that He has put at your disposal—and this includes healing too. Your belief that God wants to heal cannot be based on other people's healings, no matter how wonderful they may be. Many people sit at the side of their "pool of Bethesda," looking down, hoping for an angel to come and stir up the water (John 5:1-3), and wondering when their turn will come for a sudden healing from heaven.

However, this is not the will of God. He does not want you to wait for a possible, but improbable healing from out of the blue. Instead, He wants you to look to Jesus; who He is and what He has already done for us **all**. The sight of Him will provide the grounds you need for believing that God will perform a definite miracle in your life. God has made His will clear and plain in Jesus. What He accomplished when He walked the earth and what He achieved on the cross was the perfect will of God.

The Cross—the Grounds for all God Wants to Give You

The cross is both the starting point and the continuation of everything God desires to give you and to do with you today. It was on the cross that Jesus took your sin and paid your debt. On the cross, He died in your place. All that the New Covenant offers of life, blessing, peace, right standing before God and uninterrupted fellowship with Him, is because of the cross. The New Covenant is open and inaugurated, having been sealed by the blood of Jesus. But, it applies, only to those who acknowledge and claim the benefit of that completed work on the cross.

Every answer to prayer, every individual blessing you can ever enjoy in life, you receive on the grounds of Jesus' sacrificial death **for you**. Without the cross, there is no access to the Father. If there had been no cross there would be no eternal, abundant life. Without the cross there would be no forgiveness, no deliverance and no miracles.

Jesus' redeeming death is the condition and guarantee that God's will and blessings apply you. Therefore, you must know what His redeeming work contains. What He achieved there, is available today.

Matthew 8:16-17, says that *When evening came, many who were demon-possessed were brought to him, and he drove out the spirits with a word and healed **all** the sick. This was to fulfill what was spoken through the prophet Isaiah: "He took up our infirmities and carried our diseases."* Here, the Holy Spirit is citing, through Matthew, the prophecy in Isaiah 53, making it clear that when Jesus drove out evil spirits and healed **all** who were sick, it was a fulfillment of that prophecy.

Jesus' redeeming death on the cross is foretold in the words of Isaiah 53:2,3, *He had no beauty or majesty to attract us to him, nothing in his appearance that we should desire him. He was despised and rejected by men, a man of sorrows, and familiar with suffering. Like one from whom men hide their faces he was despised, and we esteemed him not.*

This passage refers to the cross. Jesus was despised, mocked, lashed, ridiculed and rejected. People regarded Him with disgust, a detestable offender, a corrupted and depraved wreck of humanity. But Isaiah saw further than man's view of Jesus, he saw how God, from His vantage point, viewed Him as well—and these two views were worlds apart. *Surely he took up our infirmities and carried our sorrows, yet we considered him stricken by God, smitten by him and afflicted* (Isa 53:4).

The world looked on Jesus' suffering as a penalty and chastisement from God. But it was not the case! It was **our** infirmities He bore. On the cross, Jesus took on Himself something that was not His fault. He bore it **voluntarily** for us, **so we** could be relieved of it. He became our substitute, our replacement, so that we could be spared. O, what a blessed exchange!

> But he was pierced for our transgressions, he was crushed for our iniquities; the punishment that brought us peace was upon him, and by his wounds we are healed. We all, like sheep, have gone astray, each of us has turned to his own way; and the Lord has laid on him the iniquity of us all (Isa 53:5-6).

Healing for Physical Sickness

What happened on the cross? God let our sins and their consequences fall on Jesus. He was pierced and wounded for our transgressions, He bore our sin and guilt; but not only that, He also took on Himself our infirmities and carried our sicknesses. He did it for our sakes. The punishment that brought us peace was on Him. He was penalized for us, and by His wounds, we are healed.

We have often emphasized that Jesus took our sins on the cross, and praise the Lord, He did! But Jesus did more than that. He even took our sicknesses on the cross. This truth has often been neglected, and then, men and women have not been built up in faith to receive their healing. When the foundations are being destroyed, what can the righteous do? (Ps 11:3). The cross is the foundation on which the whole of your Christian life is built. If you have only a vague and imperfect picture of what happened on the cross, then your Christian life will be just as vague and imperfect. You will not be able to fully enjoy the benefits of all Jesus has done for you.

Some even go so far as to deny that Jesus took our sicknesses on the cross, saying instead that it was the "sickness of sin," or "our spiritual infirmity" He bore. This is absolutely incorrect.

Isaiah 53:4 says that Jesus bore our griefs, our infirmities. The word is **kholee** in the Hebrew, meaning physical sickness and is the same word used in Deuteronomy 7:15 where it tells us that *The Lord will keep you free from every disease.* Disease is physical sickness. When Jesus cured physical sicknesses in Matthew 8:16-17, the Scripture asserts that Isaiah 53:4 was being fulfilled, where it is written, *He took up our infirmities*.

Accordingly, Jesus bore both sin and sickness. 1 Peter 2:24 quotes from Isaiah 53:5 where it says, *By his wounds we are healed.* The word "healed," is the Greek word, **iaomai**, and means "physically healed." It is used this way no less than 28 times in the New Testament.

We must not discredit or deny what Jesus accomplished on the cross. He paid the ultimate price for our salvation and we have no right to diminish what He has done.

Isaiah 53:4 says that *he **took up** our infirmities*. The Hebrew word is **nasa.** In Isaiah 53:12 we read that, *he **bore** the sin of many*. The same word, "nasa," is used in this text as well. In other words, Jesus took up and bore both sins and sicknesses in the same way.

Further, in verse 4 we read that *He **carried our sorrows***. This is **sabal** in the Hebrew, and the same word is used in verse 11, *and he will **bear** (sabal) their iniquities*.

Jesus Took Both Sin and Sickness

Jesus took and bore our iniquities and infirmities. One does not exclude the other. "But surely," you may exclaim, "sin must be the most important thing He bore." Well, of course, when it comes to salvation, because without such a reconciliation, we could never have had peace with God and go to heaven. The most vital truth is that a person can be saved and escape being lost forever. To be healthy all life long and then go to hell, is infinitely worse than being sick all life long and going to heaven. You should also know at this point, that it has never been a question of your first having to achieve sound health to be accepted by God for heaven. That would be terrible! God loves you just as much if you're sick as if you're well. That's not the issue. The issue is that God has accomplished a work on the cross that has taken care of both sin and sickness. He offers you both salvation and healing in the redemption. What God has joined together do not divide asunder.

Psalm 103:2, says, *Praise the Lord, O my soul, and forget not all his benefits,* meaning all the wonderful things Jesus **has** done for us. What has He done? *Who forgives **all** my sins and heals **all** my diseases* (Ps 103:3).

On the cross Jesus took every sin and crime that anyone has ever done or could do. He died for **all** the sins of **all** the people. But He also took **all** our sicknesses and infirmities, and so He can "heal **all** our diseases." There is not a sickness that Jesus did not bear on the cross, and because of that He both can and will cure them all.

In Matthew 9:35 it says, *Jesus went through all the towns and villages, teaching in their synagogues, preaching the good news of the kingdom and **healing every disease and sickness***. Matthew 8:16-17, tells us He **healed all the sick!** Why? Because *this was to fulfill what was spoken through the prophet Isaiah: –He took up our infirmities and carried our diseases.*"

Therefore, in Mark 2:5-12, Jesus could not only forgive the lame man's sins, but also heal his body. His ministry had two equally important functions. Then on the cross, He paid the price for our sickness as well as for our sins.

1 Peter 2:24 declares, *By his wounds you **have been** healed*. This means that Jesus healed us on the cross nearly 2,000 years ago in precisely the same way that He forgave us and saved us. Everything is ready and complete. Now the invitation is open and we can *approach the throne of grace with confidence, so that we may receive mercy and find grace to help us in our time of need* (Heb 4:16).

Today is "the day of salvation!" Forgiveness and healing are available to us today, because of the work Jesus **has completed** for us. The promise of healing is no uncertain one. Healing is not the result of a passing fancy on God's part or an inexplicable, haphazard bolt from the blue, but is something out of the Father's innermost being and will. The foundation for healing was laid on the cross. As His own Son was willing to pay the price, so the Father showed that it is His will and testament for healing to become "the children's bread" (Matt 15:26-28). He revealed healing as a covenant blessing and privilege when Jesus let His body be broken and His covenant blood be poured out (Matt 26:26-28).

Jesus' victory in the cross is for everyone. Each of us is God's special favorite. He loves us all. Everyone who believes will be saved. He has riches to give to all who call on His name (Rom 10:12-13).

God does not want the experiences of others, your own feelings or anything else to be the basis for your healing. He has provided the cross as the foundation for healing. This is why the devil always tries to get our eyes off it. However, when you see what Jesus has done for you, you can approach the Father with confidence and assurance of faith and take what He offers you. The Holy Spirit will be your Helper and Guide. He will encourage and strengthen you, and enable you to receive everything God is waiting to give you.

32

Healing for the People

When Jesus lived on earth, He spent much of His time healing the sick—and He did so because He was sent to do the Father's will.

In Hebrews 10:7 Jesus says, *Here I am—it is written about me in the scroll—I have come to do your will, O God.* Jesus came to earth to do the Father's will, and as He carried that out, He healed the sick. In other words, it is the Fathers will to heal the sick!

Acts 1:1 says, *In my former book, Theophilus, I wrote about all that Jesus **began** to do and to teach.* What Jesus did when He was here on earth was only the beginning of His ministry. He planned to continue doing the same things He had done while in His physical body, through His spiritual body, the Church.

In Hebrews 13:8 we read that *Jesus Christ is the same yesterday and today and forever.* He has never changed. The same things He did "yesterday on the earth," He does today and will continue to do until eternity.

He is the unchanging God. The same power and anointing for healing that worked in Him then, works in Him now. Just as miracles took place then, by the impartation of healing through His body, they take place today. When He was here, He spoke, used His mouth, touched people with His hands or let them touch His clothing. Today, healing is imparted in the same way—only now, through His body, the Church.

More people are being healed today than when Jesus was here. Now, His body is worldwide. Then, He was limited to one geographical place at any given time. Today, He is everywhere! Believers everywhere, the members of His body throughout the world, are praying for the sick and seeing Jesus do His miracles today!

Healing is Part of the Good News

Healing is part of the Gospel. The Good News is that Jesus forgives sins, frees the captives and brings blessings to every area of life. There is no other Gospel than this. If we refuse to pray for the sick or reject faith for healing, we distort and detract from the Good News that Jesus brought.

The truth is not that Jesus healed people sometimes, but usually he did not! He was always healing people. He always healed all who came to Him. You will never find an occasion when Jesus turned a sick person away with an excuse like "I can't" or "I don't feel like it."

Mark 6:56 says, *And **wherever** he went—into **villages**, **towns** or **countryside**—they placed the sick in the market-places. They begged him to let them touch even the edge of his cloak, and all who touched him were healed.*

In place after place, time after time, Jesus healed all the sick who came to Him.

Matthew 9:35 says, *Jesus went through all the towns and villages, teaching in their synagogues, preaching the good news of the kingdom and healing every disease and sickness.*

Everywhere Jesus went there were people with a multitude of complaints. The Bible does not say that He only healed a few of them who had certain ailments. It is written that He healed "every disease and sickness." This means that He cured all who came to Him, whatever problem beset them. That was Good News—that Jesus both could and would heal the sick—from whatever sickness they were suffering!

Healing: An Expression of the Father's Will

In Luke 9:11 we read that crowds followed Jesus and that *He welcomed them and spoke to them about the kingdom of God, **and healed those who needed healing**.* Can you imagine the situation? Thousands of people were following Jesus. Among them, there must have been hundreds who were sick. There was an endless number who needed healing, and "all who needed it, He healed."

Is there anyone in your family or among your relatives or in your church who needs healing? If there is, then Jesus wants to heal that person.

Once, a leper came to Jesus. He did not doubt His ability to heal but he doubted His will, or desire to do so. He said, *Lord, if you are willing, you can make me clean* (Matt 8:2). *I am **willing**,* Jesus said. *Be clean!*

With that, Jesus answered the question of God's willingness to heal the sick once and for all. *For God does not show favoritism* (Rom 2:11). If He is willing to cure one, then He is willing to cure all. Jesus did not heal on one or two occasions only; He healed everyone who came to him, demonstrating the Father's will to heal all.

Jesus came to do the Father's works. He did nothing except what He saw the Father do, so when Jesus healed sick people, it was an expression of the Father's willingness to do the same. Wherever He went, He healed the sick.

In Acts 10:38 it says, *God anointed Jesus of Nazareth with the Holy Spirit and power, and...he went around doing good and **healing all** who were under the power of the devil, **because God was with him.***

"God was with Him" because God liked what He was doing! What was He doing? He was healing **all** who were under the power of the devil! Therefore, sickness is not the Father's will, but an attack from the enemy. God's will is to break every such oppression and torment through healing. Healing is from heaven and it is ours because of Jesus.

God's will is to heal, and He showed it by letting Jesus cure all who came to Him, as it is written in Luke 6:19, *and the people all tried to touch him, because power was coming from him and healing them **all.***

Heal the Sick!
Part of the Great Commission

Healing is available today in the same way that is was when Jesus walked on earth. In His last words on earth, Jesus gave orders to the disciples (the Great Commission) to place their hands on the sick and *they **will** get well* (Mark 16:18).

The disciples did exactly what Jesus told them to do and the results are recorded for us in the Book of Acts. We read *that crowds gathered also from the towns around Jerusalem, bringing their sick and those tormented by evil spirits, and **all of them were healed** (Acts 5:16).

It was completely natural for the disciples to **preach the Gospel and heal the sick**, because Jesus had told them to do so. He had sent them out to preach the Kingdom of God and to heal the sick (Luke 9:2).

He had instructed them, *As you go, preach this message: "The kingdom of heaven is near!" Heal the sick, raise the dead, cleanse those who have leprosy, drive out demons. Freely you have received, freely give* (Matt 10:7-8).

Jesus commanded the believers not only to preach, but **also to heal the sick!** It was His will to have the sick healed!

He would never have asked us to do anything against His will. He says plainly, *Freely you have received, freely give.* You have received healing. You have been delivered. You have been blessed—make sure you pass it all on!

There is a world of sick and depressed people around us today—and the Church has the answer for them. We have the weapons, and the power—we have the goods! If we do not make use of them, judgment will come upon us. If we hold back healing from those in need, we will be called to judgment. We have no mandate to either change or abolish the Gospel. Jesus has never required us to stand up and deny or explain His Word away.

We do not have the right to blame God, or maintain things about Him that are not written in His Word, simply so we can defend ourselves and our unbelief.

Our task is to take God's healing power to the people. His power to heal will abound in any situation where the people take Jesus at His word. In situations where believers refuse to take Jesus as their healer, then, of course, it is more difficult for Him to perform miracles among them. However, where they expect Jesus to be the one He says He is and do the things He promises to do, His miracle working power is readily released.

What God needs today is not a crowd of people apologizing for the Gospel, but an army of believers who take a firm hold on His promises. He needs believers who will ignore hopeless situations and increasingly expect Jesus to manifest His will and power to heal the sick.

God is a good God. Healing in one of His wonderful gifts to the humanity He loves so much. Remember, He let His Son die for us. He wants men and women to have life to the full!

A VICTORIOUS LIFE

...who satisfies your desires with good things.

Psalm 103:5

33

Our Superabundant God

When God showed Himself to Abraham and entered into covenant with him (Gen 17) He revealed Himself as God Almighty, or "El Shaddai," which means the "God who is more than enough," the "All sufficient God" and the "Giver of Life."

The living God is the source of all life, eternal life. In John 10:10, Jesus said that He had come to give us God's abundant life, His life is full and brimming over: *You anoint my head with oil; my cup overflows* (Ps 23:5) and more than sufficent: *"The Lord is my shepherd, I shall not be in want"* (Ps 23:1).

There is no lack in God. He has a profusion of everything. Majesty, honor, might, authority, radiance and glory all belong to Him. His inner being pulsates with life and love.

When God created man, He made him in His image, to be like Him (Gen 1:27). According to Psalm 8:5, He made man a little lower than the heavenly beings and crowned him with glory and honor. Man and woman lived in fellowship with God, made in His image, clothed in glory, filled with His life and having access to His power. God is the God of all sufficiency, lacking nothing – and it was mankind's lot to live in the same abundant supply, lacking nothing. They lived in Eden's paradise. "Eden" in Hebrew means "riches, bounteousness and pleasure"—and God was the source of it all.

When man fell into sin, he lost his abundant life and the devil became his master. Man came under his satanic nature (Eph 2:1-2) and his spirit died. The devil became the god of this world and age, exercising his dominion to steal, kill and destroy. Man was now a mere slave. In his fall, he had exchanged his God-given glory and life of abundance—for sin, poverty, sickness, loneliness and death. None of these things was in the world before sin, but now they lay like a blight on all creation. None of it came from God's heart and nothing like it was ever present before The Fall.

By making a covenant with Abraham, God intended to reestablish His fellowship with mankind and restore all that man had lost in The Fall. Through Abraham, Christ was to come and through Jesus Christ, the superabundant life and fellowship with the Father, the all sufficient God, was to be restored.

God Needed a Man

What was it that mankind lost at The Fall?

1. Man lost his legal standing before God. Being separated from Him by sin, man came under condemnation and forfeited his right to approach God (Isa 59:2).

2. Man lost his Godlike life and became spiritually dead.

3. Man lost his citizenship in the Kingdom of God and became a citizen of the devil's kingdom. The curse of sin and death overwhelmed him and he came under Satan's dominion.

Man was spiritually dead. He was condemned from within, and enslaved by sin. As he stood under this curse, he was condemned by the devil to a life of sickness, poverty, loneliness and despair. Man was moving toward certain eternal death and total separation from God.

However, God had a completely different plan for mankind, and this plan led Him to establish a covenant with Abraham. It was man who had originally received authority from God to rule the earth (Gen 1:26,28; Ps 8:6), but he handed it to the devil, who thereby became the god of this age (Luke 4:6). **A man** became the channel for Satan to spread his spiritual death, and it would take **a man** to become the channel for God to spread His life, God needed a person who would obey Him before anything else. Abraham accepted the covenant and walked in that obedience of faith before God. Because of this, God could uphold the covenant on the earth and send Jesus to deliver us!

A covenant always works two ways. Each side must give himself and all he was to the other person. In our covenant with God, we give ourselves to Him and He commits Himself with all that He is and has, to us.

The covenant God established with Abraham meant that on Abraham's side, he was to love God, obey Him, follow and believe Him—in short to give his life to God. From God's side, it meant that He would give Himself to Abraham. He would protect him and lead him, comfort, bless and support him, and give him His life and bounty. We have often been taught this important truth, but it bears repeating, that all that Abraham owned now belonged to God.

For us, it is a question of our consecration and love to God that causes us to put Him first, "forsaking all others." We must be prepared to leave everything for Him. Everything is now His—home, family, work, time, money, relatives, property and so forth. These are no longer ours: they belong to God. What we've often missed, however, is the awareness that a covenant is, in fact, a **two-way agreement**. We agree to surrender ourselves to God and are prepared to pay whatever it costs. This does not mean, though, that God takes everything away from us and we never get anything from Him. No, God also has a responsibility in the covenant.

On the other side of the covenant, and the devil desperately wants to keep us ignorant of this, is God, the Almighty. God who is the God of plenty and who joyfully gives us "every good and perfect gift." Your covenant relationship with God means that He has unreservedly committed Himself to you. He has committed His bountiful life, His mighty wisdom, His supernatural power and His personal presence to you so that you, in "all things at all times will have all you need" (see 2 Cor 9:8). When in need you can call on Him and He has pledged Himself to help His partner-in-covenant.He says to us in Luke 15:31, *My son...you are always with me, and everything I have is yours.*

He who did not spare his own Son, but gave him up for us all—how will he not also, along with him, graciously give us all things? (Rom 8:32). God has life for you in every area through Jesus Christ.

Life in Every Area

God is the God of abundant life, and through Jesus He has made that life available to us. The fullness of His life and divine nature are ours through His precious promises (2 Pet 1:4). His bountiful life includes more than we can ever need, in any situation.

When mankind fell into sin, no part of our life was left unaffected by The Fall and its spiritual death. No area of our life remained in the glory of God. Everything fell. Lack and the absence of abundant life became a fact for everyone.

However, in Jesus there is a superabundant supply of life and resources for any need, and for everyone. Jesus' death on the cross and His resurrection covers every aspect of life's needs. Jesus took your sin on the cross and He paid your debt. He bore your agony. He took your sickness and He removed your poverty and want (Isa 53:3-6; 2 Cor 5:21, 8:9; Gal 3:13), replacing it all with His righteousness and overwhelming life. This is the Good News—the Gospel: God, in Jesus Christ, has life to the full for us all.

As long as God does not say a clear "No" to any area of your life, you have promises and blood bought rights to draw on in faith. The only realm about which God specifically speaks in the negative, is death. Until now death is not subject to Jesus. We will all die if He does not return beforehand. But the sting of death, with its authority and power, is broken (1

Cor 15:50-57). God, your kind heavenly Father who loves you, has ransomed you at an astronomical price.

He is the God of abundance. When you allow His overflowing life to function within you, He manifests His presence and glory. The devil loathes God's life and presence and is constantly trying to steal its accompanying promises from the saints. He endeavors to paint God as an erratic, half-vacant, unpredictable despot whom you slavishly and blindly worship. He uses not only accusations but even your own longing to love and serve God against you; to try and rob you of what God has already given you. He makes you feel guilty about almost everything you do, getting you to believe that nearly everything is taboo and that you are sinning as soon as you allow yourself the simplest little enjoyment.

But God is not like that. He is your gentle Father who loves you and bought you at tremendous personal cost. You are incomparably dear to Him. Why do you think He has given you His precious promises with Jesus? **All He has is yours, and it gives Him great personal pleasure when He sees you draw on His promises and abundant supply.**

God is prosperity itself. He does not want His children to have a deficiency in anything, including their finances. He hates selfish desire and greed, but has nothing against distributing His wealth to the needs of His children. He does not want to see them suffering lack, but is happy to see them enjoying His goodness in the financial area too. God wants His children to imitate and follow Him (Eph 5:1), and to be as kind and generous as He is.

Poverty entered the world through sin. It is not a virtue, bringing you nearer to God, but a curse that robs men and women of their health, joy and ability to help those in need.

God wants the Gospel—the Good News—to reach to the ends of the earth. He wants to bless you in every way so you too can be a channel for His glory, prosperity and love, wherever you go.

34

God Wants You to Succeed and Prosper

The words "prosperity"and "success" have become so misunderstood that we must look a little more closely at what the Bible has to say about them.

To some people, the word "prosperity" sounds somewhat suspect. Influenced by experiences in the world, we have received our impressions and often drawn our parallels from the world. We imagine a selfish life of luxury, a life of "success" for a privileged few at other's expense, or a religious excuse for leading a carnal, soulish life or even retaining a get-rich-quick attitude.

The Biblical view, of the words "succeed" and "prosper" is totally different. God does not want you to live an egocentric life for your own ends, or a life described in James 4:2-3, *You do not have, because you do not ask God. When you ask, you do not receive, because you ask with wrong motives, that you may spend what you get on your pleasures.* God makes two remarks here: 1) Asking in order to lead a selfish life, is to ask with wrong motives, and 2) the one so motivated, will not receive an answer. We see, then, that God looks on our motive when we pray. If we have a wrong motive, He cannot bless it.

However, the Bible does speak of prosperity and success, so it is important that we are aware of what God means by it. When mankind fell into sin; fear, failure and defeat became part of his experience and thinking. These things continue to influence us even after we have been born again—especially if we have not received accurate teaching from God's Word. Many Christians are left with the scars of unbelief and failure, never expecting that anything can ever go well again, or develop successfully and prosper. That is not God's will.

God does not want His children to fail in everything they do or to live in defeat. He has planned for His family to live in triumph. This is one of the reasons Jesus died and conquered Satan. The devil is extremely unhappy when things go well for you. He doesn't want to see you joyful, happy, healed, liberated and blessed. He wants to see you bound and fettered, unable to live in the blessings of God. His **only** reason for coming to you is to steal, kill and destroy in your life; but Jesus came to give you life to the full. (John 10:10).

Oppression, discouragement, defeat, poverty, sin and the curse all have their home in the world, but Jesus says, *Take heart! I have overcome the world* (John 16:33). 1 John 5:4 says, *For **everyone born of God overcomes the world***. You and I are born of God, and He has put within us the ability to overcome the world, by His Spirit. We can live in victory over every attack. This is living in success and prosperity.

The Word of God Prospered

We are not talking about a life without problems. Not at all! Rather, a life under continuous assault. The devil rages when he sees that you have really decided to take God at His word. He tries everything to stop you—but with your God, you will succeed. *If God is for us, who can be against us?* (Rom 8:31).

Since many people become upset over the word "success," I once asked the Lord what His definition of prosperity and success was, and I received this answer, **"A man or woman prospers when all that God has said and promised in His Word, becomes a manifested reality in his or her life. This is to prosper and succeed."** It is the Word which is to prosper. *So shall My word be that goes forth from My mouth; it shall not return to Me void, but...it shall prosper in the thing for which I sent it* (Isa 55:11 NKJV).

God wants His Word, the Gospel, to prosper. When it does, its power is seen and people are saved, blessed and restored. The Word prospers when many people are touched by it and the number of disciples increases rapidly.

God has always thought in terms of increase, progress, success and prosperity. It is the same with His Word. He sends it out, not to get stuck somewhere on the way, but to return to heaven after *watering the earth and making it bud and flourish, so that it yields seed for the sower and bread for the eater* (Isa 55:10). God confirms His Word with signs and wonders, wanting as many as possible to be overtaken, "struck" by as much blessing as possible!

God is kind, and does not begrudge people good things. He does not grudgingly "withhold any good thing" as some teach when they distort the Scriptures and make God out to be other than who He is. Ephesians 1:3 tells us He has *blessed us in the heavenly realms with **every** spiritual blessing in Christ*. Romans 8:32 tells us, *He who did not spare his own Son, but gave him up for us all—how will he not also, along* *with him, graciously give us **all** things?* God does not withhold from us, He **gives** to us.

God wants you to be His servant, and as His servant, to prosper. In Psalm 35:27 it says, *Let the Lord be magnified, who has pleasure in the prosperity of His servant* (NKJV). He wants you to see that when you do as **He** desires, you **will** succeed. Why? Because you are in His plans and they are already blessed. His plans are expressed in His Word which, He has already declared, "will not return to me empty," or without fruit. If you believe His Word, follow and proclaim it, it will increase and multiply, in other words, it will prosper. Blessings will come to you and all those you reach with the Gospel.

In Joshua 1:8 the Lord says, *Do not let this Book of the Law depart from your mouth; meditate on it day and night, so that you may be careful to do everything written in it. Then you will be prosperous and successful.* What does the Lord promise here? *Then you will be prosperous and successful.* **When** will you be prosperous and successful? **When you are abiding in His Word, believing it and following it** because **the Word is prospering in you!** This is not some kind of egocentric, elite thinking for the strong, brave and beautiful. No! It is all about the Word of God transforming, blessing and lifting up the lives of all those who take it to heart.

Material Needs in a Material World

The promises of God are not for just one area of our lives. Many theologians have made the Gospel so diffuse that hardly anyone dares take it literally anymore. But the Gospel speaks in concrete terms. God's blessings are for here and now and for eternity too. However, healing and deliverance are only for today, because in heaven you won't need them. You need them **here!**

Psalm 1:1-3 says that if you have your delight in the law of the Lord, you are a person like a *tree planted by streams of water, which yields its fruit in season and whose leaf does not wither. **Whatever** he does prospers.* Notice that it does not say that you will prosper in just **one** area of your life, namely, new birth, and that every other area will go up and down, or just badly, as it does for everyone else "because everyone shares the same conditions in life." No! We don't share the same conditions at all! This world lies under the curse of sin, but when you are born again and become a "hearer and doer" of the Word, your life will be blessed. You pass in under the covenant blessings, not because you are clever but because, by God's grace, you have accepted Jesus, the surety and guaranty of that covenant. Jesus is blessed and you are now **in Him**. **In Him** you are also blessed with *every spiritual blessing in Christ* (Eph 1:3) in **every area of life**.

Psalm 1:3 says of the righteous person, ***Whatever*** *he does prospers.* This means that every branch of your life will begin to sprout and become verdant. Life has come! Abundant life (John 10:10) life from God that is overflowing, increasing, developing and going from glory to glory!

Once I heard the Spirit of the Lord say "The most difficult thing I have to do is to get my people to believe I have really blessed them." We have been deceived and "brainwashed" by religious thinking instead of sitting under the teaching of the Word. We've been ashamed and embarrassed if God has blessed us and have often excused ourselves for the blessings we have received. This does not honor God. It glorifies God when we believe His Word and accept what He has for us.

Jesus says in Luke 12:15, Watch out! Be on your guard against all kinds of greed, a man's life does not consist in the abundance of his possessions. Your attitude is extremely important. If you think you must own a mass of things in order to be accepted or satisfied, you've missed it all. The important thing is to love and serve Jesus. Everything else is meaningless compared with that.

Many Christians today are living in their expensive homes, surrounded by luxurious furniture and with a stylish car standing proudly outside, while they themselves are miserable. They don't love Jesus, because if they did, they'd be doing His Word (John 14:21). They'd be witnessing about Him, speaking in new tongues, prophesying, praying for the sick, casting out demons; giving to God's work and getting involved in the lives of others. Material belongings are only of minor importance. Jesus is Number One, but He does not want you to blush when He blesses you.

God has created this earth for His children. It is a material world where material blessings are necessary. Jesus said, *But seek first his kingdom and his righteousness,* **and all these things will be given to you as well** (Matt 6:33). What are **all these things**? In the context, Jesus is speaking of food and clothing. He says in verse 32, *Your heavenly Father knows that you need them.* God begrudges you nothing! To the contrary! He blesses you in every area of life because He wants **everything** to go well for you.

"Much Fruit" for the Father's Glory

In 3 John 2 it says, *Beloved, I pray that you may prosper in all things, and be in health, just as your soul prospers* (NKJV). God wants everything to go well and prosper for you. The word for "prosper" and "succeed," in Greek means blessing, good progress and success. God wants you to make good progress and succeed so His Kingdom will be spread further through you.

Consider how many parables Jesus put forward that speak about abundance and good progress. For instance, He talked of the talents which were to increase. He took up the parable of the Word that was sown and gave a yield of between 30 and 100-fold, and another parable portraying us as fishers of men. What does a fisherman want to get? A catch! **God wants to see results and growth in his Kingdom.**

In John 15, Jesus says He is the vine and we are the branches. In verse 5 He states that *Apart from me you can do nothing*. It is true, and often quoted, but isn't it rather typical that we content ourselves with citing only that part of the verse? "Yes," we agree, "without Jesus we can't do anything" and begin to dwell on how little we can do and how few results we see. We must read the whole context! Sometimes we fundamentalists are charged with taking verses out of their context, but I maintain the opposite to be true. It is the religious traditionalists who isolate their verses. Here, Jesus says in verse 5, *If a man remains in me and I in him* **he will bear much fruit**; *apart from me you can do nothing*. We have often fastened on the negative, but what Jesus is saying here is something positive. *In me you will bear much fruit*. What is "much fruit"? Prosperity and success!

To emphasize how anxious God is for you to "bear much fruit", Jesus repeats it **several times** in the same chapter. In verse 16 He tells us He has **appointed**—that is, ordained us by design and purpose—to bear fruit that will last. In verse 8, He goes as far as to say, *This is to my Father's glory, that you bear much fruit, showing yourselves to be my disciples*. What does Jesus mean? He means that God is glorified when things go well for you and fruit is born in your life: fruit that comes from a life in Jesus, the abundant life, that reaches into **every cell and fibre** of your being.

It is the will of God that His Word, His promises and His blessing increase and multiply within you. It is His will that His plans are realized through you. So lift up your head and see how you are blessed. See that in Jesus you are a blessing wherever you go. You bear fruit and grow and "whatever you do, prospers."

Don't accept your failures as the last word on the subject. Everyone makes mistakes. **Everyone falls short and makes a false move somewhere, but don't get stuck there. Lift up your head, look at Jesus and let Him show you how He looks at you.** As you see what wonderful plans He has for you, fear, failure and a defeatist attitude will lose their grip and you will see that you are truly blessed by God!

35

Abraham's Blessing—Yours!

Now, the Spirit of God is more active than ever before. He is moving throughout the world as a tremendous period of preparation is underway for His glory to fill the earth. The body of Christ is rising up to take its rightful place, which Jesus paid for by His blood.

However, none of this will happen while the devil sits quietly by. He is already doing his worst to block the Holy Spirit's work. He is especially attacking the Spirit's influence on men and women through the Word, because it contains the power of God for salvation. The Word is the sword of the Spirit. It sanctifies, purifies and edifies the saints and through it, we participate in all God has for us. No wonder Satan hates God's Word and fights it tooth and nail.

One of his methods to fight the Word is to keep people ignorant of its promises. Another tactic is to let traditional thinking determine the limitation on their lives. Still another way he fights the Word, is to exalt human reason to the place of highest authority. The devil is an expert at explaining away Bible passages, consigning them to the past or the future. He uses either methods of deception, just as long as the believers do not avail themselves **in the present** of what Jesus has done for them, and begin to be led by the Holy Spirit to impart the Gospel of liberty to others, **right now**.

However, the Holy Spirit who is our teacher, is bringing about a change in our day. Revelation knowledge is flowing clear and strong from the Word of God, allowing the believer to clearly see the meaning of the redemption and its eternal consequences.

Satan not only attacks God's Word generally, but he also attacks specific parts of the Gospel. For example, he particularly attacks the teaching on healing. He does not want to see anyone enjoy good health. But teaching on economic prosperity especially exasperates him. This is a truth that is not only precious but enormously important in our day and generation. Jesus has commanded us to evangelize the whole world in the power of the Spirit, but we're not there yet. God wants all nations to hear the Good News of Jesus. As yet, however, not all have heard, and the Holy Spirit is earnestly admonishing us to advance on all fronts and with every available means.

Meanwhile, the devil is doing everything he can to delay us and make us inactive or listless. Unfortunately, he has partly succeeded in distorting and watering down the Gospel, keeping it inside the four walls of the church and encumbering it with unbiblical traditions. His aim is that as small a minority as possible will hear, and that the light of the Gospel will be hidden behind all manner of religious bric-a-brac.

One of his tactics has been to encourage mistaken teaching on finances, with the aim of leaving the Church without money or influence. However, the Holy Spirit is emphasizing true instruction in financial prosperity so that the Lord's money will be freed and the Church will be able to fulfill her commission: "Go into the whole world, preach that Jesus is alive and waiting to meet the needs of all creation!"

God did not Invest in Poverty

The Bible makes its position perfectly clear concerning money. Money can be used by God or by the devil. Note that in 1 Timothy 6:10 it is not money itself, but the **love** of money that is "a root of all kinds of evil." Tradition has taught us that everything to do with money and the material world is evil, but that is not what the Bible teaches. Gnosticism, an early doctrine that crept into the Church, taught disdain for material things. But the things that find their expression in gnosticism are not found in God. He created the material world and saw that it was good (Gen 1:31).

God made the world for His children. In it He placed gold, silver, precious stones and countless other treasures. Out of His own abundance, He produced an abundance in nature. The problem does not lie with the material, but in the evil, rebellious, human heart that lusts for money, and worships riches and power instead of delighting itself in the Lord and worshiping and glorifying Him.

Poverty has traditionally been regarded as a virtue, but God never introduced or invested in poverty. Poverty and lack came with The Fall, as a result of mankind's rebellion against God. At the same time, poverty, sickness and spiritual death made their appearance, through sin.

Later when God made the covenant with Abraham, He blessed him—and that blessing contained even material wealth (Gen 13:2). This same blessing was also operative in the lives of Isaac (Gen 26:12-14) and Jacob (Gen 27:28). However, when Israel was in captivity in Egypt, it was overtaken by the curse of poverty. But when God delivered them, He brought them out laden with silver and gold (Ps 105:37).

Then, when Moses received the law, he pronounced the conditions of the blessing and the curse to Israel with these words, *The Lord will send a blessing on your barns...The Lord will grant you abundant prosperity—in the fruit of your womb, the young of your livestock and the crops of your ground...The Lord will open the heavens, the storehouse of his bounty* (Deut 28:8,11,12). These blessings followed Israel as long as they observed the Word of the Lord and obeyed Him. Bread was not a scarcity—and they lacked nothing else, either (Deut 8:9). When they loved Him and put Him first, God gave them *the ability to produce wealth* (Deut 8:18).

On the other hand, the curse of the law would bring poverty and lack (see Deut 28:29,33,42,44). It would come, the Bible says, in Deuteronomy 28:47, *Because you did not serve the Lord your God joyfully and gladly in the time of prosperity.* The curse of the law brings poverty. However, when Jesus died on the cross, He was made a curse for us so that the blessing of Abraham could be ours (Gal 3:9, 13,14).

Financial Prosperity
for the Building of the Church

Jesus took the curse on Himself, on the Cross, so that we might be free. He took our sin, sickness, poverty and everlasting death so we could have His righteousness, peace, abundant life, health and prosperity. He took our place so His blessing could be ours in every area of life and God could be honored in all.

2 Corinthians 8:9 says of our Lord Jesus Christ that, *Though he was rich, yet **for your sakes** he became poor, so that you through his poverty might become rich.*

When Israel left Egypt, the people went out laden with its riches (Ps 105:37). Why? So they could wallow in luxury? Of course not! The gold and silver was needed for the building of the tabernacle where God was to be worshiped and where He would reveal His glory. The same principle is true today. Financial increase is never given so the saints can live selfishly. It is for God's temple, the Church, to be built up and for His glory to be seen. Instruction in economic blessing is the Lord's own way of satisfying the believers' needs and freeing them to give to others. In this way, God's money is distributed and the Gospel spread into all the world.

God wants to bless your life through and through. He'll give you His love—and your love will warm others. He'll give you revelation so you can pass it on. He will bless you financially so you can give your surplus to others. When your cup is full, it will flow over and bless those around you.

And God is able to make all grace **abound** *to you, so that in all things at all times having all that you need, you will* **abound** *in every good work* (2 Cor 9:8).

In 2 Corinthians 9:11 Paul states, *You will be made rich in every way so that you can be generous on every occasion.* God wants to bless you abundantly so you can give to every good work. When you see that God is your source of supply, not people, and that He has taken care of your needs in His covenant, you can relax and trust Him. He can then begin to lead your giving so that it will become a sheer joy. You do not need to be afraid. God will look after you. You don't need to hold back any longer because God's channels of blessing are open to you. Because of your obedience, the flow of His money will not be dammed up anymore—whether the hindrance was due to ignorance of the Father's will or fear of its consequences. *You will laugh at destruction and famine* (Job 5:22) because it is the Lord who is your security.

You won't give in order to get. You'll give because God wants you to be a giver, like Him. However, when you give, you will receive. Jesus says, *Give and it will be given to you* (Luke 6:38). It begins with your obedience which will release God's blessings and because you sow, you will also reap (2 Cor 9:6).

Therefore obey the Word. Let it be your guide instead of mistaken tradition. Receive what the Lord has for you and live in His promises. Any influence from a spirit of poverty will then be broken in your life and the work of God will be carried out abundantly. His workers will be able to fulfill their calling, as they receive their proper support and by your obedience, you will be blessed and multitudes reached through the Gospel. God loves a free and cheerful giver! (2 Cor 9:7).

36

The Lord Wants to Give You the Desire of Your Heart

Trust in the Lord and do good; dwell in the land and enjoy safe pasture. Delight yourself in the Lord and he will give you **the desires of your heart** (Ps 37:3-4).

The Lord wants to give you the desire of your heart. Often we think, "I know what I'd really like, but I don't know if it is God's will." Hesitancy over whether our thoughts really are the will of God can paralyze us inside and if we're unsure, we're open to attacks of doubt.

Jesus says in Luke 9:62, *No one who puts his hand to the plow and looks back is fit for service in the kingdom of God.* However, this is exactly what we are tempted to do. We feel uncertain and begin to look behind. But God does not want us to be unsure of His will. In Romans 12:2 He says that we can *test and approve what God's will is—his good, pleasing and perfect will.*

1 Corinthians 2:12 tells us that we have received the Spirit from God (our Helper), **that** *we may understand what God has freely given us.* God has no intention of keeping us outside His will. The opposite is true. He wants to reveal it to us so we can be sure of His thoughts toward us and of what He has freely given us.

Sometimes we hide behind phrases like, "God willing" or "I only want His will." Of course these are right and necessary conditions. We must be following Jesus and seeking God's Kingdom first of all. However, when you already have that attitude, God will begin talking with you and actually asking you what **you** would like. **He** would like to give you what **your** heart desires.

In Mark 10:46-52 we meet Jesus on His way out of Jericho. He passes Bartimaeus, a blind beggar. Bartimaeus has heard of the Jesus who heals. Verse 47 states that when Bartimaeus heard it was Jesus of Nazareth, he began to call out loud to Him. Why? Because he had heard of Jesus! What had he heard? He must have heard that Jesus forgave sins, drove out evil spirits, healed the sick and taught about the Kingdom of God. He would never have expected that Jesus would want to help him if he hadn't previously heard that Jesus cured the sick.

What you hear is very important. *Faith comes from hearing the message, and the message is heard through the word of Christ* (Rom 10:17). If you do not hear the full Gospel, your expectation will be limited. You cannot obtain faith for things if you don't know God's will in that area. The less of the Gospel you hear, the smaller your faith in Him. Nevertheless, praise God for the Gospel you are hearing now. It is His Good News to you for **every** area of your daily life.

What Do You Want?

Bartimeaus had heard that Jesus made the sick well, wherever He went. He began to cry out to Jesus and despite resistance from the crowd, he refused to be quiet. Jesus heard Bartimeus and called him. Bartimaeus rushed forward and Jesus put a question to him, *What do **you** want me to do for you?* He didn't just state, "This is God's will for you!" He asked the man what was in his heart. "What do you want?" He asked. Notice Bartimaeus' answer, *Rabbi, I want to see.* There will always be one or two quibbling theologians who will point out at this juncture how Bartimaeus' request was totally self-centered; how he only thought of himself and how his prayer should have been much more God-centered. Such talk is nonsense. Jesus came to help people, to lift the oppressed, liberate the captives and cure the sick. He responds to people's needs and prayers!

Bartimaeus had a request, a longing—a need; he wanted to see. It was not wrong of him to desire it for himself. It wasn't selfish of him to ask for his sight. Of course, Jesus wanted to give it to him, but before He did He wanted to know what Bartimaeus' thoughts were.

In John 15:7 Jesus says, *If you remain in me and my words remain in you, ask whatever **you wish**, and it will be given you.* He does not say, "Pray for whatever I want and it will be given you," but **whatever you wish**. God wants to give you the desires of your heart. If you are in Jesus and His words remain in you, He expects you to ask for whatever you want because your heart and mind are right before God.

What does that mean? Philippians 2:13 says, *For it is God who works in you to will and to act according to his good purpose.* God is working in us, making His own desires our longings. Bartimaeus' longing for a cure, for healing, was not a selfish matter. It was something God had put in him. However, he was first compelled to recognize and accept the longing, begin to desire it and express it in word and action, before it was made a reality to him.

God is not Begrudging

God has placed thoughts, dreams, desires and longings inside you that He wants you to accept and begin to act on. However, it is precisely here the devil most often creeps in, points the finger and accuses us. "You're selfish," he says. "That can never be God's will. You're making it up yourself. It's all 'the flesh'," etc. What is really happening is that Satan is sowing suspicion toward your heavenly Father. Remember what happened at The Fall. Eve sinned because the serpent succeeded in deceiving her mind and getting her to believe that God was holding something desirable back from her. In Genesis 3:5 the serpent says, *For God knows that when you eat of it your eyes will be opened, and you will be like God, knowing good and evil.* Or, in other words, "God is withholding things from you. He doesn't want you to be like Himself. There's something He is not allowing you to have. He's holding something back." We hear similar suggestions today.

But God is not like that! He is not holding things back from you. He is a kind and loving Father. Tragically though, many people go through life under the same impression as Eve, whom the devil had deluded—that God is unloving, stingy and generally against you. But that is wrong! God is with you! Romans 8:32 says, *He who did not spare his own Son, but gave him up for us all—how will he not also, along with him, graciously give us all things?* Many have gone through life feeling that God has begrudged them nearly everything and they have become bitter toward Him. God has become almost like an enemy to them. They know it's no use struggling against Him, He is almighty and must be obeyed. However they don't find their joy, their companionship or their comfort in Him. They imagine He is out to even steal the little joy they have. **This is terrible!** The serpent has embittered their hearts and given them a false picture of our wonderful heavenly Father.

An example of a person who had this problem was the older brother in the parable of the prodigal son (Luke 15:25-32). He became resentful when his younger brother was met with such a wonderful welcome and loving homecoming. He felt his father had never given him anything, to which the father answered, *My son...you are always with me, and **everything I have is yours*** (v. 31). The assets were there all the time but he had never come and asked for **what he wanted**. Remember Jesus' words in John 15:7, *Ask whatever you wish.*

When you have the right image of God and realize that it is the devil who has been hindering you from praying for the desires of your heart, you'll begin to come more boldly to God. When you see that it is the devil who has tabooed things that are natural for you to ask of your Father, you will begin to approach God with confidence. Just as you are physically created in a particular manner with particular needs, so your new nature in Christ has certain needs that God desires to satisfy. You are never ashamed of being thirsty. It's natural to be thirsty, hungry and tired at times. You know these are normal human needs that must be satisfied. Just as your physical body has needs that God wants to supply, your soul and spirit also have needs He wants to meet. Don't let the devil burden you with blame about them. Let your Father satisfy them instead.

Cherish Your Dreams!

God wants to give you your heart's desire. Many people squash down their desires, dreams and thoughts and try to "sober up." Don't! Accept what God has placed within you. He wants you to dream His dreams, think His thoughts, plan His plans and He wants you to begin taking steps toward their realization. They are manifested when you ask God for them and begin to act in accordance with what you prayed for. God will then begin to work in you, and He will first deposit in you the things He wants on earth. When you subsequently begin to meditate on them, pray for them and claim them and then take steps in their direction, God can bring them to pass.

That is what happened to Bartimaeus. Perhaps it began as just a thought. The thought grew to hope. Hope rose to a conviction that if Jesus came past one day something **would** happen. Then Jesus came! The conviction, longing and desire in Bartimaeus rose to such a pitch that nothing could stop him. The people couldn't hinder him and neither could his blindness. He shouted out and ran to Jesus—and what happened? He received the desire of his heart. Jesus said to him, *Your faith has healed you* (Mark 10:52).

Jesus called his persistent, importunate desire to have his need satisfied, **faith**—and He does the same in your case too. Jesus gave Bartimaeus the desire of his heart, and He will do the same for you. And what was the result? Bartimaeus followed Jesus (v. 52). Some imagine that if we receive what we wish for, we will be drawn away from God. No, it's just the opposite. We follow Him all the more closely!

In John 15:8 Jesus says, *This is to my Father's glory, that you bear much fruit, showing yourselves to be my disciples.* It brings glory to God when you bear much fruit and receive the desires of your heart. Men and women see that God is real when He hears and answers your prayers because God is obviously with you.

God is glorified when people see His Kingdom, His plans and thoughts prospering in you. He wants to see you reaching out for His promises, believing He will respond to your wishes, and that He will give you the desires of your heart. He longs for you to stretch out and reach further, to dream, plan and desire more from Him!

THE CHURCH

*On this rock I will build my church, and
the gates of Hades will not overcome it.*

Matthew 16:18

37

Dynamic Local Churches

We are living in days when the Holy Spirit is emphasizing the place and power of the Church. God plans to reach the world through His Church, and show His power and glory to this generation.

The Church is the spiritual body of Christ. When He was here on earth, Jesus did everything through His physical body. Likewise, today, He does everything through His spiritual body, the Church.

The body of Christ is manifested in different places through local churches. God wants these churches to be strong so He can perform His work on earth through them. Therefore, we must have the eyes of our faith opened to see what God can do, in and through a local church. Revelation must come to us in this area so our faith can grow for this aspect of God's will to come to full completion. Here in Sweden, we have experienced a time when the Holy Spirit has emphasized teaching on faith. Many have criticized it and worked against it, but to no avail. Many more have experienced freedom, joy, blessing and a changed life through realizing that the Word of God says, *The righteous will live by faith* (Rom 1:17).

The teaching of faith is essential if we are to walk with God, hear from Him and begin to do what He has called us to do. The Holy Spirit gives prominence to something to bless us and make us stronger in the Lord, and so it is vital that we continue with the teaching of faith. In Acts 2:42 it is written that the believers *devoted themselves to the apostles' teaching*.

The key to a breakthrough in the Spirit is **to hold** on until the victory is totally manifested. You will always hear raised voices, often from people who are frustrated themselves, saying, "Faith isn't the thing any more, now it's this or that." But that is not true!

Today God's people need to receive teaching on faith, to walk in faith, rest in faith, overcome by faith and receive by faith. The righteous will **live** by faith – that's for the whole of life, not just for a time.

Faith for the Local Church

When the Holy Spirit has emphasized victory to the individual believer and blessing in his personal life, it does not mean that God wants numerous individuals running around in different directions, keeping themselves busy with their own concerns. There is a greater purpose than that in your walk with God. When you begin to walk by faith in your own life, the Lord will help you lift your eyes off yourself, so you can receive faith primarily for two areas; for the lost to be saved and for the local church.

In the Book of Acts we see how the local church grew in a dynamic way—and it is possible for us to have the same experience today. However, we need faith for the local church, because, without it, the church will never grow. When all the believers in a local church become convinced and expectant that their church will grow, God can act and something powerful can happen.

We must understand the local church from God's perspective. This does not necessarily involve a total comprehension of the New Testament concept of church, although that is important. First of all, you must understand how God sees your local church. What does the Holy Spirit say about your church? What does God want to do through your children? What do you have faith for in this area?

The Holy Spirit wants to speak into your situation and give you a picture of God's plan and purpose for your church. When you receive this into your heart and believe it, something dynamic happens. God's Word concerning your local church creates faith in your heart that something, which may seem naturally impossible, can actually happen.

Every pastor needs to receive this revelation and have God's view of the Church engraved on his heart. If he doesn't, he will be so consumed by all the difficulties and problems, that he will become discouraged and give in to all kinds of pressures and finally give up.

However, it is not just the local shepherd who needs to have this vision in his heart. The sheep—the people, the members—must also have it. It is only when individual believers in the church have this vision in their hearts that church growth can become a reality.

God wants this to happen. That is why the Holy Spirit is anxious to speak to churches all over the world. It is time to have faith in your heart for church growth. God wants large, strong, growing churches! He never planned for one human being to do all the work alone. His work will be achieved through His people, the local church.

The Church—An Environment for Miracles

When we read the book of Acts, we can see that signs and wonders took place in the church. The church provided the environment for miracles! Today, the opposite is often true. God has to work in spite of the local church and He has to use those with ministerial gifting, from outside. That was never God's purpose.

The situation in a church is frequently as it was for Jesus when He came to His hometown of Nazareth, He could not do any miracles there, except lay his hands on a few sick people and heal them. And he was amazed at their lack of faith (Mark 6:5-6). Here was an environment that stopped signs and wonders instead of encouraging them.

However, when we read about the Church in the book of Acts, we see that signs and wonders were taking place. This occurred simply because all the believers were positive, all were involved, all believed and all were going in the same direction. This is the type of church that God will raise up in these days.

God needs strong churches like this to be able to perform His works here on earth. Therefore, it is vital that we understand God's view of the local church and then begin moving toward it, in faith.

Traditional and conventional thinking is seldom Bible based and has hindered us from having faith for church growth. This is why God is starting with the individual believer, the foundation of the church. As each one learns to trust Him and to hear from Him, it will pass on to the entire congregation. The whole body will live in an atmosphere of faith and expectation. The Holy Spirit can then use such an environment to do wonders and furthermore, it creates church growth.

Acts 2:41-47 provides an example of a growing church:

Those who accepted his message were baptized, and about three thousand were added to their number that day (v. 41).

They devoted themselves to the apostles' teaching and to the fellowship, to the breaking of bread and to prayer (v. 42).

Everyone was filled with awe, and many wonders and miraculous signs were done by the apostles (v. 43).

All the believers were together and had everything in common (v. 44).

Selling their possessions and goods, they gave to anyone as he had need (v. 45).

Every day they continued to meet together in the temple courts. They broke bread in their homes and ate together with glad and sincere hearts (v. 46), *praising God and enjoying the favor of all the people. And the Lord added to their number daily those who were being saved* (v. 47).

In the early church there was constant and multiplied activity involving many people, and it is possible for God to do the same today!

All Growth and Strength Comes from Commitment

One of the keys to life and growth is found in the words *every soul* (v. 43), *all* (v. 44), *all things* (v. 44) and *daily* (v. 46-47). This indicates that every person in the local church is to be actively involved. It is not a case of just a few going ahead, while the others grudgingly allow themselves to be pulled along. No, everyone is a participates.

In the early church all of them were motivated, all of them believed, all of them went in the same direction and all of them were dedicated. When it was time for prayer, all of them prayed. When it was time for teaching, they all received and continued in it. When it was time to give, none held back, all gave!

There is tremendous power in such a church. This kind of manifested unity is the most important of all. We will never come into unity in the body of Christ if we do not live in unity in our local churches. This unity will never come until all of us in the local church commit ourselves to God's particular plan for the church, commit ourselves to Jesus, commit ourselves to each other and commit ourselves to win our neighborhood.

All growth and strength comes from commitment. If you want to please Jesus and do what **He** wants, then He will put you in the place He has prepared and you will be a great blessing. Your commitment, love and faithfulness will spread to others and the whole church will rise in the Spirit and be even more effective.

On the other hand, if you feel that everything must be done according to your conditions, or that you must have a position and others must recognize you while you are seen at the center of everything, it will create a situation where you hinder yourself from coming into the center of God's plan. As a result, you may become critical and leave the church in bitterness and disappointment because it "wasn't good enough for you," and in the process, you miss all that God wanted you to do. This is a tragic attitude that has stopped many talented people from becoming a blessing. They were more interested in themselves than in committing themselves wholeheartedly to what God wanted to accomplish in their local church. We are living in an exciting time. God is going to build dynamic local churches and through them He will change the whole spiritual atmosphere of our nations.

It is important both for those who have ministerial gifts and for individual believers, not to glide around with a spiritual jet-set, but to commit themselves to that local church to which God leads them. God does not want you to be a spiritual nomad. He has a living, growing church for you; a church that preaches the full Gospel, expects signs and wonders and which reaches out to the unsaved. This kind of church will soon appear everywhere.

38

Spiritual Leadership

God is now laying a careful foundation for all that He will do in the future. His long term plans include a powerful onslaught against the enemy's territory, together with a shaking of kingdoms and lands so His glory can become visible to the nations.

Scandinavia and Europe in general, are specific target areas for God's power. Just as the invasion of Normandy during World War II liberated Europe from the Nazis' reign of terror, so God is going to invade Europe, showing His power. Every invasion must be carefully planned and prepared. No revival happens by chance. Detailed plans are being drawn up at headquarters and there is intense activity among the angels for the preparations of the heavenly invasion and liberation of the "European stronghold." Towering defense and whole systems of philosophies must be penetrated and destroyed. Enemy strongholds must be rooted out so that the revival can gain ground and men and women can hear and receive the Gospel.

Thousands of soldiers and a great deal of ammunition were gathered in preparations for the invasion of Normandy during the Second World War. The soldiers themselves hardly know what was about to take place. They realized that something was imminent and they were eager to get going and join battle, although they didn't know where or how they would be doing it.

Meanwhile, they trained and constantly practiced. Many became impatient and others grew critical, but it was all to no avail. They had to wait until preparations were finalized, conditions favorable, all equipment was in place and all were fully trained.

Then came the day, D-day, when the European continent was invaded. The beaches of Normandy, northern France, were filled with amphibious landing craft. Thousands of soldiers fell in the sands, but tens of thousands more established successful beachheads, forced holes little by little in the enemy fortifications and then finally broke through.

About a year later Europe was free. The invasion had succeeded through:

a) Careful planning.

b) Superior strength.

c) Coordination of troops—each one knew his place and carried out his own orders.

d) Prepared, trained and efficient soldiers.

e) A strong motivation and abiding conviction that the job could be done, and finally,

f) Capable leadership.

Strategic Planning

If all these factors are necessary for a natural army to win, **how much more important are they for God's supernatural forces! They do not fight with fleshly, physical weapons but with spiritual ones; against a supernatural enemy, Satan, who has kept Europe in captivity for centuries!**

The careful planning takes place in heaven. God then reveals His plans to the officers of His army, those with ministerial gifts in the body of Christ. **The superior strength** is ours through Jesus' victory over the devil on the cross and by our access to the power of the Holy Spirit. **The coordination of the troops** takes place when the Holy Spirit is allowed to take over in every individual believer's life, refining his motives for serving the Lord so that selfishness and thirst for power and vain glory beat a hasty retreat. **The preparation** gets under way when Christians undergo training in Bible schools and churches that are flowing in the power of God. **The motivation and conviction** that the job can be done arises when God's Word is invited to work on the heart of each believer, causing him to see that it is not only possible "theoretically" but that it **is** the will of God to attack, invade, conquer and liberate zones for His heavenly Kingdom.

The Holy Spirit and the angels are engaged in all of this, right now. An intense period of heavenly activity is currently taking place, the reverberations of which are noticeable here on earth. In your spirit and in mine, there is a restlessness and an expectancy. Like the soldiers who were waiting for D-day, we do not know exactly when or how, but we know **that** the invasion is going to take place. God is going to invade Europe with His glory. The shackles presently chaining the masses will fall away and multitudes will be saved.

In time of war, an army has bases in the field that are set up to provide food, rest, ammunition and instruction for the soldiers. Without such bases, an army's power for offensive power is reduced and it cannot maintain a continual advance. **These bases are the churches.**

The church is not a playhouse, nor is it a mutual admiration society, or a place where everyone prophesies over everyone else and all are strictly occupied praying exclusively for one another. It is not a social club for the killing of time. The church is a base where soldiers can receive inspiration and instruction, enabling them to go out, invade and gain ground in their immediate surroundings and subsequently, send out others into new areas beyond.

Some say there are too many churches being started, but on the contrary, there are too few. New churches are necessary bases providing supplies, ammunition, weapons, rest and inspiration and instruction from heaven, and they are needed in every town and city in our nations.

The spiritual leadership in churches are the officers who guide, instruct and inspire the forces to take new territory, while at the same time, caring for the wounded with the purpose of getting them back on their feet and out into the battle again.

The church is not only likened to an army. It is also a home, full of love and care. However, a family is not simply a place where care is found. It is an institution of authority, necessary for the function of a happy and harmonious unit.

The Saints do the Job

God is establishing His saints and His word is going out like never before. At the same time, He is also correcting mistaken opinions concerning spiritual leadership. God's leaders can be compared with the officers in an army. They lead in battle, inspire, instruct, train and care for the soldiers. They cannot do all the work themselves. They oversee the work, making sure that it is done properly. They help the forces, the believers, to be competent in service; but it is the believers who are to go out and take the land **and they are well able to do it!**

Looking back we can see how the devil has cunningly stopped revivals. By encouraging incorrect teaching, he has hindered many plans and crippled much that the Lord has placed in the hearts of individual believers, aborting it at an early stage.

Many have never been taught how they can be led by the Spirit. They have not realized that God loves them so much that He wants to use them to accomplish supernatural feats for His glory. Consequently, they have become passive, steered and dominated by a leadership that has discouraged, rather than encouraged, individual initiative.

Some time ago, the Lord told me that a greater number of spiritual initiatives had been aborted in Sweden during the 1970's than during the preceding years of the century. One of the causes of this was that people refused to obey the Word and start new churches.

Fear of man and mental blockages meant that people did not dare establish churches that exercised spiritual protection while, at the same time leaving room for personal initiative. An odd doctrine on collective leadership tied the hands of both the leaders and the believers, suffocating many initiatives at birth. All the leaders were to decide collectively about everything, to demonstrate some kind of unity. It sounded good, but it never worked.

Delegated Authority
and Coordination—Not Domination

God works by means of delegated authority. Each one finds his place and is handed an area of responsibility with the accompanying room to serve there. Order is then established and the workers do not become confused or crowd one another.

In certain circles, this order of authority went so far that people "entered covenant" with one another, signing under lifelong contracts of loyalty to each other and to their respective leadership.

Many have suffered under such treatment and been bewildered, because their personal relationship with the Lord and their own initiatives were taken from them. If you have been in those kinds of circles, renounce all such agreements and burn any remaining contracts.

Do not allow this kind of teaching to creep in and bind what God has initiated. We should not sit in conferences and summit meetings deciding when, how and what God is to do. **We do not believe in a national leadership that must approve everything before it is done, and screens every spiritual initiative.** The disciples in Mark 9:38-40 told Jesus they had tried to stop a man who was casting out demons in Jesus' Name but who was not one of their followers. He answered that no one performing a miraculous deed in His Name was against Him. Jesus permitted the man liberty to carry on, while the disciples wanted to decide over the activity and make the man follow them.

An old leadership often wants to have control of everything new, but God will not allow this. The Holy Spirit is in control and delegates His ministries to men and women for appointed purposes. Such commissions simultaneously provide both a freedom and a framework; freedom for the Holy Spirit to lead a believer individually and a framework in the local church for the "harvest to be brought in," the "sheep to be fed" and the "soldiers to be trained."

Now, God is establishing order in the ranks: among the individual believers, the differing ministries and the local churches. He is working with the body of Christ so that it can do the same things Jesus did when He lived on earth. Jesus preached, taught, healed the sick, cast out evil spirits—and multitudes came to faith in Him.

God's purpose for the body of Christ is the same today. The aim of unity in His body is to coordinate resources, enabling the true work of Jesus to be carried out. Only then can the masses be saved, the possessed delivered and the captives freed.

God's eyes range over the whole earth. He removes incorrect teaching so we are not limited and hindered but given liberty to spread His Gospel to the nations. He is training His armies to invade Europe and the continents of the world with His power.

Even if slight problems occur in the ranks now and then, the end result will be the same—a powerful, pure and aggressive force, occupying enemy territory and defeating him. Our best years lie ahead!

39

The Supernatural Ministry Gifts

It was he who gave some to be apostles, some to be prophets, some to be evangelists, and some to be pastors and teachers, to prepare God's people for works of service, so that the body of Christ may be built up until we all reach unity in the faith and in the knowledge of the Son of God and become mature, attaining to the whole measure of the fullness of Christ. (Eph 4:11-13).

In Ephesians 4:8, the Bible tells us that Jesus has given gifts to men. Paul explains what these gifts are in verse 11, declaring that they are ministries set by God in the body of Christ, the Church. Early in chapter 4, Paul, speaking of unity in Christ's body, points out how important it is to *keep the unity of the Spirit* (Eph 4:3). We have all heard a great deal about unity, and all of us know that it is vitally important. But what kind of unity is the Holy Spirit striving for? It is described in verse 13: *until we all reach* **unity in the faith** *and in the knowledge of the Son of God and become mature, attaining to the whole measure of the fullness of Christ.*

This kind of unity is being produced by God today, through the ministerial gifts He has placed in the body of Christ. Their task is *to prepare God's people for works of service* (Eph 4:12). They have been set in the body by Jesus Himself. It is He, not men and women, who has chosen, called, separated and anointed them. We see this clearly in the book of Galatians where Paul begins with a personal introduction, *Paul, an apostle—sent not from men nor by man, but by Jesus Christ and God the Father, who raised him from the dead.* Paul received his calling directly from God and immediately began to serve Jesus, carrying out what he had been anointed to do. In Galatians 1:16-17, he says, *I did not consult any man...I went immediately....*

The ministerial giftings spoken of in Ephesians 4:11 are supernaturally distributed and anointed. They are not polished, ready or fully developed at once. Much time can elapse before they actually begin to function in their ministries, but they are nevertheless, called by God and will be anointed by Him. The ministerial gifts mentioned in Ephesians 4:11 are apostles, prophets, evangelists, pastors and teachers. Each of these giftings is supernatural and given for the growth and expansion of the Kingdom of God.

Just as the Bible talks about the Church as an army, it is also compared to a body. This similarity speaks of interaction and fellowship and of the mutual dependency of the many cells on each other for the body's existence—in other words, we are all involved. Although these are necessary pictures of the Church, they are by no means complete in themselves. The Bible also talks about the Church as God's temple—the place of His glory. It compares it to a vine and its branches which bear an abundance of fruit. The Church is a wonderful, multifaceted, living entity.

The illustration of the Church as God's army depicts its aggressive side. We possess weapons and we are at war, so God wants us to be aggressive. We need to attack, and if we do, we will overcome. In the army of the Lord, every individual soldier must know his place and his task; he must be trained and be able to master his weapons. He cannot expect others to carry his backpack, march in his boots and shoot with his weapons. He has a particular area of the front that is his responsibility and if he fails to cover this, an opening will appear. He must be disciplined and have inner victory in his own personal life if he is to gain external victories. He must be free to act efficiently, take initiatives and make forays without being tied down by others.

The Holy Spirit is bringing this side of the Christian life into clearer focus in readiness for the last battle; the final, previously unparalleled harvest of men and women who will be swept into the Kingdom of God. The ministerial giftings are given for the teaching, practical training, correction and strengthening of the saints for these "works of service."

The Apostle

The apostle has a special commission to lay the foundation of both the teaching and the ordinances and then to supervise and encourage them, especially where he has been involved in starting the work. He cannot, however, travel everywhere ordaining people left, right and center. He may give advice, but he can only exercise apostolic authority where he has initiated the work. Otherwise, his ministry is generally of a national and wider character.

The Prophet

The prophet can have a traveling ministry, pointing out various situations in the body of Christ, coming with messages from God, correcting and encouraging. Several of those with ministerial gifts can prophesy, but that does not make them prophets. The prophet, like the apostle, can recognize and point out those who have ministerial gifts, but this is not his main task. A prophet should concentrate on proclaiming the Word, not on soulish imaginations. Although it may seem exciting to travel around, ordaining people for the ministry and prophesying over them, it can also lead to much confusion if it is not done by the Spirit of God.

You must know that God will never speak exclusively through other people to inform you of your ministry. He will speak directly to you through the Word and by His Spirit. A prophecy or a message from God is given as a confirmation of what you already know. If someone prophesies over you, and the result is bewilderment, inertia, disorder, conflict and tension, forget the prophecy instantly. If it flatters you and builds up your pride, you are on the wrong track. If it confirms what you already know, you may quietly continue.

If you have a ministry, you have work, and God wants able workers (2 Cor 3:5-6), not able braggers. If you are faithful in your present circumstances and aim at spreading the Kingdom of God, walking in faith, evangelizing, helping the saints and laboring for the Lord—God will ordain you, putting you where you best fit and where you are needed the most. What God wants more than ever are competent soldiers, not windbags. He wants servicemen who know **how** to use their weapons, not ones who just sit around in the officer's club, fantasizing over landslide victories. He wants men and women who can roll up their sleeves for the work, who know their Lord's commands, know how His power is released and who can bring healing, salvation and the baptism in the Spirit to the people. God is supernaturally down-to-earth. Having both feet on the ground, He wants to see concrete, supernatural results achieved through His people.

The Evangelist

An evangelist is not a preacher who travels around to different churches admonishing Christians. He effectively reaches out into the world, touching the untouched masses and is accompanied by miracles and powerful signs in his ministry. The multitudes are naturally attracted to him. His message is strongly Jesus-centered, and is always followed by the miraculous. There is a great need today to encourage evangelists and support them, freeing them to fulfill their task of winning souls for God's Kingdom. Evangelists may work locally, regionally, nationally or internationally. They will speak to both the crowd and the individual. Through the evangelist, people are attracted to Jesus, introduced to Him and saved by Him.

The Teacher

The teacher is not a theorizing person full of abstract expositions. He is not so deep that no one can follow him or dare ask him questions, for fear of showing their ignorance. He does not present homemade theories precariously balanced on Bible verses taken out of context. He is clear, plain and accurate, and he knows and lives what he is talking about.

Would you like to be taught by a driving school instructor who has doctored in "Ford's Financial Feat of the Forties" on which he has written tomes, but who has never driven a car in his life? No, you'd choose a competent driver, one who could pass on what he knows, so you can become efficient too. Your aim is not to fall in love with or even idolize the driving instructor, but to learn the art of driving.

The anointing on a teacher makes everything clear and plain to you. Soulish teaching can sound very impressive but it is always vague and confusing and leaves people hanging in the air. In this kind of teaching practical application is absent and the student becomes more tied to the teacher than free to move with Jesus. Instruction is better than enthusiasm.

The Pastor—The Shepherd

The pastor (shepherd) has the oversight of the local church and the authority to lead it. He is not the church's errand boy who has to comply with their every request. He is ordained and anointed by God to lead the local work. He leads the sheep. The sheep do not lead him. It is unthinkable that a shepherd would ask the sheep where they would like to go. Instead he knows their condition and their needs and also how to "gently lead those that have young."

The shepherd provides security and stability. He is not always dragging his heels, always the last one to come around, fearful of every possible (and impossible) eventuality that may or may not happen. He is out in front, as an example for the sheep to follow. The local, supernatural church should have **one** shepherd, not fifteen. Just as the universal Church has one head, Jesus, and a family has one head, the man, so the local church has one shepherd who bears the final responsibility. If the anointing is present in the church, every member will find his or her right place, a wonderful order will reign, and the glory of God will be seen. The shepherd will then be neither a misplaced errand-boy, running around serving coffee and handing out flowers, nor a dictator holding everything in an iron grip and having his finger in every pie, while no one else is allowed to lift one of their fingers without asking him permission. Such unfortunate examples have often caused believers to abandon leadership altogether. In such cases, everyone is then called to lead or there is a committee decision, even for when to buy a new pencil sharpener! No army, no company would survive a day like that. All it does is stifle initiative and encourage disorder.

The Ministry of the Believer

We will soon see the ministerial gifts becoming what God originally intended them to be—supernatural, anointed and led by Him. As men and women entrusted with these gifts take up their rightful places and are given correct freedom, the believers will be edified, unified and brought to maturity. Furthermore, the church will be built up in faith and in the knowledge of the Son of God (Eph 4:13). The whole body then, *joined and held together by every supporting ligament, grows and builds itself up in love as **each part does its work*** (Eph 4:16).

Jesus is going to strengthen and activate individual believers so that he can lead and use them in an outstanding way. As the ministerial gifts are recognized, order will be established, revelation will begin to flow, knowledge of the Son of God will increase and the saints will go from faith to faith. As each individual believer begins to walk by faith, he will attain the life of victory that is so important to him. There are many believers, though, who are not able to grasp all the great visions and dreams in circulation. They are desperately trying to gain victory in their daily lives and longing for someone to show them **how** to do it. As an individual begins the daily walk of faith, however, victory will be achieved in his life, and faith will function—if he walks in love (Gal 5:6). For this reason, he must be loving toward others, and the reward will be unity and God's glory being manifested. John 11:40 says, *Did I not tell you that if you believed, you would see the glory of God?* If the individual never learns to walk by faith; he will not see unity or the glory of God.

When the ministerial gifts come into their God-given (not humanly dictated) position, they automatically come into a spiritual unity with other ministries and all the saints everywhere. Unity is no longer a problem nor even the focus of attention. It simply becomes manifested, just as in any place of work where everyone knows his business and does his job, thus spreading an atmosphere of happiness and satisfaction.

As saints, we are duty bound to show love to all and "live at peace with everyone as far as it depends on us." We are not to be adherents of opinions, teachings, and doctrines. Unity is built on Jesus and the Spirit and goes deeper than all doctrines. The unity, however, that is based on cooperation is of a different nature. 2 Corinthians 6:14 says, Do not be yoked together (work together) with unbelievers. This means, of course, non-Christians, but it also applies if you have a vision or a commission from God. You will hardly choose partners who want to alter, delay, criticize, manipulate or stop what God has called you to do. However, you have no right to criticize or retaliate. You must love and respect them, while making sure that you keep yourself free to fulfill your own calling from God.

Unity is practical. It exists to help us work better, not dominate or keep a check on one another. When Jonathan and David made a covenant together (1 Sam 18), it was not because Jonathan wanted to bind David. It was because he acknowledged the anointing on David's life and wanted to help him in every way achieve what he was called to do. In these New Testament days we no longer make such agreements. We are all embraced in the New Covenant that God made with Christ. We are happy to hear advice, encourage one another and allow another the freedom to take God-given initiatives. In this way, we will achieve both the liberty and unity God which desires.

We live in wonderful times. God is raising up His ministers His gifts to bring blessing to your nation. He is training His army. Many victories are waiting just around the corner!

40

The Revelation Gifts

In 1 Corinthians 12:1, inspired by the Holy Spirit, Paul says that he wants us to know about spiritual gifts. God, in other words, does not want us to be ignorant about them. Unfortunately, we have been ignorant of these same spiritual gifts, for centuries. But, things are changing! The Holy Spirit is increasing revelation about them so they will be given their rightful place in the Church.

The spiritual gifts are essential and we cannot manage without them! They are mighty instruments for pulling down spiritual strongholds and for gaining victories. They are tools in the saints' hands for winning the world. Therefore the Scriptures tells us to eagerly desire them (1 Cor 14:1). The word translated "eager" means to be concerned, wholehearted, motivated and fanatical! It is the same word used of Simon the Zealot. The Zealots were full of zeal. They were zealous about driving the Romans out of their land. They were terrorists who stabbed Roman soldiers to death wherever they could get at them. They were fanatics. This is the word that is used to describe what our attitude toward the spiritual gifts should be! We are to be zealous; eager for them to be in operation. We cannot afford to be apprehensive about them or to resist their use. On the contrary, as we zealously pursue them, they will be manifested, bringing joy to many of us.

Throughout history, teaching about the spiritual gifts has often become muddled. People have confused them with natural gifting received at birth and the supernatural has been lost. However, the spiritual gifts are not the same as natural gifts or inborn abilities. They are entirely supernatural. 1 Corinthians 12:7 says, *Now to each one the manifestation of the Spirit is given for the common good.* The key word here is **manifestation**. The gifts are a supernatural manifestation and revelation of God's abilities, not a natural display of human capabilities and attributes.

When the Church was born on the Day of Pentecost, it was born into the supernatural. On that day, everyone was baptized in the Holy Spirit and began to speak with new tongues. The supernatural was manifested. After that, healing, miraculous signs, wonders and mighty deeds followed. They belonged to the natural life of the Church just as they had been a natural part of Jesus' life when He was on earth.

The signs and wonders Jesus did were a result of the gifts of the Spirit functioning in His life. The Spirit of the Lord was upon Him. That same Spirit fell on the Church on the Day of Pentecost and produced the same results. The same Spirit and gifts are available to us today, and they will produce the same results—miraculous signs and wonders. The devil is terrified of the spiritual gifts being manifested. He is afraid that we could receive knowledge about them and begin to function in them, because it would spell defeat for him. We can never defeat him with natural intelligence, natural strength and natural abilities, whether physical or mental, because he is a spirit being. But in the Spirit, with the spiritual gifts in operation, we defeat him every time! For this reason, the spiritual gifts are vital!

Supernatural Gifts

In 1 Corinthians 12:7-11, Paul lists the gifts of the Spirit. There are nine in all, the same number as the fruit of the Spirit in Galatians 5:22-23. **The fruit of the Spirit reveal the Father's character**, recognizable in His children. **The gifts of the Spirit are the Father's abilities**, also to be seen in His children.

The nine gifts of the Spirit are usually divided into three groups. **The first three are the revelation gifts**, which have the ability within themselves to reveal something. These are the word of wisdom, the word of knowledge and the gift of discerning of spirits. **The second group consists of the power gifts**, which have the ability to perform something. These include the working of miracles, the gift of faith and the gifts of healing. **The third group is the inspirational gifts**. They have the ability to say something, and because of this, they are also referred to as the oral gifts. They are prophecy and the gifts of speaking in tongues and the interpretation of tongues.

All these gifts are supernatural, and are given to believers who are baptized in the Holy Spirit for the common good. Through them, the body of Christ is built up. They are tools to be used to reach the whole world, given as the Spirit determines, not as we dictate (1 Cor 12:11). They are given to each and every one (1 Cor 12:7,11), so every one of us can expect them to be manifested in our lives as we serve the Lord. Paul thanked God that the Corinthians were not lacking in any spiritual gift (1 Cor 1:7)—and you do not need to either. Instead, you can expect their manifestation in your life.

Let's take a look now at the revelation gifts, which are the word of wisdom, the word of knowledge and the gift of discerning of spirits.

The Word of Knowledge

This gift is not to be equated with the possession of a great deal of knowledge. It is not an innate ability. The word of knowledge is a supernatural insight concerning plans, facts and people, both in the past and the present. The fact that it is called 'the word of knowledge signifies that it is not complete knowledge but only a word of knowledge, a piece of the whole. In the same way that a word is only a part of a sentence, so the word of knowledge is only a fragment of God's knowledge concerning a particular situation.

In Acts 9:10-12, the disciple Ananias is given a word of knowledge by Jesus concerning Saul of Tarsus. He is told the name of a street—Straight Street, the name of a homeowner—Judas, and the name of the one he is to visit—Saul. A word of knowledge is not always so detailed, but sometimes it is.

How did Ananias get this word? Acts 9:10 says it was imparted to him in a vision. These gifts can be manifested in a number of different ways. They can come in a vision, by angelic visitation, by a word coming to the consciousness, by an inner image or through an external or internal voice. God is the God of multiplicity and His Spirit reveals Himself as He wishes.

Unfortunally, we usually think that we know how God is going to speak, and so we miss Him. It is not often that we hear a thunderous tone from heaven. God does not primarily use this method for speaking to us in His New Covenant. You and I are new creations and His Spirit lives within us. The Spirit of God is in our spirit, in our inner man. Our inner man has a voice and God speaks from His Spirit to ours. Then, from our spirit, a word, a thought or an image begins to rise to our consciousness. The problem is that as such a thought arises we often react with, "Oh, it's my own thought. It's just me."

It is true that it is you, but not "just" you. It is your inner man picking up divine information. The fact is, your soul and flesh usually react negatively and you begin to reason, "This can't be real. I can't do that", etc. But stop and listen instead. Begin to believe the information your spirit is giving you and you will be surprised how accurate it is, even if you don't understand it all.

It may be just a single word "cancer," "headache," "nausea," or "dejection," for instance. It may seem quite minor or unspecific but for the person who is helped, it can mean the difference between life and death. Do not "despise the day of small things," but step out into the supernatural knowledge you have, however small it may seem.

As we obey and take what we are given, our capacity increases and God gives us more specific direction. On several occasions I have received unusual words, but they have always proved true. I once received a word that someone had a tube that had been surgically placed into their stomach that was causing irritation and, as a result, inflammation had set in. In an ordinary meeting you do not find many people with such an unusual complaint. It took a while, but after some time, a woman who had exactly that problem, made herself known. At another time, the Lord indicated that there was a person with a steel support in an arm, and again, someone else with a particularly deep hollow in the palm of the hand that caused inconvenience for the person. The information was found to be correct and the people were helped by the Lord. The word of knowledge gives rise to faith in the heart, making it easier for them to receive the miracle God has for them.

The Word of Wisdom

The word of wisdom is a part of God's wisdom concerning His thoughts, plans and purposes for the future. His wisdom is His counsel and planning. **A word of wisdom is the revelation of a part, a fragment, of God's plans for the future.**

In the word of wisdom we find prediction. God does not unveil all His plans, only what is needed for the present. You may compare it with receiving advice from a lawyer in a particularly awkward situation. He gives you a word of advice. He does not pass on to you all his legal knowledge, but only his counsel for your situation so you can know what you are to do. *But when he, the Spirit of truth, comes, he will guide you into all truth. He will not speak on his own; he will speak only what he hears, and he will tell you what is yet to come* (John 16:13).

The word of wisdom is a means for God to make His plans known. Such words of wisdom often come in the form of a prophetic message, usually making us think that it is prophecy. However, prophecy is primarily given for strengthening, encouragement and comfort (1 Cor 14:3), not for prediction. When the Bible says that we can all prophesy, it does not mean that we can predict the future. It means that we can all be inspired by the Spirit to prophesy for each other's edification, comfort and encouragement. Prophecy is like a cup of tea to which you can add sugar and milk. The sugar and milk can be likened to the word of knowledge and the word of wisdom. The word of wisdom, when rightly used, is a tremendous blessing that brings excellent guidance for the future.

The Gift of Discerning of Spirits

This is not the gift of criticizing everything and everyone or of lamenting over one's personal dislikes. It is the gift of seeing into the spirit world. The spiritual world is opened up and we perceive—either in a vision, or through a word, or an inner confirmation in our spirit, what is happening in the spirit realm. There are three kinds of spirit beings, 1) God's Spirit and His angels, 2) spiritual rulers and demons, and 3) human spirits.

With this gift also comes the ability to judge and discern. We must be able to distinguish and assess what we see. We should notice whether it is important and then take appropriate measures. Peter functioned in this gift when he unveiled Ananias and Sapphira's lies and hypocrisy in Acts 5:1-11. As a result, great fear came on the whole church so that they carefully avoided deception, fleshliness, rebellion, slander, a critical spirit, apathy and worldliness.

This gift was in operation in Jesus when He saw what was in Nathanael's heart and said, *Here is a true Israelite, in whom there is nothing false* (John 1:47), and when He perceived the thoughts in Pharisees' hearts as they were criticizing His words and deeds (Mark 2:6-8).

By the gift of discerning of spirits, underlying motives of both a good and evil nature can be brought to light. Demonic activity can be recognized and unmasked, Satanic plans can be annihilated and God's presence can be seen touching and strengthening men and women everywhere.

An Old Testament example of this gift can be found in 2 Kings 6:14-17. Elisha's servant was full of fear because the city where they were staying was under siege by the enemy. As Elisha prayed, the eyes of his servant were opened, enabling him to see the whole host of angels standing ready to help them. He saw into the spirit world, caught sight of the angelic activity and was strengthened and received guidance!

The revelation gifts play a vital role in the Church as they come increasingly into their own and equip it like a supernatural army to defeat Satan, wherever he dares show his head.

41

Love, Unity and Balance

Words are extremely powerful. When they come from God, they carry life and strength, but when they come from Satan, they bring death. The same word can mean one thing to one person, but something else to another person.

Words can be charged with feeling. They not only convey facts, but emotions as well. Our experience and backgrounds affect our understanding of words. Often, we don't consciously consider the meaning of words, we simply register a positive or negative response to what we hear. Therefore, it is vital that the Holy Spirit leads us into truth and frees us from prejudices about words inspired by the Lord.

As an example, examine three words; love, unity and balance. All three have a pleasant tone and awake positive feelings. They are important to everyone, not only to Christians and none would like to be accused of lacking these qualities in his life. Furthermore, all these words constitute three important truths from the Word of God.

The question is, what do we mean when we use these terms? If someone should give them meanings other than what God originally intended, they can become shackles to bind, instead of truths to set men and women free.

God always lifts people. He builds them up and gives them liberty. He restores their human dignity and makes them see that they are precious in His sight. He gives them responsibility and work and helps them take initiatives. He empowers them to accomplish things for Him—and He does it all through Jesus Christ.

Any teaching that does not result in this liberty or that inhibits or oppresses you, may have the same **words** and they may be correct, but their meaning has been altered. Such a distortion of meaning results in words that no longer set men and women free, because they no longer serve the truth.

The Love of God

Let's take a closer look at the word **love**. *But God demonstrates his own love for us in this: While we were still sinners, Christ died for us* (Rom 5:8). 1 John 4:8 says that God is love. God not only possesses love, and has demonstrated love by what He has done, but He **is** love. His being is love. All He says and all He does is love.

Jesus leads us to the Father. All Jesus says and all He does is love in action. Everything He does is **motivated by love**. This is so important. If you want to know what true love is, you cannot rely on your own ideas. You must look at what Jesus said and did in the Scriptures.

We are to love God and we are also to love one another. Jesus tells us in John 14:21, *Whoever has my commands and obeys them, he is the one who loves me.* It is only when we truly love Jesus that we can love one another. What is meant by the words "to love Jesus?" It is to know his commands and obey them. Love for God is connected with His Word. I cannot claim that I love God or my fellow men if I do not have God's Word as my authority and rule in life.

It is totally unacceptable to accept sins—fornication, adultery, fraudulence, "white lies" and so on—on the grounds of being "charitable." It is unloving to compromise, in the name of love, with what God declares to be the opposite of love, no matter how one may use the word. Love is connected with truth, and only the truth can set men and women free.

1 Corinthians 13:2 declares, *If I have a faith that can move mountains, but have not love, I am nothing.* Galatians 5:6 tells us that, faith expresses itself through love. In other words, faith cannot work without love. Faith is a conviction and a certainty. It hears and does what God directs. Faith does not ask what people think. Faith asks God what He thinks.

I may know I'm right and I may know what God has said but it does not permit me to flatten everyone around me with my foolproof arguments. What's more, conviction is not conveyed by raising my voice. It is the assurance that God has spoken, that enables me to meet resistance without fear of being wrong. I have no need to carnally promote my own plans and ideas, or persistently and zealously put up arguments to defend myself. We must also consider the almost forgotten fact that love and truth are united. Where the truth has been shrouded, a thousand-and-one bewildering ideas have sprung up. The Spirit of God, however, never sanctions human opinions and ideas, only His own Word. Therefore, many people have lacked inner assurance for their arguments. They have chosen instead to offer their mistaken ideas in an unassuming, appealing and ostensibly modest manner, but have nevertheless filled them with veiled objections to the truth.

This has been taken for kindness and love but, in reality, it is not loving at all. When anyone has declared the Word of truth among them, and in so doing, has cut through the maze of their muddled human thinking, the hearers have reacted, accusing the speaker of self-importance and arrogance. In fact, it was courage. Genuine love fearlessly proclaims both the negative and positive sides of the truth—what the devil has done and what God has done about it—both the problem and its solution. Faith has the ability to bring out the positive and emphasize the solution.

Any doctor first makes a diagnosis before prescribing the remedy, the medicine. David was an excellent example of this. His older brother accused him of being haughty because he was ready to challenge Goliath. David did not reply in bitter anger, he just continued undaunted and was eventually brought before King Saul. Saul was filled with unbelief and paralyzed by fear. When David saw it, he did not criticize the king nor did he excuse himself and back away. Faith, motivated by love, spoke through David's mouth. He said, *"Let no one lose heart on account of this Philistine; your servant will go and fight him"* (1 Sam 17:32).

The Unity of the Believers—A Testimony to the World

The next word we need to examine concerns the important subject of **unity**. Jesus prayed in John 17:22-23, *That they may be one as we are one: I in them and you in me. May they be brought to complete unity to let the world know that you sent me.*

Jesus prayed this prayer in faith, as He always did, and accordingly, God is going to answer His prayer. Jesus Himself said, *If you believe, you will receive whatever you ask for in prayer* (Matt 21:22). What a wonderful assurance! However, the questions then arise: **what** is this unity that Jesus speaks about and **how** is it to become a reality? There is really only one answer: By a miracle of the Holy Spirit.

First of all, a unity of the Spirit exists among all born again believers. It is primarily a unity of spirit, not of soul. Romans 12:2 tells the saints not to *conform any longer to the pattern of this world, but be transformed by the renewing of your mind.* As long as our mind and thoughts need renewing we will have differing views, ideas and opinions. However, if we are born again, we experience a unity in spirit (Eph 4:13), and the Lord's aim is for that unity to be the **unity in the faith** *and in the knowledge of the Son of God.*

This is the unity toward which we are growing, but we must realize that it is a process. It is produced by the Word of God and by revelation knowledge washing the soul clean from worldly and fleshly reasoning. Then we can begin to think God's thoughts. This process, the process of holiness, takes time.

You will always meet believers with differing views. This is why Paul exhorts us, *be patient, bearing with one another in love. Make every effort to keep the unity of the Spirit through the bond of peace* (Eph 4:2-3). If your heart is right, if you desire to honor, love and serve Jesus; if you follow Him and seek the Kingdom of God first, it will be easy for you to retain spiritual unity in the bond of peace. However, if you have carnal ambitions and a lust for power; if you want to manipulate and maneuver, you will make it hard. If fear and domination rule instead of faith and love, it will be difficult. If Jesus and His Word are not given the first place, it will be hard for you to keep the bond of peace.

You can enjoy unity with people without accepting what they stand for. You can learn to differentiate between the problem and the person and have a good relationship with someone, without having to agree with him. The point is, our struggle is not against flesh and blood but against spiritual rulers and authorities (Eph 6:12).

You do not ever need to hold anything against anyone, even if they show hostility toward you. If you start to hold a grudge against someone and become antagonistic toward them you will not get your prayers answered. Jesus says in Mark 11:25, *And when you stand praying, **if** you hold **anything against anyone**, forgive him, **so that** your Father in heaven may forgive you your sins.*

If you find yourself among Christians who don't think as you do and who haven't seen the truths in God's Word that are so precious and lovely to you, you can still have fellowship with them. Find out what you are agreed on and talk about that. The blood and the cross of Jesus unite all who are born again. Talk about that! Speak about what God has done and what He is doing today. Concentrate on what God has said in His Word, instead of on what divides you. It doesn't infer that you waive your convictions, but that you meet the other person where he stands.

It is a pity that the word "unity" is used as a cloak for dominance, ambition and manipulation, so that it binds rather than sets free. Behind it, there is usually someone demanding to be kept informed of every detail under the guise of "helping," while the real reason is a desire to dominate.

In Matthew 2:1-8, Herod suddenly became quite religious and attended a Bible class along with all his scribes and legal advisors. He had heard of the newly born king and was frightened (v. 3). Fear, coupled with his lust for power, drove him to amass all available intelligence on the subject. He instructed the wise men, *Go and make a careful search for the child. As soon as you find him, **report to me**, so that I too may go and worship him* (Matt 2:8). Herod was pretending. He talked of doing Jesus honor but in fact, he was planning the child's death and would have murdered the Anointed One to stop the anointing.

As soon as God does anything; as soon as He fathers some infant enterprise into existence, the same phenomenon shows its ugly head—someone wants to squash it and dam up the flow of divine anointing.

Unity is not achieved by everyone checking up on everyone else. Unity is attained as we recognize the anointing and commission on others' lives and make room for them to do what God has called them to do, even if we do not totally understand it. God cautions us about entering into a "unity" that is not based on the Word. Such "unity" will only lead to bondage and slavery—a slavery that puts an end to every enterprise of faith and to God's will on the earth, to liberate men and women.

Although all Christians are united in spirit, it does not mean they all have to work together. The Spirit imparts the same long term aims to every believer; the salvation and liberation of souls, the establishment of the Church in power and the preparation for the return of Jesus. Methods of working and commissions may vary. Therefore, instead of pulling down or correcting what others are doing, concentrate with joy and fervor on your own section of the wall! We each have a part to build!

Divine Balance

The last word to be examined is **balance**. It sounds good and seems important, but what kind of balance are we talking about? When the world talks about balance, it calls believers overheated fanatics. Is balance the absence of jumping, dancing and a loud voice? No. True balance is as God describes it. It is not a little pinch of the sermon on the mount with a large dose of "common sense," that is to say, worldliness and unbelief.

It is tragic to observe Christians stooping to drink out of the world's *broken cisterns that cannot hold water* and forsaking *the spring of living water* (Jer 2:13)—the Lord and His revelation. When human and worldly thinking begins to dominate believers, they usually cry out for balance and admonish others. But such balance is not from God. It is from a devil who is frightened of revival breaking out.

The most balanced thing anyone can do is to lie with one's face on the floor and weep over people's spiritual situations—if that is what God is calling for. Balance is to walk with God. Perfect balance is to be in God, led by God and set on fire by Him. True balance has **nothing** to do with this world.

God is longing today for men and women who will offer their lives to Him in total sacrifice (Rom 12:1) to be consumed by His fire. Then, as they rise like flames, burning and dancing to Him, they will exhibit that perfect balance found in their Lord.

True balance is to preach the whole counsel of God; all that He has promised, not selected portions only. Balance means to let God finish His sentence without constantly interrupting and raising objections. To be balanced is to fully see why Jesus came into the world.

Luke 4:18 (taken word for word from the Greek) explains why Jesus came: "The Spirit of the Lord is on me, because He has anointed me

1. **To** preach the Good News to the poor.
2. He has sent me **to** heal the broken—hearted
3. **To** proclaim freedom for the prisoners
4. And recovery of sight to the blind
5. **To** send out the oppressed into liberty and
6. **To** proclaim the year of the Lord's favor."

The reason Jesus came was to save, heal and liberate the captives spirit, soul and body. The Gospel has the answer to life! Therefore, true balance is to preach **everything that God has**—to everyone!

42

Prosperity and Maturity

Prosperity

He also said, "This is what the kingdom of God is like. A man scatters seed on the ground. Night and day, whether he sleeps or gets up, the seed sprouts and grows, though he does not know how. All by itself the soil produces grain – first the stalk, then the head, then the full kernel in the head. As soon as the grain is ripe, he puts the sickle to it, because the harvest has come." (Mark 4:26-29).

Jesus compares the Kingdom of God to a field. We know from Mark 4:14, that the sower sows the Word. The Word has inherent divine qualities. Life and spirit, power and blessing are to be found in it. Of course we also know that seed is of no use if it is not sown. In the same way, the Word of God is only productive when sown in the heart, but having been sown, its life will begin to sprout and grow and in time it will produce the *full grain in the head* (v. 28).

What is planted will grow, it will become visible—even if it takes time. When a farmer sows and lets nights and days pass, the seed will spring up, *though he does not know how* (v. 27). He does not know how the harvest comes, only that it will come when time has elapsed.

What an encouragement this parable is to us! Even if you don't yet see the results you are looking for and that the Word of God guarantees, hold on! No farmer surveys his field the day after planting, expecting to see ripe grain! It takes time, but the yield will come.

The same is true of the Word of God in your life. *Let God be true, and every man a liar* (Rom 3:4). Keep believing that God is who He says He is and does what He says He will do, even on those days when you survey the land and see nothing at all. Let nights and days pass. *All by itself the soil produces grain* (Mark 4:28). This is a promise. The earth will bear fruit. Your life will bring results, and the day when the "wheat" stands high will be a day of blessing for many.

The Lord is anxious for His Word to prosper in our lives. His Word prospers as it is given the liberty to accomplish what it was sent to do. Then, God's promises will become tangible realities in our lives.

Jesus says in John 15:8, *This is to my Father's glory, that you bear much fruit, showing yourselves to be my disciples.* According to Jesus, the more fruit we bear, the more glory we bring to the Father. "Fruit" means harvest, result, victory, success, answers to prayer, signs and wonders. This is what God wants to see in our lives—a harvest from the Word He has sown in us.

Just as time must elapse while a field appears barren, with no green shoots, no heads of grain, so there is also a time when one actually sees the harvest ripen to maturity. This is also true of your own life personally, and the Kingdom of God generally. We are going to see a great time of reaping when many will be saved, new ministries will arise and new churches will become established and grow strong in the Lord and in His power. Your country is going to be increasingly influenced by the power of God!

Maturity

When the Lord does something new, it is like the birth of a baby. A child is wonderful, lovely to look at and he or she brings great joy to the parents. However, if the child's development is arrested year after year, something is wrong. It needs to grow up to maturity.

A little child is not given much responsibility, it is given a lot of time to play. However, as it grows up, it has to shoulder responsibility and discipline itself. When a child argues, cries and fights in the sandbox, one can overlook it. But if it grows up and retains its "sandbox manners," something is wrong. All that God wants to do in and with us, is based on the assumption that we will grow up to maturity.

Even though we will always be God's children, the Bible, in 1 John 2:14, describes three stages of spiritual growth: 1) the baby stage, 2) adolescence and 3) adulthood. God does not expect us to remain lifelong spiritual babies or teenagers; He expects us to mature into responsible adults.

You will grow spiritually through God's Word, not just by hearing it, but by **doing** what God is telling you. We often deceive ourselves into thinking we have come a long way when we've been to a terrific meeting or listened to some fantastic teaching on a tape. Of course, we need both of these, but they are not enough. We need to act on the word as well as hear it, then we will be blessed (Jas 1:22-25).

We act on the Word as we lay aside all fleshly behavior. When you are a newborn Christian, there is a lot that God overlooks, simply because you are a baby. But as you grow and want to begin serving the Lord in earnest, you cannot continue behaving in the same way. James 1:26 says, *If anyone considers himself religious* (a servant of God) *and yet does not keep a tight rein on his tongue, he deceives himself and his religion is worthless.* In other words, if you suppose yourself to be powerful and of great importance to the Kingdom of God, with a mighty anointing and highly specialized ministry, and yet talk behind others' backs, gossip, criticize and tell lies, your religion is **worthless**.

People often see only skin deep and they are easily duped by externals, but God looks on the heart and the desires, searching to find His qualities of godliness, holiness and purity rooted there.

God demands that you and I refuse to live in a carnal manner, use our tongues against one another, jockey for position or put on a front. He wants us to approach Him honestly, laying aside whatever may be hindering us from coming to maturity and walking in the Spirit. People and ministers who refuse to comply with this rule will notice that their lives begin to go downhill instead of up. However, when we submit ourselves in every area of our lives to God's Word, our strength will be renewed and we will find a new joy and maturity.

Miraculous Signs and Wonders

Jesus has promised to confirm His Word with miraculous signs and this too is governed by the law of sowing and reaping. Miracles do not grow on trees like apples. The Word must first be sown in our hearts and faith given time to grow, before we can begin to witness signs and wonders in greater measure. But praise the Lord, it is growing all the time!

Faith is expectancy. The level of people's expectation that Jesus will prove Himself to be the one He says He is, is much higher now than before. Dead religiosity is losing its grip on them, and "denial theology," that disgustingly calls God in question, has lost its power. The devil's main weapons: fear, pride and unbelief, are effectively being taken out of his hands. As the battle in the spiritual realm is won, conquests will be all the easier in the physical realm.

We will witness more healings, miracles, signs and powerful deeds than in the past. God is anxious to show men and women that He is alive! The whole world is sick spiritually, physically, emotionally, socially and materially. Doctor Jesus has the answer, and He is going to perform miracles in your country as never before.

Signs and wonders are blessings of the Kingdom of Heaven that we are invited to take by force. This means we are to have an aggressive attitude, not to sit passively at home. We are to be like the woman with the issue of blood and press on toward Jesus and what He has for us. Your miracle is there. Go and secure it!

Unity

Much has been said on the subject of unity, both good and bad. Some have hidden behind the cry "keep the unity of the faith" when they should have been daring and stepped forward with God in His new moves. Others have used the word unity to manipulate and force people into a position of submission. But true unity is still vitally important to God.

The power of the early church in the book of Acts, came from the Spirit, but also from the unity enjoyed by the Church. In John 17, Jesus intercedes for unity among believers, and before His return it will be manifested among *those who call on the Lord out of a pure heart* (2 Tim 2:22). The lack of this unity will hinder and delay His return. We cannot organize true unity into existence, but we can pray it into being, and we can ensure that we live in unity on a local level in our own situation.

We are experiencing an increasing spiritual and heartfelt unity. Those with anointed ministries who have, in the past, not understood one another are beginning to understand and receive one another as never before. They are recognizing and accepting the other's anointing, where previously they only looked questioningly on the outward appearance.

Ministries with concurrent emphasis on the work of God will be prompted by Him to find one another and flow together toward common goals. As a result, the strength of the anointing will increase on everyone so joined. When a bridge is to be built the individual pillars are first erected. When they are in place, the bridge and traffic lanes are laid over the top. From that point on, the individual pillars are not so much in focus, though each remains standing firmly in its place with its particular function. The traffic now becomes the focus of attention. Jesus has bridged the gap between heaven and earth with His Gospel and power.

Wonderful days lie ahead. Regardless of what the devil says to you, remember you are involved in something wonderful. You are in the body of Christ. You are a member in particular. You are needed, your capacity is necessary and you are of value to the Lord and to your brothers and sisters. Never forget that you are in the greatest invasion force that has ever existed; and remember also that the invasion is gathering a momentum unparalleled in history.

Heaven is invading earth and the Kingdom of God will be declared with power to every nation under the sun. A tremendous harvest is ripening, so lift up your eyes and praise your God!

Arise, shine, for your light has come and the glory of the Lord rises upon you. See, darkness covers the earth and thick darkness is over the peoples, but the Lord rises upon you and his glory appears over you (Isa 60:1-2).

43

Faith for an Overcoming Local Church

His intent was that now, through the church, the manifold wisdom of God should be made known to the rulers and authorities in the heavenly realms (Eph 3:10).

I am writing you these instructions so that, if I am delayed, you will know how people ought to conduct themselves in God's household, which is the church of the living God, the pillar and foundation of the truth (1 Tim 3:14-15).

When God wants to do anything, He does it through His Church. The Church stands as a unique institution; it is both the Body of Christ and the channel through which God's power and glory are revealed to the world.

There are two institutions established by God for the protection and well-being of mankind: One is the family and the other is the Church. When God created the family, he took the woman out of the man's side, only to unite them forever in lifelong partnership. Similarly, God took the Church out of Jesus' open side that was pierced by a spear. The weapon thrust into his heart, bringing a sudden flow of blood and water. The Church came from Jesus' heart. This was a mystery that had been buried deep in the Father's heart until the day He chose to reveal it.

The Church Came out of Jesus' Heart

He made known to us the mystery of his will according to his good pleasure, which he purposed in Christ, to be put into effect when the times will have reached their fulfillment – to bring all things in heaven and on earth together under one head, even Christ (Eph 1:9,10).

The revelation of the Church emerged from God's heart. It was founded on the redemption—the blood—and confirmed by the Spirit—the water—that flowed from Jesus' sacrificial death on Calvary. The Church was taken out of Jesus' side so it could be reunited with Him on the Day of Pentecost and become one flesh and spirit with Him.

Therefore, the Church is absolutely unique in world history! It was a mystery even to the disciples until Jesus' ascension and, although the Church was born on the Day of Pentecost, its true identity and purpose was revealed much later, mainly through Paul.

God's dealings had previously been with His people, the Jews, but at Pentecost, a new era began in which God included all nations. The Times of the Gentiles had begun. This era is also called the Day of the Spirit, The Church Age, The Age of Grace and The New Covenant! Never before had men and woman been able to know such a deep relationship with God. The Holy Spirit no longer came on only a select few—the kings, priests and prophets of the chosen people, Israel, but on any person in any nation who called upon the Name of Jesus. **God was now reaching out to all the world. Furthermore, men and woman could receive a completely *new heart* and be born again**. The Spirit of God, who had previously confined Himself to the temple in Jerusalem, entered everyone who confessed Jesus as Lord and the Church became the new temple.

In other words, the Church is now the place of God's manifested presence in the New Covenant, just as the temple was in the Old Covenant. His presence, however, is manifested more clearly now than it ever was in the temple. The glory of the New Covenant is greater than the glory of the old.

In 2 Corinthians 3:7-11 we can read, *Now if the ministry that brought death, which was engraved in letters on stone, came with glory, so that the Israelites could not look steadily at the face of Moses because of its glory fading though it was, will not the ministry of the Spirit be even more glorious? If the ministry that condemns men is glorious, how much more glorious is the ministry that brings righteousness! For what was glorious has no glory now in comparison with the surpassing glory. And if what was fading away came with glory, how much greater is the glory of that which lasts!*

God now revealed a formerly hidden ministry, and released a much greater glory on earth than ever before, through the Church. At Pentecost, Joel's prophecy that the Holy Spirit would be poured out on all flesh was fulfilled—*Your sons and daughters will prophesy, your young men will see visions, and your old men will dream dreams (Acts 2:17). The Spirit of God was poured out on all people. He entered those who believed, and the Church became a vessel, an abiding place, for His presence. God's glory is His manifested presence, and by His supernatural love, knowledge, wisdom and power, His presence abounds in the Church today.*

The Church is an extremely powerful institution on the earth, and a mortal threat to the devil. The Church is not merely a collection of individuals coming together in Christ. It is a united body with a special collective anointing, making it a rock solid, powerful victorious Church at which the devil cowers. His primary aim therefore is to attack, divide, weaken and profane the Church of the Living God. If he succeeds, the glory will fade, the manifestation of God's presence will recede, and the devil will gain the upper hand in this world. Thus, the raging battle over the Church of God today.

The Overcoming Nature of the Church

For this reason, the Church is called God's army and the believers, the soldiers of Jesus Christ. It is commissioned to use its powerful spiritual weapons (2 Cor 10:4-5) to break down Satan's strongholds, to make God's counsels known in the spirit realm (Eph 3:10) and to manifest His presence by miraculous signs, wonders and miracles. The Church is also commissioned to determine the spiritual atmospheres of nations, regions, cities, towns and villages and to win men and women for God.

All this will arouse demonic resistance, so the Church must be filled with God's presence, and be able to flow in the supernatural. It must be firmly founded on His Word and know how to use its weapons. Today, God is raising up supernaturally equipped churches, prepared and ready for the time ahead.

It has always been God's plan for revival to flow out through the church—the local church, that is. The Church is the Body of Christ that is made up of every born-again believer throughout the world and its primary expression is through the local congregation. God wants us to have faith for local church growth. He wants strong, influential local churches available to everyone, everywhere. It is because the church is such a dynamic force that it comes under such concentrated fire. The devil does his worst to weaken and confuse the church and to hinder it from achieving the fullness of its calling, to reach out to the region over which God has placed it. This hindering work of the devil is also the reason behind much of the strife, jealousy, backbiting, rebellion and worldliness that has crept into local churches. The enemy does all he can to sow division and rebellion, to weaken and cause adversity and setbacks among the members of the local church so they do not go forward.

Today, God is raising up many new churches, and He plans for them to enter His fullness. However, there is a price for every one of them to pay. Each church has a heavenly vision but it will only be strong enough to attain it when the individual members identify themselves with that vision, not just in word, but in heart. Each particular plan is God's strategy for that local church. God's plans are anointed, and as they are accepted and received by the church and its members as their own, the anointing comes upon them to fulfill it.

Consecration Creates for Strength

Sometimes, people find it difficult to see this truth, so they try to promote their own personal plans and ideas, using the church as a platform. When it doesn't work they become critical and resistant, blaming the leadership for lack of understanding, inflexibility and of being autocratic. In fact, they are accusing God for not blessing their ideas when in reality they ought to lay them down at His feet, identify with His plan and assume their place in the local church. Then there will be greater strength, increased anointing and greater satisfaction. They must overcome their fear of losing "their own vision" in the church, then God will bring them greater opportunities and use them in an even mightier way.

God has a special place for each person in the local church. No one is unnecessary. It may take a little time to find your place, and your final role may not appear right away, but everyone can give himself immediately and wholeheartedly to work for Jesus. Some people think that the church only exists to serve their needs and they themselves are "consumers," but that is not the case. It is true that Jesus ministers to men and women in the church, but the church is more than a place where "I get things given to me." I give of myself there too. If I am not willing to give of myself and serve others, then I am misguided as to the purpose of a church and to my place in it. God wants to remove the concept of the church as a home for the chronically ill and remind us we are an army on the march, with every one in his place and at his post. If we are to achieve all that God has planned for the years ahead, it is vital that we submit to Jesus and obey Him in His church, where He manifests Himself to us and we receive Him with love and loyalty. Love and unity are never far away where such faithfulness and dedication are found. Fresh vitality and power are at hand and the church will be able to reach out farther than ever.

Dedication and consecration to Jesus—to what He is saying and doing in the local church—will create the unity and strength necessary to keep the enemy from driving in a wedge of division or causing confusion and weakness. Instead, it will grow in strength and influence, so that Jesus can be seen everywhere in the church neighborhood. God wants powerful, influential and authoritative churches, aggressively and effectively spreading His Gospel. He wants churches touching every area of human life and need. He wants them stamped with His presence, power and revelation. Such churches do not arise overnight—but they do arise.

Unite your heart with God's vision, His revelation of the local church. Accept His plan and aim for your local congregation and join your faith to it. See with the eye of faith what God wants to do through your local church and it will come to pass. Then, you will see as God sees and recognize how He works. You will notice that the building, though not yet complete and ready, is at least under way. You will stop pointing out its weaknesses and complaining about your ideas never being accepted. Instead, you will become a laborer who, while spreading love and unity around you, will be used by God to build the most choice and precious thing He knows—His beloved Church.

44

The Church of the Future

The Bible depicts the Church in many different ways: The Church is God's house; it is a spiritual temple, a nation of people, God's family and His army. It is also the Body of Christ and His bride. The Church is not one of these only, it is all of them. The Holy Spirit emphasizes its different aspects at various times to provide a total picture of the fully developed Church, clearly showing its aim and identity and its many functions.

When the Holy Spirit stresses any particular aspect of the Church, it is important that we accept His emphasis; that we comply with it and draw on the benefits it brings. It is unwise to suppress it or preach against it or try to balance it out, regarding it as a dangerous extreme. The Holy Spirit is well able to take care of excesses, but will hardly do so before men and women have come to the obedience of faith and wholeheartedly received what the Lord wants to give them.

When instruction and prophetic messages are given through God's servants, the Lord speaks of things to come. It we immediately try to balance it out, or interfere with it and alter it, we are setting ourselves up as judges, rather than meekly receiving the word. True spiritual discernment and judgment never dulls the prophetic word.

This is important because God will be speaking to His people in the future and it is vital that the message comes through clear and plain and that it is received into willing and ready hearts. When the prophetic word comes from heaven, it has tremendous power. It is an authoritative and creative word. God wants His words to be obeyed and then they create exactly what He has intended and said. Never in Church history has it been more important that the Church listens carefully to the Holy Spirit; and not only listens, but also obeys what He says.

This not only applies to the body of Christ as a whole, but also to every individual church and each individual believer. We must obey God and do as He instructs us. We must not do anything He has not told us to do, even if it seems right and good. He has planned that someone else will do those things, so we must stay with what God has spoken to us.

When we discover our identity and become secure in it, we are free to take up our position in the Kingdom of God and give Him our undivided allegiance. We are called to do what God says, not what others think we should do, or not do. As we find our rightful place and meet others in theirs, we can work together accordingly. This can only be achieved through a clear genuine prophetic word. It is not enough for it to be someone's "prophetical" opinion or a commentary on the present spiritual situation from a person who is nothing more than a spectator.

During the 70's, the revelation of the body of Christ came as a blessing to the Church, but just because some excesses may have occurred does not mean that the revelation should be forsaken or relegated to the 70's only. The whole counsel of God is relevant in every age, though each discovered revelation can play a different role at different times.

Faith Has a Militant Side

During the 80's, the teaching of faith came as a great encouragement and blessing from the Lord. Throughout the Bible there is an emphasis on faith. *The righteous will live by faith* (Hab 2:4; Rom 1:17; Gal 3:11; Heb 10:38). *Without faith it is impossible to please God* (Heb 11:6). Believers need to hear the eternal truth in such areas as faith, healing and righteousness. They must understand their authority in Christ and the meaning of the redemption. Without such knowledge they become confused and impotent, easy prey for Satan. Weak believers make weak churches where compromise provides a ready foothold for worldliness and where the enemy can gain the advantage. Therefore, the Holy Spirit needs to continually lead believers into the whole truth of God's Word showing them their position and privileges in Christ Jesus.

Belief that the Church can now do without faith would spell spiritual suicide and be the same as a return to "Egypt." The opposite is necessary. The Spirit of God must increasingly lead believers into the reality of what faith in God can achieve. This can be achieved in various ways, however, because God Himself acts in a multitude of different ways.

One of faith's characteristics is its **aggressiveness**. There is a militant side to faith that God's Spirit has been increasingly emphasizing for several years. Some have misunderstood it, some have been fearful of it, but many more have seen the truth of being a soldier of Christ and have begun to use their spiritual weapons to drive the enemy out. As believers begin to advance in this way, the Kingdom of God can be increasingly manifested and spread abroad.

We must realize this important truth—we are soldiers in God's army. We must not object to this. Today, we need a spiritually strong, divinely equipped army, ready with holy aggression to take the camp of the enemy, break down his strongholds and deliver his prisoners from captivity and oppression.

The Holy Spirit's emphasis on the Church as the army of God stands firm. Every believer must be sure of his place in this army, he must know the weapons at his disposal and learn to master them under the guidance of the Holy Spirit. I would be foolish to pretend that there is no enemy or to refuse to speak of him for fear of overemphasizing him. No army at war is so poorly trained that it neglects to gather intelligence on the nature and movements of its enemy or its strength and strategy. The same is true of the army of God; the only difference being that our victory is a foregone conclusion because of the death of Jesus on Calvary. These truths are of utmost importance and we must not allow the enemy to deceive us into letting them fall into oblivion. On the contrary, we must keep on the move, rout him out and set his prisoners free.

The Church—The Devoted Bride of Christ

I am convinced that the Lord is about to bring to our attention yet another truth—the picture of His Church as the Bride of Christ. Other areas of the church that have been emphasized by the Holy Spirit, will then form a complete whole. Everything will supernaturally fall into place and the Body of Christ will appear.

As the Holy Spirit begins in earnest to give her prominence, it will mean that the time of Jesus' return is rapidly approaching; and we will recognize four special, distinguishing features that identify the Church as the bride for whom Christ is waiting:

1. **Devotion**. A bride-to-be has a heart and eyes for one person alone—her bridegroom. In the same way, Jesus will become the one and only attraction for His Church as the attraction of the world and its thinking habits are broken over it.

There will be a rising tide of expectancy amongst the saints who will be occupied with His return. Just as a bride begins to make herself ready for her wedding and happily busies herself with preparations for the great day, the Church will lay everything else aside and be wholly occupied with its great and consummate aim—its union with Jesus.

2. **Purity**. The preparation for the coming revival and glory will be characterized by both purification and purity itself. The radiance of a bride-to-be is her purity and virginity. She is free from other relationships and every impure motive. The bride marries for love and has kept her virginity for lifelong faithfulness to one man. The same is true of the Church. Unclean motives, lust for power and vain glory, the love of money, prestige and worldliness will be swept away and be replaced by unswerving faithfulness to her bridegroom.

3. **Order**. When the bride is ready for the wedding, everything is arranged and in position. Her crown, veil, jewels and flowers are all as they should be and all serve their special purpose. The same is true of the Church. The revelation, teaching and doctrines will all have their place and function, with love crowned in the highest place of all.

The gifts will be poured out as intended, unpolluted and through purified vessels. The graces, the ministerial gifts, will be given their rightful place and granted liberty to flow unhindered in their particular anointings, without fear of being stopped or exceeding their God-given limits. There will be a revelation of order in the Church, giving security and protection to those who find their places under its shadow. Power struggles, jealousy, domineering attitudes and personal ambitions will all have to give way to the advancing truths of the Holy Spirit.

4. **Attraction**. No one is as attractive as a bride making her way to the altar. The most hardened hearts usually soften at the sight of a bridal couple giving their lives to one another before God. This is the scene the world will see as they observe the beauty and glory of the Church and the attraction of her Gospel. The Church will have favor with the majority of people, who have been searching for God in their hearts, wondering where He is to be found.

This attraction will result in revival for thousands when they see the devotion, purity, order and unity in God's Church which He Himself is bringing about and for which He alone will receive all the glory. Jesus is going to fortify and beautify His Church, His bride, and the gates of Hades will not be able to hold her back. She is not going to be a passive, wan, introverted bride, but a Church full of strength and love's own passion, clearly manifesting the presence of God in the future right up until Jesus comes back!

BACK TO BASICS

The grass withers and the flowers fall, but the word of our God stands forever.

Isaiah 40:8

45

Is the Bible Really God's Word?

God sent His own son, Jesus, into the world. We are told in John 1:14 that The Word became flesh and lived for a while among us. Jesus is called "The Word" because He is God's means of communication. We cannot communicate with one another without words and Jesus is the Word through which God communicates with men and woman.

Words are important to God and in His words there is unparalleled power. By His words He created the world (Gen 1). The whole universe is sustained by Jesus' word (Heb 1:3). Words from heaven have unprecedented power. We are born again through the spoken Word of God (1 Pet 1:23). When Jesus spoke a word, the officer's servant was made well. When Jesus said *"Ephphatha,"* the ears of a deaf man were opened (Mark 7:34). Words from God cure, heal, liberate and restore. They can bless, warn and guide.

Yes, words are immensely important when they come from heaven. Hebrews 1:1 says, *In the past God spoke to our forefathers through the prophets at many times and in various ways.* God **spoke** through the prophets. They wrote down all that they received from heaven and we have them in the Bible today.

The Bible is a controversial book. For many it is just a book, but for Christians in every age, throughout the world, it is the Word of God. God reveals Himself to men and woman through its pages. He teaches them about themselves and shows them the way to salvation through faith in Jesus Christ. This has never been disputed among Christians but something remarkable has happened recently. A whole barrage of divergent opinions on the authenticity of the Scripture has emerged amongst Christians. This is a new phenomenon in Church history and something we must take seriously.

People talk of different "views of the Bible." They think it is permissible to look on it as one likes, selecting the particular "views" that suit one best. However, the Bible has its own view of itself. you may not read it as you please, taking from it whatever you wish. True, there are old religious sects, just as there are so-called "new spiritual" ones that take verses out of context; but they all fall, without exception, on their denial of basic Bible truth, or on the inconsistency and contradictions in their claims.

The danger today is the creeping denial within Christendom itself of the fundamentals of our faith. Faithfulness to the Bible as God's written Word has been so seriously undermined in some quarters that another gospel entirely is being presented and they often try to disassociate the Bible from Jesus, accusing Bible reading believers of bibliolatry. How false! How foolish!

God Watches over His Word
to See That it is Fulfilled

Every Bible believing Christian believes **in Jesus just as the Bible describes Him**. Therefore, the teaching of the Scriptures as God's Word is of paramount importance. If the Bible is not the Word of God, we have no true and reliable image of who Jesus is, what He has done or what he is doing today, and neither do we know how we can worship Him properly. But thanks be to God, the Bible is its own commentary on itself. It is not a hodgepodge of disjointed fragments from different ages, thrown together into a document, much of which is missing or incomplete, and which remains totally irrelevant for our day anyway! **The Bible is inspired, collected and arranged by the Holy Spirit and God is watching to see that His Word is fulfilled** (Jer 1:12).

2 Peter 1:21 declares, For prophecy never had its origin in the will of man, but men spoke from God as they were carried along by the Holy Spirit. In Jeremiah 1:12 the Lord says, You have seen correctly, for I am watching to see that my word is fulfilled. The Holy Spirit inspired prophets and authors to say just the words they said and to write exactly what they wrote.

David says in 2 Samuel 23:2, *The Spirit of the Lord spoke through me; his word was on my tongue.* In Jeremiah 30:2 the Lord says to the prophet, *Write in a book all the words I have spoken to you.*

We continually find in the Bible that the Lord told the prophet to write down all His words as He spoke them. This means that the words God said to them became the Scriptures—nothing else, no adulteration of His statements, but exactly what He had said.

In Acts 28:25 Paul says, *The Holy Spirit spoke the truth...when he said through Isaiah....* He spoke the truth, and it came to pass just as He had said, because God inspired the words and watched to see that they were fulfilled.

Jesus Confirms the
Historical Validity of the Scriptures

Today, in our so-called scientific age, a rampant academic pride is causing people to reject the Bible on very inconclusive evidence and from an exclusively human standpoint. The Bible is regarded as any other book, full of mistakes and contradictions, written by people encumbered by weakness. The writers were certainly not perfect, and for this reason they were aided by the Helper, the Holy Spirit, who supervised the whole work, making sure everything included was true, authentic and from God.

Jesus says of His Father's words in John 17:17 Sanctify them by the truth; your word is truth. We have the Father's words in the Bible and they are true. They may contradict people's limited knowledge, common sense and experience or even their morals and ethics, but that does not make them any less true. A refusal to believe in the Bible is never based on an intellectual principle which cannot allow it, but on morals which will not allow it. A loose lifestyle needs the support of a lax theology. They both deny and reject God's Word.

It is interesting to see how Jesus handled the Scriptures! People often ask, "What school of Biblical thought do you belong to?" I answer, "The same one as Jesus!" He is God's Son so He ought to know best. It is logical for a Christian to have the same opinion on the Scriptures as Jesus Christ. He is the very heart of the Scriptures, their center and goal.

Notice that Jesus placed His words on equal rank with Himself. In Luke 9:26 we read, If anyone is ashamed of me *and my words, the Son of Man will be ashamed of him when he comes in his glory and in the glory of the Father and of the holy angels.*

Jesus often quoted the Old Testament. In these scriptures we see that He:

1. Believed that Adam and Eve were once physically existed (Matt 19:4; Mark 10:6),

2. That Noah lived and built an ark (Luke 17:26),

3. That Jonah's experience in the large fish was real (Matt. 12:40),

4. That Sodom and Gomorah existed (Matt 11:24),

5. That Moses wrote the Pentateuch (Mark 10:4-5; John 5:46,47), and

6. That Daniel wrote the book of Daniel! (Matt 24:15).

All this and much more was obvious to Jesus. He believed it all, even though every one of the above mentioned points and many more are rejected by numerous theologians and pastors today. Jesus is God's own Son and He knows the truth better than anyone else; and if He believes it, I believe it too. He knows better than every liberal theologian how things are. I would much rather side with Jesus than with some academic who denies the beliefs of my Savior.

Paul says in Acts 24:14, *I admit that I worship the God of our fathers, as a follower of the Way, which they call a sect.* **I believe everything** *that agrees with the Law and that is written in the Prophets.* Paul believed the whole of the Scriptures, counting it his duty to God to do so—and God wants us to do the same today. He wants us to be faithful to His Word, accepting it and obeying what He says.

Bible Faith is Returning

These days there is a clear distinction between Christians as whole denominations move to disassociate themselves from the Bible and thereby, from the God who inspired it.

Such a climate of apostasy has become a hotbed for the most bizarre ideas and objections. Church leaders and theologians have come out with the oddest theories, trimming their sails to every wind as they are blown about in the world. But this is coming to an end. Bible faith is returning. Men and women from every sector of society are opening their hearts to Jesus and discovering how easy it is to believe in His Word!

The objections of liberal theology are collapsing like a house of cards. **There is no power in its liberal denials! The power is in the Word of God!** The power is in the Gospel! The power is with our risen Christ who is the same today as He was when He was on earth and He still performs miraculous signs, wonders and powerful deeds. Today, Jesus is doing the things the Bible says He did yesterday and promises He will do tomorrow!

You can rely on God's Word! Do not be afraid if anyone questions your faith in it. His Word is like a lion. Do not discuss its existence or qualities. Let it loose! God's power is in His Word:

So is my word that goes out from my mouth: It will not return to me empty but will accomplish what I desire and achieve the purpose for which I sent it (Isa 55:11).

God's promises stand firm! He keeps His Word! His power is real, and He loves to do miracles! One of them is His own Word—the Bible—and it will prove itself true to the end, right up until Jesus comes back!

46

The Boundaries are Drawn

We are standing at a crossroads in time. Never before has the true Christian faith been so challenging and so challenged.

God is meticulously preparing for the manifestation of His glory and it is vital that Christians are firmly rooted in His Word and outspokenly loyal to Jesus.

In recent years, there has been an almost uninterrupted turbulence among the Christian churches. Many have praised God for it, while others have turned against it completely. There has been much discussion, a variety of rumors and a great deal of scandal in circulation. Can God really be in all this stir and commotion somewhere? Yes, He can, without doubt!

God is rooting out blatant, deep-seated ungodliness and dealing with backslidden behavior, attitudes and lifestyles. He has made up His mind to reveal Himself as He is to the people and bring a charge against those who live in the land (Hos 4:1). First He is going to come in righteous judgment and then with blessing.

This is not primarily a case of taking sides for or against particular persons, churches or movements. That would be far too convenient. No, the choice is between false religiosity and ungodliness on the one hand, and God's Word and the Spirit's work on the other. Fundamentally, it is a stand for, or against God.

These are the positions that are currently being drawn up and the cause of the present, sharp conflict and confrontation. It has been many years since the Gospel was last headed on such a collision course with the spirit of the age in our society and God made such demands on believers to stand up for Jesus, rally around the banner of His cross and do battle for their Lord. If we heed Him, we will see a mighty unparalleled breakthrough!

Therefore, it is tragic when both preacher and people choose the path of compromise with this world. The carnal longing to please people and gain their approval is a poor substitute for pleasing God and witnessing a breakthrough for His Kingdom.

As the Gospel has advanced throughout history, there has always been confrontation, persecution and fierce resistance. However, if we are prepared to pay the price of being misunderstood and misrepresented, even to the point of being openly hated for following Jesus and taking Him at His Word, then we will see some wonderful breakthroughs and the glory of the Lord will appear!

Gradual Decline of Biblical Christianity

For years the devil has been preparing the world to go his way and follow his directives. Similarly, the Church has been lured step by step into the most demeaning desertion Christianity has know for centuries. Its opinion of the Bible has swung so drastically that our former pioneers of revival, venerated by the denominations, would feel like perfect strangers.

There has been a gradual movement away from the Bible as God's Word, so that now, the most absurd contradictions are heard from our pulpits. The concept of God, the virgin birth and Jesus' work on Calvary are entirely different from what they once were. Most of the fundamental principles of our faith, cherished by the Church throughout the centuries, are now being flagrantly denied.

Bombastic denouncements of the faith revival can be heard from these quarters. Misleading indictments and so-called dissertations containing the most amazing allegations and inferences have also come from these same sources. The leadership of several denominations has risen up in this area and encouraged their chief theologians to lay grievous charges against other believers, while vast numbers of them are members and supporters of their own churches. Many of these saints hardly dare voice their desires openly for fear of being linked with groups publicly banned by their leaders! This is nothing less than the spiritual violation of thousands of people. However, praise the Lord for the thousands who are beginning to have their eyes opened to what is going on around them and who see what the battle is really all about.

The flare-up over "popular spiritual movements," "prosperity," "para-church organizations" and the like, is really nothing more than a barrage of invective from an apostate church against the work of the Holy Spirit. No hatred is greater than hatred from a backslidden church. A backslider is one who has tasted of God but then turned away. He is not reckoned among those who hold back from God through ignorance or fear. He is aware of the divine gift, having once *tasted the goodness of the word of God and the powers of the coming age* (Heb 6:5), yet he has decided to reject them. As a result, when others have a powerful meeting with God, he experiences jealousy and a desire for revenge. He feels compelled to oppose and resist what he once experienced himself but later abandoned.

It may seem incredible but it is nonetheless true, that many of the more influential positions within the established churches today, and many of the higher positions in society, are occupied by such people. They are pushing for a worldly, humanistic "gospel" from which the supernatural has been carefully dismantled and thrown out.

These are the circles in which sin is defended and God's Word denied. When a Swedish priest, well known for his radio broadcasts, returned from a journey to Easter Island, a leading evening newspaper reported that he had a small, invisible creature sitting on his shoulder, guiding him and telling him what to say! (Aftonbladet, 17 April 1988). These people said nothing, but on the other hand, they rant about Christians who dare to mention the devil and demons!

Only One Gospel!

The former rifts between denominations are rapidly becoming obsolete and their contentions out-of-date. Now other, much more fundamental issues are at stake, and it is crucial that we move the battlefront forward. It is our evaluation of God's Word and the Holy Spirit that is going to determine where the line is to be drawn today.

The question you must ask yourself as a Christian is whether the preachers to whom you are listening are declaring Bible truth or preaching another gospel. Equally, do they acknowledge the work of the Holy Spirit today as it is presented in the life of Jesus and the Acts of the Apostles? The Gospel is the supernatural Good News that Jesus has promised to confirm by miraculous signs and wonders.

In some circles, lip service is paid to Bible truths while they deny Jesus' words by their deeds. They never expect miracles, never pray for the sick nor seek the baptism of the Holy Spirit. They despise speaking in other tongues, explain away the gifts of the Spirit and are critical of evangelism in its power. They resort to the world for help instead of God, for the means His Spirit offers.

This is the scene of battle today. These are the questions on which positions are being drawn up, and the final outcome will be an apostate or an apostolic church. The issue is about one part of so-called Christendom falling away to false doctrine;

backslidden religiosity, worldliness and syncretism—one universal, world religion—while the other part returns to the original Gospel, to Jesus, Calvary, to Bible faith and the work of the Holy Spirit.

Some think that by merely regulating a number of outward behavioral patterns we will arrive at unity. No, the sword of God's Word must cut still deeper, separating spirit from soul, truth from falsehood and light from darkness.

The Church is Rising Up

Today, the light of God is exposing the influences of the spirit of antichrist and the world on the Church, so that the New Testament Church can rise up in all her glory, free from worldliness and compromise, and be all that Jesus wants her to be.

We are going to witness a period when the Church shakes off her "Babylonian captivity" and returns to Zion. For this reason the Lord says to her, *Arise, shine, for your light has come, and the glory of the Lord rises upon you. See, darkness covers the earth and thick darkness is over the peoples, but the Lord rises upon you and his glory appears over you* (Isa 60:1-2).

What we are witnessing in our countries is not negative but positive! It is positive that we are taking a radical stand for God against ungodliness wherever it appears, whether in the Church or in the world. It is positive that thousands are marching out to freedom, joy and power because they have chosen to follow Jesus as the Bible presents Him. It is positive that the presence of the Holy Spirit and supernatural manifestations are becoming more visible in the Church.

It is positive that Christians everywhere are taking their faith to heart and confessing with their mouth that they believe it possible to change the spiritual atmosphere of their lands. It is positive that the saints are beginning to see that together with Jesus, their countries can be saved!

No wonder the devil is growing nervous and trying to suppress everything. Like Pharaoh, he is using threats and flattery to hinder the children of God from escaping to freedom and from serving Him as he requires. But just as Moses did not deviate from his purpose nor bend before resistance, neither do we. Liberty and joy, with the presence and power of God in our lives, are far too high a prize to be sold for a bowl of lentils or exchanged for the fleshpots of Egypt.

God offers us something far greater, worth every ounce of resistance we can muster, to keep ourselves from compromise. We are living in wonderful times; times when the boundaries are being drawn so that the blessing and liberty God has in store for us can become a reality for the whole of our land.

47

Eight Signs of Revival

All true believers long for revival. It is a burning desire within their bones, desperate to burst into flame.

Revival is the one and only solution to the problems of both the individual and society. Jesus says in John 15:5, *apart from me you can do nothing.* An individual or a society without Jesus is headed for downfall, for neither can survive on "Christian values and principles" alone. What we need is fire from heaven, conviction of sin and conversion. We need men and women who will fall before the face of the Almighty and call on Him for mercy, cleansing and help, refusing to cease until the flames engulf them. *For our "God is a consuming fire"* (Heb 12:29). When that fire fills us we will be burning in spirit, sanctified in our lives and courageous in our deeds. We will be on fire for our Lord!

Right now the Holy Spirit is more active than ever preparing, purging and working toward revival. The world needs it, the Church needs it and God wants it. Anyone who is willing to receive revival can have it. We often think of revival as a bolt from the blue, without any cooperation from us—but it is not like that. Even at Pentecost, the Spirit could only be given after the disciples had prayed. Of course, it is the will of God that we should always have revival. If we take hold of His will and apply His principles for revival, it will come and flow constantly through our lives and churches just as He desires. Today, we can already see many signs of approaching revival.

1. An Awakening and Restoration Among Believers

God takes wonderful care of every individual believer. A crowd consists of individuals. A church consists of individual people. A chain is made up of links and every single one is necessary. All church work, organizations and government must have the needs of the individual as their goal. Anything else will lead to a hierarchy sitting way up at the top, leading its own artificial life and nursing its own contrived problems, without contact with the people or the needs of the individual. Today, God is making every believer strong in Him. He is showing him his position in Christ, his rights and privileges, his work and responsibilities and his tools and resources. The Holy Spirit is extremely active, equipping God's army and every individual soldier in it.

2. The Revival of Teaching

The Holy Spirit is our Helper and the one who will lead us into all truth. He is the one who inspired the Word of God and who can interpret it for us. During the 1900's there have been formidable attacks against the Bible. Without exception, every fundamental doctrine has been undermined in the most serious way. Liberal theology has taken a heavy toll from deep within the ranks of the nominal church, and robbed men and women of the power of God.

The first thing we discover about our enemy is that he sows doubt concerning God's Word. In Genesis 3:1 he said to Eve in the garden, *Did God really say...?* and he has continued ever since, to query the Word of God in the same way. Paul warns in 2 Corinthians 11:3, *But I am afraid that just as Eve was deceived by the serpent's cunning, your minds may somehow be led astray from your sincere and pure devotion to Christ.* The devil knows that power, salvation and liberty are to be found in the Word of God. If he can sow doubt there, we will become powerless, defeated individuals, totally impotent in a world where we are to be as salt. Therefore we praise the Lord for the Holy Spirit who is inspiring a supreme confidence in "that which is written" in the hearts of men and women.

When a person makes Jesus his Lord, the Bible automatically becomes his authority on life. His limited intellect and experience are no longer the criteria by which he judges what God is saying and doing but, as a true servant of his Lord, he exclaims, *Do **whatever** he tells you* (John 2:5).

Signs and wonders are no problem to the person who is devoted to his Lord. He knows that God is a wonderful counselor, almighty and loving. He is acquainted with His personality and knows He will do what He has promised. When a person is saved, his ego no longer claims the final word and acts as god in its own right. He does not stop using his God-given common sense or drawing on his limited experience, but he ceases to use them as his final authority. When head knowledge and experience conflict with revelation or the will of God and His Word, then it is the Word that must decide. Jesus is Lord of his life and mind, and it is there that confidence and reliance on the Word begins to take root. Doubt, scepticism and carnal rebellion toward the Word have to go. There can no longer be any unclean motives for remaining in the pleasures of sin.

A person whose heart is thus softened, whose spirit is sensitive and who is committed to his Lord's conditions, not his own, can be taught in the Scriptures by the Holy Spirit. God has much He wants him to know so he can live in victory. Righteousness then becomes a concrete reality to him and condemnation dies away. Faith no longer consists of pious, religious platitudes. Now it forms a functional, practical part of his daily life. Jesus is seen to be real, helping real people in real life situations and doing real wonders and miracles because He is the same, *yesterday and today and forever* (Heb 13:8).

3. Manifestations of the Gifts of the Spirit

The Church was born in the supernatural, where it must continue to live and flow. Only in the Spirit do we have the advantage over the devil. We are to walk in the Spirit (Gal 5:16) because our struggle is not against people of flesh and blood, but against authorities and powers (Eph 6:12), and our weapons are not fleshly but spiritual (2 Cor 10:3-5).

If the devil can draw us out of the spiritual realm into the soulish arena, he can defeat us. Our fine intellect, will power or rich emotional experiences cannot gain us the victory. It is our faith in Jesus and the power of His Spirit, it is the baptism in the Spirit and the spiritual gifts that make all the difference.

Victory can only be decided by our dependence on the Holy Spirit and the use of His power in our lives. We are totally dependent on the gifts of the Spirit if we are to complete the Great Commission. Without them, we are like a supertanker out of fuel—huge, bulky and impressive to the eye—but empty. God wants every believer to be baptized in the Holy Spirit, flowing in what is normal and natural to us—the supernatural.

Many Christians have been fearful, or even cuttingly critical of spiritual manifestations. This has always been the case but there has never been a revival before the Spirit has been allowed to work freely on people's lives. He needs to bring them to repentance and conversion, to purity and holiness, to power, wonders and miracles. God wants the stamp of His supernatural power, wisdom and presence to be on His children.

Neither the world nor carnal diplomacy must be allowed to put a stop to the Spirit's manifestations. Prayer in the Spirit is indispensable for supernatural results.

4. Conviction of Sin and Repentance

In times of revival God always begins with the church. It must first be awakened if it has fallen asleep. (The world is dead and needs to be born again, not simple awakened.) Backsliding, apathy, carnal pride and reliance on former success must all go. Then, the saints will burn in their spirits and their Lord can send them out to win souls. **There is no revival without soul winning.**

Today, the Holy Spirit is poured out over **all** people (Acts 2:17) and He is working in every nation. They all need to hear of Jesus Christ, of the cross, the blood, our inheritance and the power and glory of God. The Holy Spirit works mightily on the unsaved in every revival, drawing them to the cross. We have never had a better opportunity than now. People have never been more receptive. Religious discussions and controversies are filling the air. People have so many questions. Make use of the opportunity and meet them where they are. Take their questions, prejudices and ideas and direct them all to Jesus.

No one is indifferent to Jesus today. Do as Philip did in Acts 8:35. The Ethiopian chancellor, just like a lot of people these days, was reading Isaiah 53 without understanding what he read. What did Philip do? Did he start a heated, religious debate and rain arguments on the head of the Ethiopian? No. *Then Philip began with that very passage of Scripture and told him the good news about Jesus.*

5. Holiness and Purity Among the People of God

When the Church is aroused and led back to the Bible, true holiness becomes natural. Where revival breaks out we see the presence, power, wisdom and glory of God more clearly than ever. Hebrews 12:14 says, *Make every effort to live in peace with all men and to be holy; without holiness no one will see the Lord.*

The devil is doing his worst to blur the outlines between the world and the Church, the kingdom of darkness and the Kingdom of God's dear Son. However, as the light dawns, the contrast with darkness becomes all the more obvious and reveals any uncleanness, falsehood or lukewarmness that is lurking there. Previously hidden rebellion, lust for power, greed and ambition are unmasked in all their crudity, so that strife, jealousy, hatred, obstinacy and pride can all be exposed.

In revival, the fear of the Lord comes on the believers and a constant awareness of the presence of God makes them conscious that certain behavior, is now no longer acceptable.

Sanctification is not primarily something external. For example, it does not mean dressing in the style of the former generation or talking in a forced manner. Holiness starts with the inner man and expresses itself in purity.

Sanctification calls for utter devotion to the one who is making me holy. I do not abstain from things in order to appear great, but I refrain from anything that hinders the flow of the anointing in my life. I make myself free from dependence on material things, for Jesus means more to me than everything else. When blessing subsequently comes to me in every area of life, I do not become attached to any of it. I can receive it because I know who I serve. I am not afraid, because I know my motives are pure and God is getting all the glory!

6. Disputes and Controversies

This may seem a strange sign of revival because we know that, as believers we are to work toward unity. Jesus, in fact, prays in John 17 that we may be one. However, this unity, which is of a spiritual nature, can only be brought about by the Holy Spirit when we exalt Jesus, believe His Word and do as He says. A refusal to submit to God's Word, while simultaneously talking about unity, will only produce carnal attempts at achieving unity, through manipulation. Such carnal efforts result in bondage. Remember David's brothers who tried to squash his courageous faith venture by their fleshly insinuations that Goliath was probably unconquerable? But David believed God and lived in the covenant promises. He knew the power in the name of the Lord of Hosts and acted on it.

The Holy Spirit brings a spiritual unity that makes room for people to fulfill their calling. As long as we are here on earth, we will never all have exactly the same opinion on every point, but we can, nevertheless, enjoy unity in the Spirit.

When you see what the Lord is doing in a person's life you look on him or her through "spiritual glasses." You may not agree on every detail but you notice the anointing and allow the person liberty to go forward with his calling.

Constantly watching, correcting and checking up on people in the name of unity will not produce the genuine article; but rather, fear and passivity. All God's people acknowledge the importance of unity and agree that no one has a monopoly on the truth, but that does not mean they are to compromise what God has shown them to please others. They should allow genuine freedom and multiplicity, while standing firm on what they have personally received from the Lord.

No Christian wants strife, but it constantly occurs anyway. In fact, a number of these disputes are nothing more than a healthy sign of life. Jesus Himself said in Matthew 10:34, *Do not suppose that I have come to bring peace to the earth. I did not come to bring peace, but a sword.* The sword Jesus is speaking about is God's Word. Hebrews 4:12 says, *For the word of God is living and active. Sharper than any double-edged sword, it penetrates even to **dividing soul and spirit, joints and marrow; it judges the thoughts and attitudes of the heart.***

The Word of God always has a separating effect. Jesus promised to uproot everything His heavenly Father had not planted, because only that which comes from God and is born of Him, overcomes the world (1 John 5:4).

Jesus wants an overcoming Church, and therefore everything that opposes Him and His Word must be removed. However, we must take care to differentiate between the problem and the person. If you are in the Spirit, you may see and suffer much that is fleshly, but this does not give you the right to react in a fleshly manner by proudly condemning others or carnally defending yourself when in the line of fire. If you are spiritual you can mix with anyone, be kind to everyone and be at peace with all, as far as it depends on you. This does not imply that you compromise your position or cease to follow your convictions. It only means that you can distinguish between the person and the problem, so that if you should ever feel like Daniel in the lions' den, faith in your God will rescue you and bring you through to liberty.

Many people think that revival times are nothing but outpourings of latter rain, refreshing, rest and joy. No, they are times of intense spiritual warfare! They may look a bit untidy, like buildings under construction, but the end results are good. So live by faith while the dust is flying! Remember, when God was doing one of His greatest miracles, dividing the Red Sea, Pharaoh and his army were at the point of their **greatest** activity; but they were defeated anyway. Hallelujah!

7. Courage and Enterprise

Revival implies an awakening, a stirring and the **start of activity**. Today, believers are becoming more active than ever. Suddenly, they are realizing that Jesus has commanded **them**, not their neighbor, to fulfill the Great Commission. The needs of the unsaved, coupled with hunger for more of God, are urging them to take many new initiatives led by the Holy Spirit, the Spirit of liberty, who is inspiring them with thoughts, plans, ideas and projects like never before.

For hundreds of years, despotic religious spirits have attempted to dominate, manipulate and paralyze the people of God but they are not successful during times of revival. Then, the Holy Spirit anoints people with new ministries and they advance with power and fearlessly step out into new areas. They are people of faith who have found a completely new confidence in God and who say, "God is with **me**, He can and will use **me**."

8. New Churches

We are living in a new age. A new generation and a new harvest is awaiting us. God is shaping new tools to gather it in and He is erecting new storehouses. This does not mean that He is forsaking His old methods. He will use anything and everything that is available for use. But this does not prohibit God from building new equipment, which is exactly what He is doing and there is room for much more.

If we believe in the harvest, we must also believe in new and growing churches. God wants churches where the Word is preached and confirmed by signs following. He wants congregations praising Him in the liberty and power of the Spirit. He wants churches where prayer is a clear and rising flame and where believers are actively going out into the world. He wants churches where the newly converted receive proper care and follow-up and where the sheep are led to green pastures in which they can feed and grow.

We have entered an intensively spiritual era. God is preparing a harvest throughout the earth and we praise Him for it. Zechariah 10:1 says, *Ask the Lord for rain in the springtime; it is the Lord who makes the storm clouds.* Let us call on God for a spirit of prayer and revival to fall on the whole body of Christ and then prepare ourselves for a harvest. *He gives* **showers** *of rain to men, and plants of the field* **to everyone**.

48

Times of Refreshing

When Jeremiah the prophet looked on the devastations of Jerusalem, he wept. He saw the walls in ruins, the gates desolate and the people were gone. No one came to keep the feasts and the enemy was in power.

In Lamentations 1:6 Jeremiah recorded that *All the splendour has departed from the Daughter of Zion.* As the prophet viewed the terrible destruction, we read of his response in Lamentations 2:11, *My eyes fail from weeping, I am in torment within, my heart is poured out on the ground because my people are destroyed, because children and infants faint in the street of the city.*

Israel had caused her own misery by transgressing the commandments of God and giving herself to idolatry.

My people have committed two sins: They have forsaken me, the spring of living water, and have dug their own cisterns, broken cisterns that cannot hold water (Jer 2:13). Their backsliding brought all kinds of misery on the children of Israel.

This is clearly stated in Jeremiah 2:19, *"Your wickedness will punish you; your backsliding will rebuke you. Consider then and realize how evil and bitter it is for you when you forsake the Lord your God and have no awe of me,"* declares the Lord, the Lord Almighty.

The Consequences of Sin

Sin is a terrible thing, and it must never be taken lightly. It always has consequences. *For he who sows to his flesh will of the flesh reap corruption* (Gal 6:8 NKJ). God, however, paid the ultimate price to redeem us from sin. None of us can understand what Calvary actually cost Him.

The consequences of sin are far reaching, both for individuals and for churches generally. Israel's backsliding and rebellion affected not only the entire nation but also its land. Similarly, today, when individual churches or even whole denominations depart from God, the consequences are so great that they affect a whole people. The Church is the light of the world and *the salt of the earth. But if the salt loses its saltiness…it is no longer good for anything, except to be thrown out and trampled by men* (Matt 5:13).

There is nothing worse than a backslidden church, guilty of compromise and spiritual whoredom with the world, which permits itself to be seduced by the spirit and example of this age. Degradation within the church has always caused widespread rejection of the Gospel and wreaks havoc in the lives of thousands.

When Eli was priest of Israel, his sons, also priests, lived in backsliding and fornication, They forcibly took the sacrifices from the people for their own use and slept with the women who served at the entrance of the Tent of Meeting (1 Sam. 2). The results were disastrous. 1 Samuel 2:17 tells us, *This sin of the young men was very great in the Lord's sight, for they were treating the Lord's offering with contempt.*

Sin in the camp taught the people to disrespect God and as a result, the glory of the Lord withdrew from Israel. Eli's sons went to war, under the illusion that the ark would save them, only to be defeated because they had lived impure and unholy lives (1 Sam 2:17).

The Strength of the Church Lies in the Supernatural

In every generation, Satan desires to rob the Church of its glory through compromise, sin and apostasy. The Church was born in the supernatural and it should live and function in the supernatural. The power of the Holy Spirit and His varying manifestations are the vital force by which it lives.

In normal Church life God's Spirit is manifest, the sick are healed, the oppressed freed and an uninterrupted flow of revelation leads to salvation for many souls. The devil hates all of this and does his utmost to oust the Church from its natural element, namely the supernatural, for it is there its strength lies.

The strength of the Church is not found in its members' intellectual capacity, their deep emotional experiences or will power. These all lie in the soul realm and are only of use as they are submitted to the Holy Spirit. Our strength lies in the supernatural. We can only achieve success and effectively reach out to the masses with salvation, through the Spirit. Therefore, Satan's main concern is to hinder this. He is thoroughly shaken and nearly scared to death whenever the Church begins to flow in the power of God.

In our times, apostasy and idolatry have made many inroads into the Church. As the decades have passed, the world has strongly influenced it and bound it. But that will soon end and great changes are already under way. Backsliding will now be replaced by restoration and defeat will give place to victory. People are coming back and the departed glory of God is returning. God is going to visit our lands and show His mighty arm! Urged on by His love for the people, He is going to reveal Himself as the God He is.

However, revival does not come without a price. There must be repentance from sin and every idol must be destroyed. This can only happen through the Spirit of God. We cannot feign spiritual unity. We must confess and forsake sin and cease walking in the ways of the world.

Idolatry is not simply the erection of an altar to a god, but any form of religiosity where God is said to be worshiped while His Word and commandments are taken lightly. An idol is not always a statue. It can be any figment of human imagination about God, which does not have support in the Scripture. Idolatry is the same as having a form of godliness while denying its power.

People use words like, "God," "Jesus," "atonement"and "love" while meaning something totally foreign to the Bible. They legalize the sins of fornication, sodomy, abortion and so on, while outlawing the virgin birth, the resurrection, conversion, the new birth, a holy life, a final judgment and hell. This is nothing but apostasy and idolatry, and those who are party to it will come under the wrath of God. They may continue in their pride to occupy their priestly offices, like the sons of Eli, but there will be no accompanying glory and the wages of their sin will be death.

God is Restoring His Church

We live in days when the devil thought he had almost succeeded in robbing the Church of all it had. But praise the Name of the Lord from everlasting to everlasting, God knows better! Where it has suffered loss and been desecrated, the Church is going to be built up again.

The restoration of the Church is at hand. God is not sitting idly by, watching while the devil tries his tricks. No, He is busy gathering an army that fears nothing but Himself. He is building a Church that loves righteousness and hates iniquity (Heb 1:9); that loves the sinner but hates his sin and that longs for God's presence and the Spirit's power like the deer pants for waterbrooks. His Church confesses Jesus as Lord, has His Word as her only guide and refuses all compromise, whatever the cost.

The Spirit's restoring work is threefold:

First—The teaching. If we have incorrect information, we will not be able to act correctly. For years, the devil has insulted, blasphemed and reviled the Word of God and caused many saints to be ashamed of the Bible and not dare to take it seriously. Nevertheless, God's Word is still true, reliable and valid. It is active, powerful and liberating; and if you believe it, you will have what it proclaims. God says of His Word, *It will not return to me empty, but will accomplish what I desire and achieve the purpose for which I sent it* (Isa 55:11).

Second—The Life. The Holy Spirit is restoring Life to the Church. People are beginning to experience lives of separation to God, in holiness and purity. They are developing a hatred of sin and they are walking with meticulous care before the Lord Jesus. This does not mean they are introverts, searching for every possible shortcoming sin, feeling remorse over missed opportunities. Neither are they idly waiting to become "holy enough." On the contrary, it means they are firmly established in the righteousness of God and particularly in their daily lives with Him, avoiding compromise and worldly behavior. They are living for Jesus and expecting His glory to be displayed in every situation, while their lives become increasingly filled with the presence of God.

Third—The Ordinances. God's order in the family, the Church and society will be successively restored. God is going to raise up large churches in our time that will become oases in a troubled world; churches where the power of God is present to solve men and women's problems and pave the way for the blessing of the Lord to meet their every need. I am convinced that just as the devil has despised and demeaned the Church, God will raise it up. Churches wielding spiritual influence are going to rise up and shake not only their own countries, but others too.

In the time ahead we will see spiritual churches appearing, equipped to be channels of God's presence, power and revelation as never before. The devil hates the Church because Jesus prophesied in Matthew 16:18 that the gates (the authority), of Hades would never overcome it. The time is now at hand when spirit rulers and powers must bow their knees to the Church of the Living God!

49

A New Generation

When the children of Israel stood at the brink of one of the greatest miracles in history (the entering and conquest of the Holy Land), they turned back. Moses had sent twelve spies into the country to find out the prevailing conditions and to prepare the invasion. When the spies returned, ten had a negative report and two were positive.

They agreed with God, in principle, that the land was good. *They gave Moses this account: We went into the land to which you sent us, and it does flow with milk and honey! Here is its fruit. But the people who live there are powerful, and the cities are fortified and very large. We even saw descendants of Anak there* (Num 13:27-28).

They saw that the country God had promised them was good and that what God had said about it was true, but still they raised their objections: "Of course the Word of God is true, but circumstances are bigger and harder. Anyway, it isn't possible to get what God has promised."

Many people say the same today: "Of course the Bible is true; of course everything Jesus says is true—but I am not sure whether I will get answers to my prayers. Of course Jesus can answer prayer and perform miracles, but I'm not sure He will do it for me. Of course there is victory, but I can't live in it."

What a discouragement it must have been for God to see His people so close to the goal and then compromise, back off, excuse themselves, act in unbelief and lose everything God had intended for them.

The Spirit of Faith

For we also have had the gospel preached to us, just as they did; but the message they heard was of no value to them, because those who heard did not combine it with faith (Heb 4:2).

Unbelief rose up with all its carnal excuses and stole the victory from an entire nation. We cannot agree with God in principle and then bring our excuses—"in my special case" and "in my particular situation." We cannot look at our circumstances and then use them to explain why God's promises cannot become a reality. This may be sufficient in theological committees, but never before the presence of Living God.

God means what He has promised. He is faithful to what He has said and He will do what He has decided.

Among the twelve spies there were two who did not eradicate the promises of God with a big "but." God never intended that we should say, "This is what God promises, but..." Instead, He wants us to declare, "This is what God promises, Amen." The promises of God in Christ are Yes and Amen (2 Cor 1:20).

The two spies, Caleb and Joshua, had a different spirit. Numbers 14:24 and 2 Corinthians 4:13 call it the spirit of faith. This spirit of faith was on Caleb when he suggested. *We should go up and take possession of the land, for we can certainly do it* (Num 13:30). But the other spies reacted strongly against this and replied, *We can't attack those people; they are stronger than we are* (Num 13:31).

The spirit of faith on Caleb made him trust in what God had promised. Caleb knew that if God had promised them the country, then He was well able to give them the ability to overcome all resistance and every foe, so they could gain all that God had promised them.

Whatever God plans, He blesses. Caleb knew that because of this, they could possess the land. However, the people listened to the unbelief of the ten and became filled with fear, wanting instead to choose a leader and return to Egypt.

A Whole Generation Died in the Wilderness

God had done wonder after wonder, miracle after miracle and yet the people wanted to return to the slavery of Egypt. Ten times the Lord had spoken to His people and ten times they had refused to listen to His voice, though they had seen His glory.

As a result of this repeated disobedience, the people spent forty years in the wilderness. God could not bring them into the country because they did not want to go in. They told Him they would rather die in the wilderness, and they received exactly what they said: *As surely as I live, declares the Lord, I will do to you the very things I heard you say: In this desert your bodies will fall—every one of you twenty years old or more who was counted in the census and who has grumbled against me* (Num 14:28-29).

A whole generation died in the wilderness because of their unbelief and refusal to take God's promises seriously. God's promises are true and they cannot be treated any way you like.

Isaiah 1:19 says, *If you are willing and obedient, you will eat the best from the land.* God wants His people to eat the good of the land. He wants us to receive all His blessings.

In Christ Jesus we have received a spiritual inheritance. We have been blessed in the heavenly realms with every spiritual blessing in Christ (Eph 1:3), and we are to claim our inheritance by faith. It is not sufficient to agree in principle that the inheritance is available through the death and resurrection of Jesus. God expects a people who reach out and actively make the inheritance their own by possessing it in faith, in the same way that God wanted the Israelites to possess their promised land.

Just as the spirit of faith came on Caleb and Joshua, it has come on us. They were the only ones out of that old generation who possessed the promised land. By walking in faith, they became leaders who guided the people into the blessings of God.

A Whole Nation Obedient to the Faith

Since a whole generation refused to walk in faith, God raised up a new one. It was a generation that had not been brought up in Egypt, a generation that had not made a golden calf and who had not hardened themselves ten times against God's voice. This new generation was willing to follow God.

When Joshua took over after Moses' death, the people were no longer rebellious. Previously they had made trouble. They had quarreled and rebelled against Moses until God wanted to start again with Moses alone, but now Joshua was leader, they were completely with him. *Then they answered Joshua, "Whatever you have commanded us we will do, and wherever you send us we will go"* (Josh 1:16).

They had come into the obedience of faith. Joshua is a picture of Jesus, the Captain of our salvation. The people had arrived at the place where they were willing to obey everything God said. There were no "buts" left. All their reservations were gone. The promises of God were true, no matter what some people thought or said—What God had promised was valid!

This was a totally new generation, a totally new group of people. They were not a few lonely, misunderstood heroes of faith. They were an entire population who believed God, a totally new generation of people who were different. They spoke different, looked different, sang different, prayed different and acted different. And there were a lot of them!

They were the generation that took the land because they marched together *with* God, not *against* Him. They were conquerors with God in everything they did. They saw God keep His Word and they saw Him do miracles. They saw the power of their Lord in action and they saw the supernatural. They possessed their inheritance and they received the blessing and the abundance of the Lord. They saw that, *Not one of the Lord's good promises to the house of Israel failed; every one was fulfilled* (Josh 21:45).

This was the kind of people God wanted. They were a people who refused to compromise, a people who were willing to pay any price to follow God and partake of His blessings. They were a people who saw that God really is who He says He is and does what He says He will do.

God wants a people like this on the earth at all times. Today, He is raising up such a generation—a totally new generation of believers that will spread His Kingdom to every part of the globe. Where people have turned back and compromised in unbelief; this new generation is rushing forward into the breach and taking the Kingdom of Heaven by force.

A New Generation that Will Not Keep Silent

An entirely new generation of young people is rising up. They are not a generation indoctrinated with unbelief and dead religion, nor are they infected by "denial theology." They have never learned to repudiate the gifts of the Spirit and supernatural manifestations. They have never heard that Jesus was wrong when He healed everyone. They have never heard that demons do not exist. They believe Jesus is the one He says He is, and that He does what He says He does. They understand that Jesus means what He says and says what He means.

This new generation knows that the Kingdom of God is not in word but in power. They know what it is to speak with new tongues and pray for the sick. They know that everyone has to be saved and that the Gospel will be proclaimed in every nation with signs and wonders following. They know that Jesus has defeated their enemy, Satan, and that they have authority over him in Jesus' Name. They know that the gates of hell cannot prevail against the Church and that the Kingdom of God is spreading everywhere. They know that the Gospel contains the power of God to bless all people everywhere, to solve all their problems and meet all their needs. A totally new generation is arising!

They will not be threatened to silence nor will they back off in unbelief. They will go all the way with God. This generation is God's reply to the problems of mankind. It is a generation filled with the love and compassion of God; a generation that cares for suffering people and which is a channel for God's power to change them completely.

This generation is rising up to exert its authority in the spirit realm. The body of Christ is coming into its real function—to be a channel for the power, presence and revelation of God in a dying world.

God is showing His mighty arm, and His people will proclaim His awesome deeds more boldly than ever before in the history of mankind.

LAND AND NATION

O Land, land, land, hear the word of the Lord!

Jeremiah 22:29

50

What Kind of Country Do You Want?

From one man he made every nation of men, that they should inhabit the whole earth; and he determined the times set for them and the exact places where they should live (Acts 17:26).

God originally set borders. He is the one who has granted people lands and nations in which to live. When God created Adam. He allotted him an area to administrate—the paradise garden in Eden. Later, in Genesis 10:35, we read that God divided the earth into its nations. He has appointed a country for you to manage, just as we have been given our country, Sweden. Whenever God delegates an area of responsibility to people, He invests it with pride. Hence, when the responsibility centers on lands and people, nationalism appears.

However, there is a true and a false national pride. False national pride expresses itself in expansionism, boastfulness and contempt of others and is used by the devil to stir up conflicts between nations. True nationalism, true patriotism, is entirely different. It expresses itself in thankfulness to God for the limits He has given us. It is a willingness to take responsibility and care for our land, defending it against everything that would break it down and destroy it.

God has decreed and set up ordinances. He has ordained rules for people's private lives, for marriage, for the Church, for the society and for the nation. These ordinances have the twofold purpose of protecting the individual and of making the knowledge, power and presence of God available to the inhabitants. Of course, God's rules constitute a direct threat to the devil, which is why he does all he can to destroy their influence and by that, get at the people.

Divine ordinances for nations are obviously the targets of the devil. One such ordinance is true patriotism, a genuine pride, joy and sense of responsibility for one's land. For years, the devil has been working to destroy individual responsibility and solidarity in my nation. He has created a false political, economic and ideological internationalism in Sweden, not founded on Christian values. As citizens in the Kingdom of God, we have brothers and sisters all over the world and feel at home everywhere. Nevertheless, God has given us all a particular area of responsibility, our country, and this is why we unashamedly make it our prime concern.

God is Re-establishing True Nationalism

Let me take my country as an example. God is giving Christians and other citizens, a fresh awareness of Sweden, as a land in its own right. An individual has an identity and so does a nation. We need to rediscover our identity in Sweden. We may be small numerically, but we have exerted a proportionally larger influence abroad and we will continue to do so.

Ministry gifts in the Church cover different areas of responsibility, they cannot be compared or contrasted with one another and it is the same with nations. In Sweden we have to accept the particular charge God has given us for Europe and the world. Our task from God is to train workers and send them out into Europe and every other nation, and this is exactly what we intend to do. God has given us resources and people whom He wants to use mightily in all the earth. The devil knows this and is not only actively opposing individual Christians but also the entire nation.

Freedom is God's gift to individuals and nations. Paul says in Galatians 5:1, *It is for freedom that Christ has set us free. Stand firm, then, and do not let yourselves be burdened again by a yoke of slavery.* When you received Jesus you were made free. The devil loathes it and does everything he can to bind, manipulate, dominate and stop you from increasing in it. This is equally true for nations and peoples. The devil does all he can to block economical, political and ideological freedom in the land. The spirit powers he has positioned over your country are fully absorbed, trying to strip its people of their liberty and creativity.

God has told us to pray for kings and all those in authority (1 Tim 2:1-2). Romans 13:1-6 tells us that all governmental rule comes from God, who has instituted authority so that a land will not dissolve into chaos. We do not have the right to grumble, complain, criticize or break these rules. We are to pray for the authorities and those in power, especially so that the right people are in these positions. If we do not take the responsibility and initiative, someone else will.

51

Living Faith Versus Humanism

Someone once said that what philosophers think becomes a way of life within a few generations. What was originally just a philosophic reflection later becomes the everyday habit of a populace without their really knowing why. In many respects this is true of the culture in which we live today.

Why do people behave, think and speak as they do? Often, they don't know why! Certain opinions come into vogue and they are accepted as modern "facts" that few dare to question or trace methodically to their source in order to examine the basic thought behind them.

A flood of "isms" affects people's conscious and unconscious thinking habits. Often we do not know why we think in a certain way. We have been influenced in one direction or another and frequently manipulated there against our will.

The Bible declares that your mind is a battleground. *Do not conform any longer to the pattern of this world, but be transformed by the renewing of your mind. Then you will be able to test and approve what God's will is—his good, pleasing and perfect will* (Rom 12:2). In other words, your mind needs to be renewed. Why? Because you have been exposed to strong influences and manipulation by the devil to cause you to think and feel in a way that furthers his purposes. If a whole generation can be swayed to think in a certain way, that entire generation can be won.

This is part of the devil's strategy to conquer the minds and thoughts of men. One tragic example of this is provided by Hitler's hate propaganda that ensnared a whole generation of disillusioned people. Today, his shameless purposes seem grotesque and monstrous but at the time, they sounded reasonable and a whole generation was thus led astray. This was no exception. The devil constantly bombards people's minds to accept a particular way of thinking in order to make it easier for him to expand his domain.

Therefore, we ought to stop and periodically ask ourselves "Why am I doing this?" **Often we are completely unaware**

of the basis and consequences of our thinking—and nothing can be more ominous.

Relativism—The Absence of Permanent Values

Our situation today is like a seething cauldron of differing thoughts and ideologies which lead people to conclude that "Everything is relative and so we must accept this diversity of ideas." We must accept that there is a diversity of opinions and ideas but it does not mean that we are to accept the thought that everything is relative.

As Christians, we love and respect everyone without taking their views and opinions into account, but that does not mean that we accept everything they hold as true. In a society where everyone has taken it for granted that "everything is relative" it almost causes offence if someone maintains a divergent opinion to be true. However, we cannot simply swallow the popular notion that "everything is relative" and therefore more or less right and acceptable. Not at all!

All knowledge is acquired from some source or another. We learn about our surroundings by gathering information through our senses and examining these facts in the light of our experience. We then draw logical conclusions and form our outlook on the world around us. We are all aware, too, that our knowledge is limited. None of us knows everything. Not even science which specifically concentrates on the accumulation of information, knows everything, and we often change our opinion in the light of further evidence. Even scientific theories are subject to correction or rejection.

We all have the same experience when it comes to knowledge about the world in which we live. But problems arise when someone claims "The world is only what we see and feel, there is nothing else. We cannot reckon with a God, only with ourselves."

Then, because we are all similarly limited and frequently subjective and contradictory in our judgments, we conclude that "everything is relative; there is no objective truth." The majority of people think this way today and, as a result, we become a law unto ourselves, or at least, that which others have taught us becomes our rule of thought.

Christianity, is entirely different. The Bible plainly states that God exists. He is an objective reality, and because He actually exists He can do real things. He created heaven and earth at a certain point in history. He sent His Son, Jesus Christ, at another definite point in time. It is a historical fact that Jesus died and rose again. God is working in time and space and doing real things for real people in real places.

Since God created us, He wants to have contact with us and talk to us. Everything He says is true because He is just and true. He really speaks, and what He says is truth.

God's Word—Objective Truth

Everything that God has spoken throughout history, is in our Bibles today. It is his inspired address to every person in every age. The Bible is true, relevant and practical because it is God's unadulterated Word.

God and His Word provide an objective anchor for every thought and view of life. Here we find an objective truth from outside ourselves, revealed by a God who exists. Such knowledge is known as revealed knowledge.

For hundreds of years, people have generally accepted that God exists and speaks and that what He says is relevant truth. Today however, recognition of these facts has been gravely undermined. Millions of people live in a strongly secularized, post-Christian world where Jesus is only among numerous founders of religion and the Bible is only one of many religious books, neither better nor worse. For these people, belief in the existence of God is nothing more than an interesting opinion; salvation is all right for some but not for others.

Thus, God is no longer objective truth but merely a subjective thought. Nothing suits the devil better. He can even allow religious people a little room to practice their beliefs so long as he can induce the masses to believe that theirs is only one among a great variety of alternative outlooks on life, and that they are free to pick up and choose what best suits their own interests and inclinations. "Everything is only relative anyway." "Nothing is really better than anything else." This is the thinking he propagates!

The devil has been sowing these thoughts in the minds of men and women for centuries so that he can reap a bewildered and blighted generation in our day and age. The corrupt seed-thought which lies underneath all this is "humanism."

Humanism—Man, the Universal Standard

When discussing humanism we must clarify and distinguish certain terms. The word "humanitarian" simply implies "fellow-human" and is recognized by Christians and non-Christians alike as something good and right. By the word "humanities" we mean the scholarly study of literature, language, music and art etc., as devised by human ability.

We are not against either of these. What we object to is "humanism" in the sense of a philosophy of life whose fundamental premise is that man himself is the fulcrum and center of existence, and the yardstick by which he measures everything. Humanism's cornerstone is a self-existent universe, not created by any God. At every opportunity, it guards against the very thought of the existence of God and flatly rejects Him as the guaranty of eternal and unchanging moral values. Humanism preaches that man cannot know or act on anything other than what he reasons out himself; none of his knowledge comes from an external, supernatural God.

As early as the renaissance, the battle cry of "Man, the measure of everything," was heard. It was revolutionary, unfamiliar and it seemed dangerous at the time. The clergy of that day responded with force and banned it, but today the idea is commonplace. People gradually rejected the concept of an objective revelation and shifted to accept **only** what man can "prove," think or feel, regardless of whether it was compatible with Biblical truth and morals or not.

Science became a new kind of guru, a savior that would liberate mankind through information, knowledge and insight. The only problem was that scientific theories superseded one another in rapid succession and contradicted each other as new facts emerged. The optimistic attitude toward science began to then give way to a number of more pessimistic, philosophical views, such as relativism and existentialism.

People accepted a fundamentally materialistic position supposing that it was impossible to acquire knowledge of anything other than the material around oneself. They said, "Man is not created in the image of God. Man is not a spiritual being, he is only material like everything else around, no more and no less."

Consequently, man was devalued; he was no longer a unique being, but merely a chance product of so-called "natural selection." His life has no purpose and his history and existence, no goal. Man must try to fill his days with meaning as best he can. There is nothing to tell him what is better or worse, or right or wrong (society now governs these variable moral standards). Man and society decide for themselves.

This means that man can live anyway he likes, calling it freedom of choice. However, it is really only the absence of aim, purpose and norms, and because no one is able to prove objectively what is right or wrong the majority decision rules. If, for example 51 per cent are for free abortion and 49 against, the 51 per cent majority decides what is true, right and legally valid—quite irrespective of what is objectively right and true because "everything is relative anyway."

This has resulted in the total breakdown of morals and the deep spiritual misery of living for experiences. People have cast restraint to the wind in an attempt to fill life with meaning and make something out of themselves. They are like a car with water instead of gasoline in the tank, lacking genuine security and a sure foundation. They pretend that all is well, while their God-given conscience keeps witnessing against them and they think that the guilt and anxiety they feel daily, is something everyone has to live with.

A Life of Conflict

Such a life presents a tragic dilemma for modern man: He is created for fellowship with God, to see God's divine plans realized in his life. However, he lives as though God does not exist, as though there is no objective truth on which his life may rest and as though there are no norms to attain. Instead of eternal values, he creates his own arbitrary standards, only to alter them as the need arises.

Man is created in the likeness of God, but lives as though he were a lump of clay with neither meaning nor aim. His God-implanted conscience speaks of high ideals, while all around him he observes rife egoism, brute desire, and abounding weariness and emptiness. He is caught in a deep quandary, living far beneath his privileges and rights as a human being, created and loved by God.

Thousands of men and women are inwardly destroyed today because of the resulting stress. They have been fed a lie and swallowed it, believing that man is the standard of everything. Everything is relative! Man is his own savior and God does not exist!

Where has man received this? Who has given him this lie that has so debased him and robbed him of his happiness, purpose and human dignity? What devilish doctrine is it? **An earthly, humanistic and materialistic philosophy of life that denies the existence of God; that man fell into sin and needs to be restored; that Jesus Christ is the Savior of all men and that what He says is the objective truth!**

By starting with the mistaken idea that man is basically good, then linking it with the assertion that there is no God who has a plan for his life, man made himself his own savior, independent of God. Thus he rises in out-and-out rebellion against his Creator, cuts his own life line and plunges into further spiritual darkness. In his gloom he ever tries to enlighten himself by knowledge and experiment **but never succeeds because his basic premise is erroneous.**

However commendable human claims may seem, they echo emptily and all their fine sounding phrases are impotent. Calls for more involvement, increased solidarity and greater effort, along with attempts to educate and inform people have proved fruitless, regardless of the time and money spent on them. How right Jesus was when He said, *Apart from me you can do nothing* (John 15:5).

Education is good and meaningful, but it must be based on genuine knowledge and founded on the true view of mankind. In the Christian view of humanity there is no disparagement of knowledge, only a realistic attitude toward it. To the Christian, Jesus is the Savior; to the atheistic humanist, knowledge is the means of salvation. But if that knowledge disallows divine revelation, it becomes a proudly towering Babel and a futile imagination, erected against the knowledge of God (2 Cor 10:4-5).

Man has the ability to gather and collate information but needs outside help to rightly sort through his pile of material. Hence, the importance of God. Without Him, we have no blueprint of the universe, no compass in the shallows and however much evidence we think we have, we still can't interpret it correctly and come to right conclusions.

A broad and comprehensive knowledge of a high, academic standard is essential, but, without Christian values in life, it is like shifting sand. It becomes like a table spread with both delicacies and deadly poisons with nothing to indicate which is which, and with no one to advise either, because "everything is relative anyway."

Truth alone brings freedom of choice

In John 14:6, Jesus makes His most categorical of all statements, *I am the way and the truth and the life. No one comes to the Father except through me.* He says that He is the truth, He **is** the way and He **is** the life.

There is no **real** life without Him. He has something to say about **every** part of it, for both the individual and society. He created man, and He knows how man functions best as an individual, in a family, in a society, at work, in church life, in government, in politics and international relations.

Jesus is reality. He alone understands how the reality He has created works best. He is not a little religious section tightly fitted into one hour on a Sunday morning. His Word and power transform individuals, families, schools, places of work, towns and nations, wherever they are given freedom of action.

Where Jesus is opposed and His Word despised, the very foundations of that society tremble. Total confusion

reigns and lawlessness is legalized where men make themselves the criterion and become a law unto themselves. In such a society, it is the duty of every believer to stand for objective truth, regardless of contrary winds of opinion.

The truth in Jesus Christ and in God's Word is like a battering ram. *The gospel...is the **power** of God for the salvation of everyone who believes* (Rom 1:16). The commission of the Church is to trumpet forth the Word of God. As we speak the truth in love, the real Jesus appears to men and women providing them with an opportunity to choose. They begin to see that everything is not relative and grey, but black and white. Truth is seen to be truth and falsehood is also seen for what it is. Men and women can then make their choice.

Non-Christians are more positive toward believers who have a standard and a faith than to those who make everything relative and deny the Gospel. If the devil has attacked society through humanism he has also used such perversion of the Gospel. His onslaught against Christians has been aimed at making them afraid to hold opinions contrary to the surrounding world, causing them to mix human thought with their preaching and turning the Gospel into something other than what the Bible says it is. The devil is afraid of the supernatural and has done everything he can to strip the Gospel of its power.

Tragically, Christians have run the devil's errands, and not dared to believe in the reliability of the Bible. They have denied signs and wonders, the creation story, the virgin birth, Jesus' resurrection and even everlasting life. All that remains is mere humanism dotted with pious phrases. The Gospel and its power are absent. All that is left is a religious administration and empty church benches.

But praise the Lord, despite all these humanistic theologians, the people of God are rising up as never before. They are believing in Him and His revelation, acting on it and taking their stand in the spiritual battle. They are becoming a defense for the whole of their country and altering its destiny.

God has made us the salt of the earth and heavenly lights in the world. His Word is not bound, but a force to be reckoned with in the spirit realm. He wants us to wield it as the sword of His Spirit and cut His enemy, Satan, to pieces so that his influence ceases to dominate our land. Then a wave of liberty will sweep over the whole of the nation.

52

The Foundations of Freedom

> *The Spirit of the Lord is on me, because he has anointed me to preach good news to the poor. He has sent me to proclaim freedom for the prisoners and recovery of sight for the blind, to release the oppressed, to proclaim the year of the Lord's favor* (Luke 4:18-19).

Jesus spoke these words as He stood in the synagogue at Nazareth in Galilee, reading from the scroll.

He came to proclaim the Good News of freedom for the prisoners. Notice that both **freedom** and **release** are mentioned in this short quotation from Isaiah 61. Why? Because God looks on freedom as something exceedingly precious and essential.

God created man for freedom. He was to live and work together with God but he fell into sin. Through Satan's temptation he lost his liberty. He was tempted to be like God while becoming independent from Him and, instead of gaining more liberty, he entered the captivity that has marked humanity ever since—the bondage of sin.

Sin does not consist primarily of individual acts, but is essentially an attitude of heart. The word "sin" means "transgression of the law," "rebellion," and "to miss the mark." This was precisely what happened when man wanted to become independent from God. He missed the purpose of his existence and went astray.

This is the fundamental Biblical view of mankind: Man was created by God to live in fellowship with Him, and his life is only satisfied through this relationship.

The Bible definition of freedom is not synonymous with total independence and a selfish lifestyle. Biblical liberty means entering the calling for which God created you. When a man kicks against his calling and goes his own way, he loses his liberty. A car can only function as designed. If someone ignores the instructions and fill up with water rather than fuel, he loses rather than gains.

When man fell into sin, he lost his life and fellowship with God. He walked from liberty into captivity—but Jesus came to free us from this very captivity.

Selfish Freedom results in Slavery

The Biblical view of mankind is that *all have sinned and fall short of the glory of God* (Rom 3:23), but salvation, restoration and freedom have been made available, through Jesus Christ, to all who believe in His name.

The freedom man lost at The Fall affects every aspect of life. He went into total captivity—spiritually, psychologically, physically, socially and economically. Therefore, the Gospel touches every area of life as well. Salvation in Jesus Christ is not only concerned with man's spirit, but with every part of his existence. This was the liberty Jesus came to proclaim when He declared, *The Spirit of the Lord is upon me...to preach good news.* Jesus died for our release. He also came *to proclaim the year of the Lord's favour* (Luke 4:19). His words here can be traced back to the year of jubilee described in Leviticus 25:10: *Consecrate the fiftieth year and **proclaim liberty throughout the land** to all its inhabitants. It shall be a jubilee for you; each one of you is to return to his family property and each to his own clan.*

Jesus came to proclaim this year of jubilee. He died and rose again to establish this period of grace. **Freedom is one of the cornerstones of the Gospel**. Wherever it is preached and received, people are set free. Jesus declares: *If the Son sets you free, you will be free indeed* (John 8:36).

Freedom for a non-Christian, is often freedom of choice, that is, the ability to examine several alternatives and choose one of them. The decision is made on the grounds of personal preference, dictated by aims and interests. This is all right when it concerns a choice of toothpaste etc! Lack of choice in that area would be a restriction on normal human rights. No government or majority vote ought to be allowed to curtail such basic human rights.

The average person reacts against such infringements and impositions just as any healthy person would about being put under guardianship. There is an inherent need for space within human nature, which allows freedom of choice and scope for action. However, the liberty we all need must have a foundation. Its aim is not maximum freedom for everyone to do whatever they like in a lax society.

Within every human being there is a God-given need for freedom. When this is not directed toward Him but instead, given over to the devil in defiance and independence of God, it no longer achieves freedom, but slavery.

Exponents of humanism often fervently advocate freedom while maintaining a completely different outlook in life from that which is in the Bible. Ideologies influenced by humanism are based on the false idea that man is innately good and that all he has to do is develop himself. Thus, every form of hindrance to his self-realization is regarded as potentially injurious and destructive.

This is why humanism show tolerance toward more or less anything and everything. It is agreed that people must decide for themselves and because everything is relative, there is no-one to say what is right and wrong. If a man chooses to have five women or practice homosexuality, we must respect his choice because we have no underlying norm to say what is right or wrong.

We should be allowed to choose, they say, and what we choose is up to each of us. In this way humanism is tolerant and accepts just about everything—except the Gospel and Biblical faith. In these areas it shows utter intolerance because, it is argued, the Bible denies people their self-fulfillment by its prohibition of certain behavior. How deceitful and wrong!

Freedom and Truth are Inseparable

In the city of Sodom where people lived deep in sin and practiced sodomy, (homosexuality), they felt Abraham's nephew, Lot, to be a threat and provocation. Even though Lot did not have victory in his own life, he was still righteous according to 2 Peter 2:7-8, and troubled by all the unrighteousness he saw. However, the people of Sodom felt he was judging them and said to him, *Get out of our way!* and *This fellow came here as an alien, and now he wants to play the judge!* (Gen 19:9).

Despite the fact that Lot was not at all bold, but rather backslidden, his life caused them to be aware of their ungodly lifestyle in and they accused him of judging them.

This still happens today. The world and compromising Christians alike shout cries of "Judgmental!" "Legalism!" "Unloving and severe!" because the purity in the Gospel and the saints pass judgment on their sin. Suddenly, the sinner cannot continue to sin undisturbed.

Therefore, every form of humanism reacts with hatred and rebellion toward the Bible as God's Word because it not only reveals the truth, but also exposes sin and warns of its consequences.

The liberty Jesus proclaims is not licence to do whatever we like, however and wherever we wish. No! This freedom comes as we discover God's purpose for our existence and find our place in His plan. Only when a person is set free in the very depths of his innerman does he becomes a true human being and then, he can begin to release others too.

Freedom and truth are inseparably joined. True freedom means finding the place for which you were created and functioning in the way you were made. Liberty is not just freedom of choice but the ability to choose correctly and avoid the awful consequences of having chosen erroneously.

The Word of God Creates Freedom

In 1 Timothy 3:15, the Church is referred to as **the pillar and foundation of the truth.** As mentioned earlier, there is no real freedom unless it is linked with the truth. The truth sets us free (John 8:32). The commission of the Church is to preach the Gospel of truth—the full Gospel.

The Gospel is to be preached to different groups of people: to the saints to feed and satisfy them and to the world, so they can be saved. The Gospel, God's Good News, must also be prophetically proclaimed to all in authority and government so they know what God has to say about their work. Finally, the Gospel must be declared in the spirit realm so that evil spirit rulers and powers are held at bay and are reminded that they are vanquished and under Jesus' feet!

The truth, God's Word, has the capacity to achieve all of this. His Word feeds the sheep and, at the same time, works in the spirit world, keeping the devil in place. When the Church preaches the uncompromising Word, regardless of the world's reaction, she is then the pillar and foundation of truth and can create the freedom men and women need.

When the saints proclaim the truth of God's Word they may collide head-on with the concepts and values of their society. If they then water down the Gospel to make it more palatable to a secularized world, they make the worst mistake possible, because they actually take away the foundation and cornerstone of the Gospel. They remove its basic power to bring liberty to the captives.

Only God's Word can liberate men and women. If we remove the Word, or cease to live according to it, we can talk about liberty as much as we like and promise it left, right and center, but people will never experience it.

2 Peter 2:19 refers to false prophets who live in sin themselves. With fair speeches *They promise them freedom, while they themselves are slaves of depravity—for a man is a slave to whatever has mastered him.*

But when the Church boldly proclaims "Thus saith the Lord!" for every part of life, the prerequisites are created in the spirit realm for true liberty for everyone.

When the Church openly declares what the Word of God says, it has an enormous effect in the spirit world. His Word is creative and creates liberty wherever it is received, The Word of healing creates healing. The Word of forgiveness creates forgiveness and the Word of liberty creates liberty where it is received into open hearts.

The enemy is aware of this and tries to keep the Word away from people so he can hold them in slavery. But, praise the Lord, the enemy can no longer can hinder and pervert the Gospel, unchallenged.

The Word of God is spreading and being boldly proclaimed as never before in world history. As a result, we are going to see a greater freedom than ever—especially as the Lord has found a people who refuse to compromise, who put liberty before security and self-advantage, and who value freedom more than the applause and praise of men.

When believers refuse to compromise their freedom in Christ, spiritual deliverance will come to their land as a result. Liberty is at your door!

53

Revival—A Divine Attack on Society

Revival is not something that happens in a corner. Revival affects the entire community and touches everyone on all levels of society,

Acts 2:6 describes a roaring and a moving, *When they heard this sound, a crowd came together in bewilderment, because each one heard them speaking in his own language.*

What had happened? The Spirit of God had filled ordinary people who had the calling of God on their lives. They brought the power of God out from their own company and on to the street, so that the unsaved were confronted with God's power. Revival had come with a roar! There was activity and life that caught people's attention. It was challenging and it was powerful.

Now, many people are crying out for peace and quiet. They want tranquillity, they want to be cared for in calm and comfort. But we are not living in a time of spiritual tea parties! We are living in a time when God wants to make the whole world aware of the fact that Jesus is alive and that His resurrection power is available to them all.

We are living in times of both spiritual visitation and spiritual confrontation. This is a time of spiritual advancement—heaven is invading earth. Revival is here! Contrary to what you may think, revival is a divine attack on society and God is preparing for this! Revival has never come without confrontation. Revivals are times of spiritual warfare. The spirit of God is cleansing us to prevent the world system and the spirit of Antichrist from further dominating the Church and the world around us.

The Fruits of Revival in Church and Society

Revival means many things. It can change the spiritual atmosphere of an entire nation. The Lord has repeatedly told us that it is possible to change the spiritual atmosphere in our country, and we will see it happen!

Revival draws multitudes of people into the Kingdom of God, out from the mire of sin and away from the eternal, irreversible agony of hell. Revival is a spirit of love that pities the poor and the underprivileged and reaches out to lift them up and restore them.

Revival is a spirit of commitment and self discipline that hinders believers from living carnal, apathetic and egotistical lives. Revival is a spirit of moderation that stops sin spreading in society. The Spirit of God brings the fear of God into the community so that lasciviousness, alcoholism, occultism, pornography, immorality and abortions diminish, and sometimes end entirely.

Revival is a spirit that affects corruption, lawlessness and political power concentration. It causes righteousness to dominate in the government and promotes freedom in every area of life.

Revival is impossible without God. Man does not have the ability himself to bring it about, but God has. He wants to do it and He will do it. The glory of God and His presence will once again shake, confront and mark people here on earth, before Jesus Christ returns to take His bride, the Church, back with Him to be with God forever in heaven.

Revival is primarily salvation for the people, but it is also the restoration and reformation of the Church. Right now we can observe an ongoing work of reformation in the Church throughout the world and the result will be a great visitation of the glory of God. Many preachers follow the trends and are quick to give their opinion about which way this or that development is heading. They talk repeatedly about "the latest move."

Personally, I do not care for it. God works efficiently and carefully in preparing for a revival. He restores, reestablishes and follows a definite path that incorporates many different aspects. However, each aspect is not a new wave or a new revival; everything is connected and related. If some, for instance, emphasize praise and worship or strong intercession or deliverance from demons, then this is not a new wave or a new revival but a continuation of the revelation of faith. Believers should embrace all these aspects of the Church and not separate them, placing them against each other. They are all necessary and often follow in succession.

The Restoration of Life and Power

The Church must wake up and be reformed so the world can be saved. God is restoring three important areas within the Church:

1. Doctrine. God builds His Church on the foundation of sound, accurate teaching. The Church can never become alive and strong without a revival of teaching. Jesus said that if we hold to his teaching, we will know the truth, and the truth will set us free (John 8:31-32).

We must realize that in many different areas, Christianity has completely fallen away from the Word of God and has listened instead to the doctrines of evil spirits. There is an enormous falling away from fundamental Christianity all over the world. It has crept quietly upon us but now it is confronted, its horrible head appears and we can hear the hissing of the serpent.

An unfortunate misunderstanding exists among believers. Some people say, "We should not quarrel, we should be in agreement." However, such a suggestion is insidious. No spirit-filled believer wishes to quarrel with other believers. Our battle is not against flesh and blood, but we must defend and proclaim the truth, confronting apostasy and unbelief.

Revival cannot be released and grow in strength without confronting and cleansing unbelief. Unwillingness to do this indicates an attitude which would rather please men than God. Unity can only exist on the foundation of the Word, the blood and the Spirit, with the Biblical Jesus as Lord.

2. A Life of holiness. Revival is impossible without a life of purity, holiness and love. God's Spirit only uses committed, pure vessels. We are not talking about perfect people, but about committed people. A committed person, who is consecrated to God, has no interest in watching pornographic or worldly videos. A committed person has no problems with gossip or slander, bitterness or disappointment. A committed person has no problem with spiritual sluggishness or apathy He does not go in for tax evasion, slyness, cheating, stinginess and greed. A committed person does not shy away from prayer meetings or taking time with God in private. A committed person never has a dusty Bible.

Spiritual lethargy, grumbling and complaining, criticism or bickering will never result in revival. Revival comes when people are hungry for God and willing to do whatever, however and whenever. When people surrender their reservations, stop telling God how, when and through whom, He should work and just call on Him to bring revival, then He will do it.

3. Restoration of God's power. Revival is a public demonstration of God's power. Many think it will come like a thunderbolt out of the sky but it won't. Gradually, the tide of signs and wonders will rise and the glory will increase by degrees. Step by step, people will be saved in increasing numbers.

Therefore, it is foolish to stay at home doing nothing while criticizing others for not being spiritual enough, performing enough miracles or seeing great healings. If you have not seen many miracles but have prayed and seen some healings, rejoice! Do not let anyone, who complains and criticizes about not seeing enough, rob you of your joy! Know that God uses you and He rejoices in you because you are willing and available for Him.

Revival is a Result of Prayer

Many so-called spiritual experts and analysts readily offer their opinions and they are almost always tinged with negativism. Don't listen to them. They seldom do anything themselves. Continue what you are doing! Each day you will have increasing faith, boldness and joy as you live out and practice the Word God gives you.

Let no one rob you of your joy. Reach farther! Stretch out for more of God's power in your life. Don't be frustrated because you are not yet like Peter. Have faith that more of the resurrection power will flow in your life. Don't give up! Don't let Satan paint pictures of disappointment and resignation before your eyes. Jesus is on the throne and He has promised an outpouring of His glory and power in the end times. You won't miss it if you want it!

Throughout the Bible we see that revival comes because of prayer. So pray! Let no one hinder loud and dedicated prayer to the Father for revival. Give yourself over to prayer, and the spirit of prayer will come and fill you and help you give birth to the revival that will purify and sanctify your country, God wants to use everyone, so He will use you! Get organized, get together and pray!

Pray without ceasing! Pray for the authorities, pray for a breakthrough and for revival. Reach out beyond your own prayer needs and God will bless you! Pray for your country and God will shake it and correct it, and blessings and joy from heaven will flow over your nation again!

54

A Transformed Country!

Then Daniel praised the God of heaven and said: "Praise be to the name of God for ever and ever; wisdom and power are his. He changes times and seasons; he sets up kings and deposes them. He gives wisdom to the wise and knowledge to the discerning. He reveals deep and hidden things; he knows what lies in darkness, and light dwells with him" (Dan 2:19-22).

God alone created the universe. He alone has the power to do as He wants, because He is the one *sustaining all things by his* powerful word (Heb 1:3) *He has reconciled all things to* himself through Jesus Christ, whether things on earth or things in heaven, by making peace through His blood, shed on the cross (Col 1:20).

God is the one who not only rescues and saves individuals, but changes the spiritual climate of entire nations. Right now, God is altering and transforming countries. He wants cities and lands to be springboards for His revival and divine glory to reach the nations of the world. He wants to raise an army of innumerable believers who will take the Gospel to the whole sea of humanity who have never heard the Good News of Jesus, their Redeemer, who has abundant life and blessing for them.

When a person receives Jesus as Savior and Lord, the blessing of God comes into his life and God begins to do miracles. His supernatural power, the same power that raised Jesus from the dead, starts working in that person's life, restoring him and making him into what God intended him to be. He receives a completely new identity. He begins to enter God's plan for his life and realize what real freedom means. He begins to notice that sin and selfishness have lost their grip; they have been replaced by God's abundant life and overflowing blessing, and he is able, in turn, to be a blessing to others.

You have been released through Christ Jesus, so you can take God's life and power to the people around you who need a miracle—and everyone without exception, needs a miracle, The wonderful thing is that God; who is so good, wants to do it for them. Jesus came to release the captives: *"The Spirit of the Lord is on me, because he has anointed me to preach good news to the poor. He has sent me to proclaim freedom for the prisoners and recovery of sight for the blind, to release the oppressed, to proclaim the year of the Lord's favor"* (Luke 4:18-19).

As mentioned in the previous chapter, Jesus talks about freedom and release. The Good News that Jesus brought was liberty in **every** area of life. We must preach it fearlessly, unabridged, undiluted and uncensored. When a person is set free, liberty expresses itself in his life and surroundings. His release affects his spirit, soul and body. His freedom affects his family, finances, neighborhood and his country.

Believers—God's Channel of Blessing to the Land

God wants His blessing to reach out and touch a whole land. *When the righteous prosper, the city rejoices.... Through the blessing of the upright a city is exalted* (Prov 11:10-11).

When the righteous thrive, the people rejoice; when the wicked rule, the people groan (Prov 29:2). *Righteousness exalts a nation, but sin is a disgrace to any people* (Prov 14:34). Believers carry the blessings of Jesus Christ to their surroundings and as they follow their Lord, they become a blessing to the land in which they live.

During the time of Elijah, the people suffered from famine. 1 Kings 16:30-34 tells how King Ahab and his wife Jezebel fell into idolatry and in 1 Kings 17:1 we read that consequently, the vital blessing of "rain in its season" (see Lev 26:4) failed in the land and the result was blight, poverty, starvation and misery.

In Hosea 4:3, the Lord says, *The land mourns, and all who live in it waste away*. Why? Because *there is no faithfulness, no love, no acknowledgment of God in the land. There is only cursing, lying and murder, stealing and adultery; they break all bounds, and bloodshed follows bloodshed* (Hos 4:1-2).

The whole land felt the consequences of sin and apostasy, When godlessness becomes the norm in a country, ungodliness is promoted and legalized. When the Gospel is opposed and misrepresented, its preachers ridiculed, slandered and persecuted, negative repercussions for a whole land follow in its wake.

God told Abraham and his descendants (which includes every believer today), *I will bless those who bless you, and whoever curses you I will curse; and all peoples* (nations and generations) *on earth will be blessed through you* (Gen 12:3). We understand from this scripture that when authorities and powers begin to make it easy for believers to spread the Gospel, their land reaps reward in the form of blessing.

The Word of God frequently points out that divine blessing is available to nations, through its believers. Therefore, it is vital that Christians do not sleep, but take up their responsibility. If there had been ten righteous people in Sodom, God would have saved it, and there are certainly more than ten righteous people in your country. There are thousands at least!

Righteousness—A Defense for the Land

It means a lot when you realize that the righteousness you have received through Jesus Christ, is a blessing to the whole of your nation. You have become a shield of defense for your country. Do not let the devil tell you that you are nothing; that your thoughts are meaningless and your prayers and actions are a waste of time. That is wrong! You are important! Look at 1 Samuel 14:6-15, Jonathan and his armor-bearer overcome the Philistines and caused utter confusion amongst them, because Jonathan had declared, *Nothing can hinder the Lord from saving, whether by many or by few.* Your prayers and actions are not insignificant. You are a blessing to your country!

It is one hundred per cent possible for God to transform the spiritual climate in a land. It is totally possible for a country to begin walking in God's ways instead of the devil's. Many believers hardly give credence to this fact, and that is just what the enemy wants! But it is possible—if you will believe it.

2 Chronicles 7:14 states, *if my people, who are called by my name, will humble themselves and pray and seek my face and turn from their wicked ways, then will I hear from heaven and will forgive their sin and will heal their land.* God can heal and restore a whole nation. He does not single out favorites among individual people or lands, but He does have different thoughts and plans for them. I am convinced God wants to use my country to finance and send out workers who will preach the full Gospel and ignite the flames of revival over the whole of Europe and many other parts of the world.

This is why we must humble ourselves and pray for our own country; so that God's vision—not the devil's—is fulfilled. Paul urges us in 1 Timothy 2:1-4, *first of all,* that is to say, before we pray for anything else, we are to *pray for kings and all those in authority, that we may live peaceful and quiet lives in all godliness and holiness.*

This does not mean that we pray and then expect to sit at home in peace and quiet, drinking tea and coffee. It means that we should pray for powers and authorities so that their actions do not prevent Christians from practicing their faith in accordance with their convictions.

God wants believers to be free to own Jesus as Lord and to live freely according to the Word of God. God is anxious for the Gospel to be spread uninhibited, and to be proclaimed by every possible means without being hindered, misrepresented or persecuted. Why? Because *God wants all men to be saved and to come to a knowledge of the truth* (v. 4).

Authorities that obstruct and oppose the freedom and right to present the Gospel in all its fullness, cause the worst kinds of bondage. They cause spiritual bondage as their subjects are denied liberty and are lost eternally. This is why it is so important that **you** take your responsibility and pray for all in authority! If you do not, you open the door for the devil to take advantage of the powers-that-be to legislate for his purposes—and doing it all while you're asleep!

The Bible says we are not to grumble and constantly complain about the authorities but we should bless and pray for them. We should lift up our rulers in prayer, so they can make wise and right decision and, if they refuse to do so, to pray that they are replaced by others who will. God wants a governing body that is both a blessing for its land and that is open to the Gospel. This does not necessarily mean that those in authority will personally be believers but they can still acknowledge the fundamental truth of the individual's rights and liberties, for which the Gospel stands. God has given you the responsibility to pray such rulers into office.

Use Your Democratic rights

Those of us who live in a democratic society know that this implies that, as responsible adults, we are free to elect our own representatives. In a democratic society, these representatives—our authorities—are put in power by the people. It is our responsibility to act in such a way that the right people are elected; those who can govern in a way that blesses the land and who do not transgress or disallow the commands of God or obstruct the spread of the Gospel. If a government passes laws that clearly conflict with the Word of God, the believers must act.

We are held responsible by God to act in three ways:

1. We must humble and examine ourselves and then **pray** for all in authority. We are not to slander, despise or hate them. We are to show love for them and pray for them.

2. As the servants of God, we must speak His Word, **confront** open ungodly legislation and declare, "Thus says the Lord."

3. We must use our democratic rights as citizens to **vote** a governing authority out, whose ideology is fundamentally ungodly and who works toward a society estranged from the influence of the Gospel.

Believers are not to preach politics. We are to preach the Gospel—the Good News of freedom for the captives, but we must not be naive and to ignore the world around us. God has a word for every area of life and He has given us responsibility for our country. When we pray for it, He can do miracles and "depose kings and set others up" (Dan 2:21). He can change the spiritual atmosphere in an entire land so that the Antichrist loses his grip on the people and room is created for the Holy Spirit to draw the masses to Jesus.

Only the Gospel, accompanied by signs and wonders, can draw men and women to Jesus, not politics and philosophical outlooks on life. Only believers filled with the Holy Spirit, boldly preaching the whole counsel of God with signs and wonders following, can bring people to the Savior.

Elymas the sorcerer attempted to stop the proconsul on Cyprus from being saved. However, Paul pronounced the Word of God and Elymas was removed from power. Likewise, there are blockages in the spiritual world that the enemy has placed in our societies, to hinder salvation from coming to the people. As you pray and act under the guidance of the Holy Spirit, you force a passage for the power of God to reach the masses. So they can see that Jesus is their real Lord and Savior, and that God is a good God who desires to bless them in every area of life.

Therefore, take up your responsibility and allow yourself to be led by the Holy Spirit as you regularly pray for those in authority, as you confront error and injustice (as you are obliged to do), and when you vote. Every Christian ought to vote and ask God for guidance when doing so! God has a wonderful plan for your country. View it in the Spirit as a transformed land, believe in what you see, pray for it and you will receive it.

Other Books by Ulf Ekman

The Authority in the Name of Jesus
When you receive a revelation of what the name of Jesus really means, you will have boldness like never before.
Booklet, 32 pages

Destroy the Works of the Devil
Jesus came to earth to destroy the works of the devil. His death on the cross struck Satan a death blow. Jesus triumphed over him and won the victory for YOU! Booklet, 32 pages

Faith that Overcomes the World
Explains how faith arises, how it becomes operational, and what makes it grow. 144 pages

Financial Freedom
A thorough, biblical study on money, riches and material possessions.
128 pages

God, the State and the Individual
God not only deals with individuals, but with nations and governments. You can change the destiny of your nation! 112 pages

God Wants to Heal Everyone
Discover the wonderful fact that God's will is to heal everyone—including you. Booklet, 32 pages

The Power in the New Creation
A new dimension of victorious living awaits you. The Lord is with you, Mighty Warrior! Booklet, 32 pages

The Jews—People of the Future
Clarifies basic truths about the people and the land. Historical facts and Biblical prophecies combine to reveal the fulfillment of God's End-time Plan. 160 pages

The Prophetic Ministry
"Provides essential guideposts for the operation of the prophetic ministry today." From the Foreword by Demos Shakarian. 224 pages

Available from your local Christian bookstore, or order direct from the publisher:

Word of Life Publications
Box 17, S-751 03 Uppsala, Sweden
Box 46108, Minneapolis, MN 55446, USA
Box 641, Marine Parade, Singapore 9144